A
SKELETON
AT THE
HELM

THIS BOOK IS DEDICATED TO

Elaine Molina

John Richard Stephens wishes to express his appreciation to Elaine Molina; Martha and Jim Goodwin; Scott Stephens; Marty Goeller; Terity, Natasha, and Debbie Burbach; Brandon, Alisha, and Kathy Hill; Jeff and Carol Whiteaker; Christopher, Doug and Michelle Whiteaker; Pat Egner; Gabriel, Aurelia, Elijah, Nina Abeyta and Justin Weinberger; Eric, Tim and Debbie Cissna; Norene Hilden; Doug and Shirley Strong; Barbara and Stan Main; Joanne and Monte Goeller; Irma and Joe Rodriguez; Danny and Mary Schutt; Les Benedict; Dr. Rich Sutton; and to his agent, Charlotte Cecil Raymond.

Compilation © 2008 by John Richard Stephens

Cover illustration © 2008 by Tim Foley

Cover and interior design by Jo Obarowski

See p. 346 for art credits.

2008 Metro Books

ISBN-13: 978-0-7607-9302-2
ISBN-10: 0-7607-9302-6

Printed and bound in China

10 9 8 7 6 5 4 3 2 1

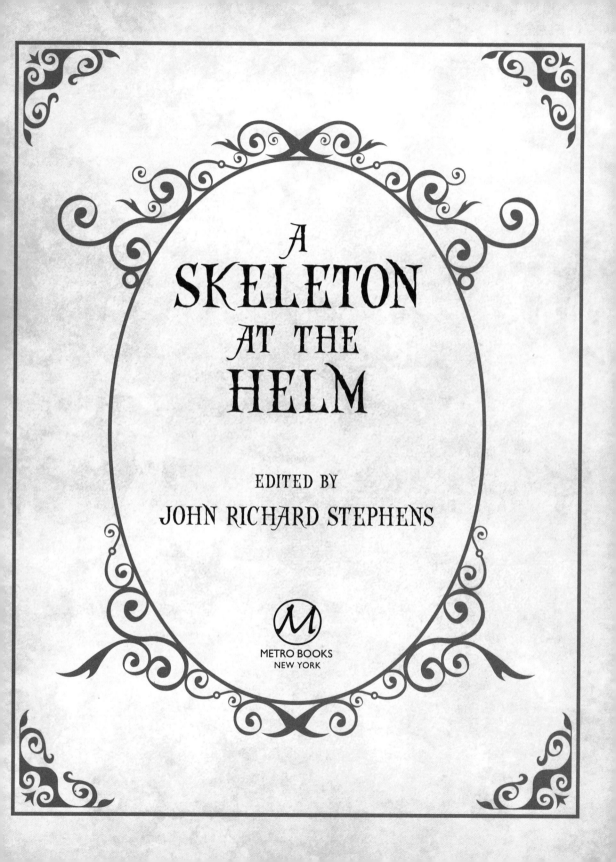

A SKELETON AT THE HELM

EDITED BY

JOHN RICHARD STEPHENS

METRO BOOKS
NEW YORK

Contents

DANGERS ON THE SEAS

INTRODUCTION BY JOHN RICHARD STEPHENS

There is three times more ocean on the earth than there is land. Vast, seemingly empty stretches of water, much farther than the eye can see. If something happens to you out there, you could be hundreds or thousands of miles from help. And while the ocean can look calm and peaceful when you are floating on it in a boat, it can be full of dangers—and many mysterious things can happen.

Countless ships have vanished without a trace over the centuries, taking their crews and passengers with them. Lloyds of London has detailed registers listing over 4,000 missing ships, including some lost during wartime. Even in these days of satellite radios and global positioning devices, ships continue to inexplicably disappear every year. A senior scientist at the GKSS Research Center in Geesthact, Germany, Wolfgang Rosenthal, says that an average of two large ships disappear without warning every week. Between 1978 and 1998, at least 200 supercarriers—each more than 219 yards long—were lost to the sea.

Some commonly accepted nautical stories that are initially presented as fact will turn out to be fiction on further research, but confirming the veracity of a tale can be difficult. This is especially true when there were only a few witnesses and nothing in the way of documentation. On the other hand, there's often no way to prove these accounts are *untrue*. Each tale must therefore be examined on its own merits.

There is one lost ship that may actually have reappeared, albeit very briefly. The *Columbia*, a schooner from Gloucester, Massachusetts, vanished without a trace, along with her crew of twenty, during a gale on August 24, 1927. No flotsam was found. The story goes that on January 1, 1928, the fishing trawler *Ventosa* caught her nets on something near Sable Island. Pulling up the three-inch steel cables from a depth of ninety feet, they found they had the *Columbia* hanging from the winch at the stern of their ship. Her masts were intact, her deck covered in mud and seaweed, and there appeared to be a corpse shackled to the helm. The *Ventosa*'s Captain Myhre and his crew stared in astonishment as their catch slowly swayed back and forth, until suddenly the cables snapped and the *Columbia* sank back down to her watery grave.

TEMPESTS

The primary suspect when a vessel goes missing is almost always bad weather, with cyclones being particularly dangerous for ships. In the Atlantic, a hurricane becomes a major hurricane when winds over 114 miles per hour are sustained for at least a minute—more than enough to wreck havoc on the largest ship—but gusts of wind have been recorded at well over 200 mph. The winds in a tornado (or a water spout, as it is called when over the ocean) have been known to exceed 300 mph.

Out at sea, smaller storms can develop very quickly, without warning, and dissipate just as rapidly. These unpredictable storms can produce large waves, cross-seas, and howling squalls that are as dangerous as they are frightening to behold.

ROGUE WAVES

Scientists have found that monstrous, so-called rogue waves—also known as freak or monster waves—are much more common than previously thought. When one of these rogue waves hits a ship along her side, it can flip her upside down. If a ship is not flipped, she can take on so much water that she sinks. If the wave hits the ship head on, the ship will first drop down into the trough, before being raised back up. For very large ships, this can snap her in half. According to C. Linwood Vincent, an oceanographer at the Office of Naval Research in Arlington, Virginia, when a ship drops into one of these troughs, "it's like riding a down elevator."

Survivors often report that a hole opens up in front of some rogue waves. In 1974, a Norwegian tanker named *Wilstar* was hit by a wave that tore off the tip of the ship and twisted the I-beams in her frame. A witness said, "There was no sea in front of the ship, only a hole." And then she slammed into a mountain of water.

The Roman poet Virgil vividly described such a wave in the *Aeneid*, recounting the legend of Aeneas. Virgil wrote:

> A squall came howling from the north, catching his sail full on and raising the waves to the stars. The oars broke, the prow was wrenched round, and as they lay beam on to the seas, there came towering over them a sheer mountain of water. Some of the ships were hanging on the crests of the waves; for others the waters opened and in the troughs could be seen the sea-bed and the seething sand.

Modern ships are designed to handle waves up to fifty feet in height. A wave this size can hit a ship with a force greater than six tons per square meter. Thirty tons per square meter will dent a ship. But waves up to 112 feet—as high as an eleven-story building—have been recorded hitting ships, lighthouses, and oil platforms. Research suggests some waves can exceed 132 feet from trough to crest; waves this size can blast a ship at more then 100 tons per square meter, enough force to rip open the bow of a ship. A 100-foot wave can form within eleven minutes, travel up to 45 mph, and then disappear almost as rapidly.

MUTINY AND PIRACY

Mutiny and piracy are among the first things that come to the minds of authorities when a ship goes missing. Though not as common as in the 18th century, ruffian crews do still mutiny and cruel captains do still exist. This is more common on commercial vessels—such as Asian fishing boats. Conditions on some boats are abominable. In an article on human trafficking in its March/April 2006 issue, *Mother Jones* magazine reported that some Third World poor are actually being sold into slavery on fishing boats where they are kept pumped up on speed so they can work practically around the clock. They slave away like this for several years before finally burning out. Then, one of the ship's officers puts a bullet in their head and unceremoniously dumps the body overboard.

And piracy, too, still exists, although modern pirates are more likely to use AK-47s and RPGs than cutlasses and flintlock pistols. They're even known to attack large cargo freighters and tanker ships. Pirates are most active near Bangladesh, around Africa—particularly the western coast and near Somalia—and on the major shipping lanes of the Singapore Straits and the Malacca Straits of Indonesia. Hundreds of acts of piracy are reported each year, and probably many more go unreported. According to the International Maritime Bureau, pirate attacks around the world tripled between 1993 and 2003. In late 2005, a luxury cruise liner with hundreds of tourists and crew members on board was attacked with machine-gun fire and rocket-propelled grenades off the coast of Somalia by heavily armed pirates in speedboats. The liner took evasive action and escaped.

The old adage "dead men tell no tales" still holds true today. If pirates simply murder all their victims and sink the ships, then who's going to report what happened? As far as anyone knows, they just vanished without a trace.

WHIRLPOOLS

Whirlpools—also known as maelstroms—are a real danger. Many ships and sailors caught in them are pulled down into the sea. Often the corpses are never found. Some of the more famous whirlpools are the Corryvreckan, in Scotland; the Saltstraumen, near Bodø, Norway; the Naruto Whirlpool off the island of Shikoku in Japan; the Old Sow near the Maine-New Brunswick border; and the original Maelstrom, which gives them all that name—the Moskstraumen, in Arctic Norway. These whirlpools are relatively permanent, though they appear and disappear, depending on the tides. Other whirlpools may suddenly appear without warning, swallowing whatever ships happen to be nearby.

SEA GAS

Australian researchers found in 2001 that giant methane bubbles rising from the ocean floor could sink a ship. Large deposits of methane, in solid form, are created under the enormous pressures at the deep bottom of the ocean. Like icebergs breaking off a glacier, large pieces of methane break off from the deposit and turn into gas form as they rise to the surface. If far enough from the rising bubble, or directly over it, the ship would be safe. But if the ship was anywhere in between, she would disappear into the ocean.

Lots of tiny bubbles, like in champagne, could be even worse. If there's enough of them, the rising bubbles can take away a ship's buoyancy, causing her to drop straight to the bottom. Being directly over a burst of tiny bubbles would be the worst place to be.

TRAPPED BY ICE

Once it was not unusual for ships to be caught in polar regions by the first storms of winter. If a ship becomes icebound, she may remain that way until the spring thaw. Before global warming, a ship could be trapped for years. Sometimes the ice pressure against the ship can become too great and the hull can be crushed, sinking the ship. Other ships survive to emerge from the ice as abandoned derelicts. (Another dangerous side effect of global warming for ship captains are the huge chunks of ice breaking off ice shelves at both poles, sending icebergs into seas where they had never been seen before.)

The following is a story that appears to be true and can be traced back to 1861. On September 22, 1860, the schooner *Jenny,* from England, was found drifting in Drake Passage—between the southern tip of South American and Antarctica. It's said that a boarding party found the *Jenny*'s captain seated at his table with a pen in his hand—he was frozen solid. A total of seven people were aboard, including one woman, plus a Newfoundland dog. According the ship's log in front of the captain, the ship had become trapped by sea ice in 1823. The last entry in the log read, "May 4, 1823. No food for 71 days. I am the only one left alive." The ship had been locked in ice for 37 years before she was found.

Since the 15th century, explorers had searched the frozen regions north of Canada in an attempt to find the fabled Northwest Passage that supposedly connected the Atlantic and Pacific Oceans, but ice always prevented it. All of the expeditions failed and many ended in disaster, until 1906, when Norwegian explorer Roald Amundsen finally made it through in a 47-ton converted herring boat. The voyage took him three years to complete. It wasn't until 1944 that a Royal Canadian Mounted Police schooner was able to make the trip in one season. History records these as the first to achieve what was essentially the Holy Grail of maritime voyages for almost four centuries.

But it's possible that Amundsen might not have been the first Westerner to make it through the Northwest Passage. There is an unverified account that a ship with a crew of frozen corpses made it through about 130 years earlier. That ship was the *Octavius*, an English trader that attempted to return to England from China by way of the as-yet-undiscovered Northwest Passage. The ship's log told of how they became trapped in sea ice roughly 200 miles north of Point Barrow, Alaska, on October 25, 1762.

Thirteen years later, on August 11, 1775, the snow- and ice-encrusted *Octavius* was discovered drifting near Greenland by the whaler *Herald*. Captain Warren and his boarding party found 28 frozen sailors on board, with the frozen captain seated at his desk in his cabin—a layer of faint green mold growing out of his face, obscuring his features. In a nearby cabin they found a frozen woman lying on her bed, her open eyes staring across the room at a young man sitting cross-legged on the floor who had vainly attempted to kindle a fire, while under a jacket was the corpse of a ten-year-old boy.

ACCIDENTS AND FUNERALS AT SEA

On ships there is always the danger of falling overboard; this is much more common than people realize. Even on today's cruise liners, people fall overboard or mysteriously disappear. An unofficial tally from personal and media sources by Dr. Ross A. Klein, a professor at the Memorial University of Newfoundland, shows that at least 32 people went missing between 1995 and 2006, while an additional 21 went overboard, some possibly suicides. Many more people disappear from smaller vessels.

Accidents are, of course, a very common danger at sea, especially on commercial or military ships with heavy machinery. Living and working in a constantly moving environment makes accidents more likely. When accidents do happen at sea, access to medical care is usually limited to first aid or the care of the ship's doctor. Only the largest ships have hospitals on board.

Because of the length of voyages, it was a maritime tradition to bury sailors at sea. In *Sailor Life on Man of War and Merchant Vessel* [sic], Charles Nordhoff described a typical funeral thusly:

> When a sailor dies at sea, his corpse is sewed up in the hammock which has
> been until that time his bed, and now becomes his shroud. A couple of
> thirty-two-pound shot are enclosed, next to his feet, to bear the body down
> to the depths of the ocean, which is his grave.

It was also a naval tradition, when stitching up the shroud, to put the final stitch through the dead sailor's nose. Apparently this was done as a precaution to avoid accidentally dropping someone to the bottom of the sea who was actually in a state of catalepsy. The hope being that passing the thick needle and thread through their nose would be enough to snap them out of it. If there was no response, the corpse was considered well and truly dead.

After consigning a mariner to the deep, you can almost picture the dead man, sewn in his shroud, planted vertically on the sea floor, held down by the cannonballs at his feet—gently swaying back and forth with the ebb and flow of the water, in a slow-motion dance with the seaweed.

SEA MONSTERS AND GIANT SQUID

As any mariner will tell you, the seas are full of mysteries—many of them dangerous. For centuries there have been tales of deadly sea monsters, ranging from giant sharks and homicidal whales to serpents and krakens, the last of which are essentially colossal calamari that don't seem to mind devouring sailors as snacks. Although ancient maps were often decorated with such monsters of the deep, most of these were of course imaginary. But there are many sightings of hitherto unknown creatures that could well be authentic. Bernard Heuvelmans' heavily researched 1968 book, *In the Wake of the Sea-Serpents*, contains hundreds of these firsthand accounts.

For years scientists ridiculed reports of giant squid, but now that they've been captured, scientists would now no doubt ridicule you if you attempted to *deny* their existence.

Giant squid often get into life and death struggles with sperm whales and the skin of the whales sometimes get badly scarred in the process, leaving large circles from the suction cups on the squid's tentacles. In 1875, Frank Bullen saw one of these battles from the whaling ship *Cachalot*:

A very large sperm whale was locked in deadly conflict with a cuttle-fish, or squid, almost as large as himself, whose interminable tentacles seemed to enlace the whole of his great body. The head of the whale especially seemed a perfect net-work of writhing arms—naturally, I suppose, for it appeared as if the whale had the tail part of the mollusc in his jaws, and in a business-like, methodical way, was sawing through it. By the side of the black columnar head of the whale appeared the head of the great squid, as awful an object as one could well imagine even in a fevered dream.

Occasionally neither wins the deadly battle. A dead whale was once found that had bitten the head off the very squid that had killed it.

Apparently squids don't always feel a need to kill their prey. Sometimes they seem happy to bite out a few large chunks and swim away before being harmed themselves. While they may look soft and squishy, they are actually ferocious carnivores. Using their two longer tentacles—each of which has a club on the end—they can seize prey with lightning speed. The suction cups on the clubs are lined with sharp circular-saw-like sucker rings, swiveling hooks, or both for holding the prey as they draw it down amongst their eight shorter tentacles. These limbs help hold and position the prey while squid rips off chunks of flesh with its large razor-sharp beak.

A seven-foot squid can bite clean through the tough skin of a fourteen-foot shark and tear out a fist-size chunk of its flesh. Recently a colossal squid—so called because they're thought to be larger than giant squid—was caught off New Zealand that was 33 feet long, weighed half a ton, and had eyes the size of dinner plates. In comparison, the largest known sperm whale was 59 feet long and weighed about 45 tons.

Squid are very intelligent and *can* be very gentle, but they'll also attack just about anything—even ships, perhaps thinking the ship is a whale. They do go after humans and it's claimed they have killed people—mainly fishermen. Squid are cannibals, and, given the opportunity, will quickly attack and eat each other. They also hunt in teams: Sometimes one squid will try to distract a diver, so that one or two of its partners can sneak up from behind. Once they seize the diver, they'll try to drag him or her down to greater depths in order to help subdue their victim.

Squid are just one of the many dangerous species mariners might encounter. Every year marine biologists discover strange new creatures in the ocean's depths, while admitting we only know of a small fraction of what's out there.

THE UNKNOWN

There are also many other strange phenomena attributed to the sea. Occasionally there are reports of islands being found where there should be none and reports of very unusual weather phenomena. There are accounts of UFOs that hover over ships before plunging down into the sea, as well as many stories involving precognition of impending disasters and even claims that mummy curses were responsible for sinking a number of ships (see my book *Into the Mummy's Tomb* for more on this supposed phenomenon).

While the mummy curse stories don't stand up well under scrutiny, they are often retold. The one most widely repeated is that a mummy (or sarcophagus) caused the sinking of the *Titanic*. A few versions say that the mummy's owner, Lord Canterville (or parapsychologist William Stead), bribed a bunch of people and rescued the mummy on one of the *Titanic*'s lifeboats. It then made its way to America, where it continued to wreak havoc, and so was sold to a millionaire in Montreal, Canada. The millionaire then decided to ship it back to England in 1914 onboard the *Empress of Ireland,* which collided with a Norwegian ship on the St. Lawrence River, causing 1,029 people to drown. Deciding it best to send the mummy back to Egypt, the millionaire then shipped it on the *Lusitania,* which was sunk by a German torpedo in 1915, taking 1,198 people with it. Of course, all this is pretty far-fetched, but who knows, perhaps there is a grain of truth in some of the stranger stories.

Some bizarre seafaring tales are difficult to categorize. For example, there is a curious incident that happened to the Coast Guard cutter *Yamacraw* at around 1:30 A.M. on August 8, 1956. They were cruising in the Sargasso Sea, east of Florida, under a clear, starry sky, when the radar operator cried out, "Large land mass dead ahead. Range: 28 miles." On checking their navigation equipment they found they were still on course and actually about 165 miles from land (or more than 800 miles, depending on the account). They soon found that the mass wasn't moving and appeared to be a straight line on their radar.

An hour and a half or so later the *Yamacraw* cautiously approached whatever it was they had seen. Switching on the three-foot carbon arc searchlight, the crew could see the mysterious brownish-gray mass. It was reflective and the light was unable to penetrate what still looked like a solid landmass on the radar. Extending, like a huge wall, from horizon to horizon from northeast to southwest and up into the sky as far as they could see, blocking out the stars, it appeared to be hovering about two feet above the water.

Slowly turning so they were sailing parallel to the strange mass, the cutter slowly moved closer and nudged into it with the starboard wing two or three times. Nothing happened, so they resumed their normal cruising speed and entered the object. Visibility dropped to zero. Even when looking directly at the high-intensity searchlight, only a dull glow could be seen. There was no change in temperature or the feeling of dampness one would get if it had been a fog bank. Some of the 51-man crew said it had the texture of dust or very fine sand, but there was no breeze. The air was dead, with no movement at all, which ruled out a sand storm.

Some of the men began having trouble breathing and their eyes started to burn. Soon the engine room reported they were losing steam pressure, which caused their speed to drop to about four knots. Greatly alarmed, Commander William Strauch decided it was time to make a quick exit from whatever it was they were in. By this time it was nearly dawn. As the sky lightened, they were still unable to see the top of the mass and the light didn't seem to penetrate it. Then when the sun rose over the horizon, the eerie mass vanished.

Cruising around the area, they were unable to find any sign of it. It was no longer visible on radar and there wasn't even any dust or sediment on their ship. The officer of the watch, Ensign Frank Flynn, later said, "Now, as to what we might have encountered that night, I really have no way of speculating. Over the years after this happened I talked to many oceanographers, and none of these people could shed any light whatsoever on what it might have been."

HAUNTED SHIPS

Tales of hauntings and ghostly phenomena on ships are almost too numerous to count. Some claim one of the most haunted places on earth is the R.M.S. *Queen Mary*, which was launched in 1936 and is said to be home for more than 150 spirits.

In her day she was faster than the *Titanic* and was almost twice as large, weighing in at more than 81,000 tons. Now she's permanently docked in Long Beach, California, as a tourist attraction and floating hotel. Among her many ghosts are Sir Winston Churchill, a lady dressed in white, a lost little boy, a girl with a teddy bear, a baby who died shortly after birth, a bearded engineer, an 18-year-old sailor who was crushed to death when an automatic door came down on him, and some of the more than 300 British soldiers who died during a World War II accident when the *Queen Mary* sliced the British cruiser H.M.S. *Curacao* in half. Because wartime orders prevented the *Queen Mary* from stopping, the floundering soldiers from the *Curacao* were all left behind to drown. They are often said to be heard banging on the outside of the ship's hull, as if wanting to be let in. A woman was seen about to dive into an empty indoor swimming pool, while a child's wet footprints have also been found near the empty pool. The ship herself was nick-named "The Grey Ghost" when she was painted battleship gray during the war, though some also attributed the nickname to the speed with which she was able to navigate through U-Boat-infested waters without ever once attracting fire. Ghost tours are conducted on the *Queen Mary* at least four nights a week.

Another haunted vessel is the U.S.S. *Hornet*—the most decorated American World War II aircraft carrier, which also served in the Vietnam War and picked up the *Apollo 11* astronauts from the ocean after they walked on the moon. Since being converted into a floating museum at Alameda, California in 1995, the *Hornet* has had around 200 ghost sightings.

S.S. *St. Paul*

Due to a very strange coincidence, some people suggest a ghost or ghosts may have been responsible for sinking the S.S. *St. Paul.* A liner that was sometimes requisitioned by the U.S. Navy during wartime, the *St. Paul* was the ship that ferried Teddy Roosevelt's Rough Riders to Cuba in 1898. During a snowstorm the *St. Paul* collided with the British warship R.M.S. *Gladiator.* Twenty-seven sailors died. This happened at 2:38 P.M. on April 25, 1908. Ten years later at 2:30 P.M. on April 25, 1918, the *St. Paul* sank with the loss of four lives.

The *St. Paul* had once again been requisitioned and had just finished being refitted for use as a troopship during World War I. While being moved to a pier, she suddenly fell away from the pier, snapping the mooring lines that had just been set. It was later found that because the *St. Paul* lacked her usual ballast, she rode high in the water and was listing slightly to port. For some inexplicable reason, an ash hatch—which was used to dump ashes from the boilers—had been opened. This caused the boiler room to flood. Investigations into the possibility of sabotage or negligence were unable to find any reason why the hatch was opened, causing some to suspect vengeful ghosts.

S.S. *Watertown*

One of the more unusual stories of hauntings concerns the tanker S.S. *Watertown*. This is one of those stories that is hard to confirm or to locate primary documentation. Apparently the tale first appeared in 1934, ten years after the fact, in a small journal for the Cities Service Company—the shipping company that owned the *Watertown*—and was later recounted by Dr. Hereward Carrington, the director of the American Psychical Institute. The incidents are said to have begun in December 1924, while the ship was sailing from San Pedro, California, down the Pacific Coast toward the Panama Canal.

Seamen James Courtney and Michael Meehan were cleaning out a cargo tank when they were overcome by oil and gas fumes and died. Their bodies were buried at sea on December 4th in 1,400 feet of water off the coast of Mexico. The next day, late in the afternoon, one of the crew spotted the faces of the two men in the waves formed by the bow of the ship passing through the water. The faces would rise to the surface for about ten seconds, before being swallowed back up by the waves, only to later reappear. They were seen by several members of the crew. Captain Keith Tracy said, "We were doing about ten knots and they kept reappearing and keeping up with us."

This continued every day until they reached the Panama Canal. Some versions of the story say that once they were in the Atlantic Ocean, the ghostly apparitions were not seen again until the *Watertown* reentered the Pacific Ocean on her return trip. Others say the dead seamen followed the ship to New Orleans and then on to her destination in New York City.

When the *Watertown* arrived in New Orleans, Captain Tracy reported what had happened to his employers and they suggested he buy a camera, just in case the

"The crew spotted the faces of the two men in the waves"

faces appeared again. The faces did reappear and the captain took eight (or six) photographs, locking the camera in the ship's safe until he could get it to a commercial developer. The first frame of the negative was blank. The next two were blurs, while four more showed blurry water. It's claimed the dead crewmen can be seen in the final frame.

Crew members continued to see the ghostly faces, though less frequently. After the third voyage, the crew changed and the faces were no longer seen. The photograph hung on wall of the shipping company's offices for years until it was reprinted in the company's journal. The original photograph is long gone and all that remains are the widely reprinted reproductions from the journal.

PHANTOM SHIPS

They can sail against the wind with full billowing sails and speed against currents with their sails furled. Sometimes they even sail backwards and a few are seen flying through the sky. Some bring fog with them. Often they are totally silent, while on others the sounds of a party or fighting can be heard from far off. Many appear as normal ships, while others are luminescent or on fire. Sometimes their planks are missing, with just their bare ribs and tattered sails remaining. They may have a skeleton for the figurehead and specters swarming over the rigging, while on their decks other specters play dice for their victims' souls. Others have skeletons for the crew, while some have no one aboard at all.

There is a report in China of a phantom pirate junk seen looting her way up the Yangtze. Captain Kidd's ship, *Quedah Merchant,* has been spotted battling another ship in Long Island Sound, while Jean Lafitte's heavily armed pirate schooner *Fame* reportedly appears in Galveston Bay. It's said that after Lafitte's death, his crew loaded $7 million in treasure aboard the *Fame* and then proceeded to get rip-roaring drunk. The subsequent shipwreck dragged the treasure and most of the crew down with her to the bottom of the sea. The best-known sighting of the *Fame* was by two ships in 1892. One of the witnesses said the ghost ship almost ran his ship down and that the *Fame*'s crew looked like the living dead. The master of the Norwegian ship *Fair Hilda* said the *Fame* missed hitting his vessel by inches and that the crew of the luminescent schooner totally ignored his ship. He also noted that the ghost ship cast no shadow.

Sometimes ghost ships appear for no apparent reason. Others are said to appear on the anniversary of their setting off on their final voyage or on the anniversary of their destruction. Some are omens of death, while others bring destruction in the form of shipwrecks, disease, or madness. Almost all ghost ships came to some tragic end or were involved in foul play before becoming phantoms. On the other hand, sailors in Granada believed vessels became "spirit ships" when one sinks without taking any of the crew or passengers with her. Such a ship would rise to haunt the oceans, searching for a crew to man her. Horace Beck, in his book *Folklore and the Sea,* adds, "As insurance against such an event, some shipmasters in the area do not attempt to rescue all hands when a vessel is lost."

Mariners also tell of the "ship of death"—a ship with black sails that can sail out of the water and over land to retrieve the souls of sailors condemned to rot in hell.

The Flying Dutchman

The most famous phantom ship story is, of course, the Flying Dutchman. This legend tells of the stubborn Captain Hendrik van der Decken (or Vanderdecken) of the Dutch East India Company, who in 1641 (1680 or 1729 in some versions) defied God and his crew while rounding the Cape of Good Hope, on the southern tip of Africa, during a fierce storm. Though making no headway against the strong winds, he refused to put in to shore and swore he'd round the Cape even if it took him until Doomsday. Thus van der Decken was cursed to ceaselessly sail the Seven Seas in his decaying vessel, the *Voltiguer*, in the midst of a perpetual storm, without ever touching land. Some say he hails many who see his ship, asking them to deliver letters for him. Those who take the letters are doomed, though some believe anyone who sees the Flying Dutchman is about to perish. Others say they see him standing all alone and bareheaded at the helm of his ghost ship. Still others claim to have seen a crew of skeletons dancing in the rigging.

A few see him in a more positive light, believing he is warning those who sight him of impending disaster so they can prepare for it or try to avoid it. Others take the more sinister view that the Flying Dutchman is the direct cause of the eminent destruction of everyone who sees him.

Nautical folklore contains several similar versions of this tale. A German medieval legend tells how Captain von Falkenburg was condemned to sail the North Sea, unable to steer his ship, until Judgment Day, while forced to play dice with the devil for his soul. Then there is the Dutch East India man, Captain Bernard Fokke, who also haunts the Cape of Good Hope. Captain Fokke was known for the rapidity of his voyages from the Netherlands to Java in the 17th century, leading some to suspect he was in league with the devil. It's said his ship, the *Libera Nos*, is crewed by skeletons. And then there's a Norse saga of a Viking captain named Stötte who stole a magic ring and is cursed to sail for eternity as a flaming skeleton, perched on the mast of his black-hulled longship.

In early Dutch versions of the story, the Flying Dutchman is named Van Straaten. In others, he's called Van Demien. He is usually seen around the Cape of Good Hope or Cape Horn (the southernmost tip of South America)—both are notorious sailors' graveyards because of their hazardous icebergs, strong winds, turbulent currents, and large waves—but he has been spotted all over the world.

During World War II, German Admiral Karl Dönitz said, "Certain of my U-boat crews claimed that they saw the *Flying Dutchman* or some other so-called phantom ship on their tours of duty east of Suez. When they returned to their base, the men said they preferred facing the combined strength of the Allied warships in the North Atlantic than know the terror a second time of being confronted by a phantom vessel!"

Perhaps the best known sighting was by a group of thirteen that included the young prince who was later crowned King George V of Britain and his brother, the Duke of Clarence, both of whom were naval cadets serving on the H.M.S. *Inconstant.* The sighting occurred on July 11, 1881, as they were rounding Cape Horn. The prince, himself, recorded what he saw in his diary, and later reprinted the entry in his book, *The Cruise of H.M.S. "Bacchante," 1879–82*:

> July 11th.—At 4 A.M. the *Flying Dutchman* crossed our bows. A strange red light as of a phantom ship all aglow, in the midst of which light the masts, spars and sails of a brig 200 yards distant stood out in strong relief as she came up on the port bow. The look-out man in the forecastle reported her as close on the port bow, where also the officer of the watch from the bridge clearly saw her, as did also the quarterdeck midshipman, who was sent forward at once to the forecastle; but on arriving there no vestige nor any sign whatever of any material ship was to be seen either near or right away on the horizon, the night being clear and the sea calm. Thirteen persons altogether saw her, but whether it was the *Van Diemen* [sic] or the *Flying Dutchman* or who else must remain unknown....
>
> The *Tourmaline* and *Cleopatra*, who were sailing on our starboard bow, flashed to ask whether we had seen the strange red light.... At 10:45 A.M. the ordinary seaman who had this morning reported the Flying Dutchman fell from the foretopmast crosstrees on to the topgallant forecastle and was smashed to atoms. At 4:15 P.M. after quarters we hove to with the headyards aback, and he was buried in the sea. He was a smart royal yardman, and one of the most promising young hands in the ship, and every one feels quite sad at his loss. (At the next port we came to the Admiral also was smitten down.)

Jonahs and Jinx Ships

While sailors are probably no more superstitious than landlubbers, they are famous for their superstitions and folklore. Since sailors work in such a hostile and unpredictable environment, the idea of having good luck can be very important, while avoiding bad luck is even more important.

In maritime superstition, a "Jonah" is a person, thing or act that brings bad luck on a ship, like the ancient mariner who kills the albatross in *The Rime of the Ancient Mariner*. This belief comes from the Bible's account of Jonah, who refuses to become a prophet and flees on a ship. God threatens the ship with a terrible storm. On casting lots, his shipmates discover Jonah is the "Jonah". Jonah admits as much and says the storm will cease if they toss him overboard, which they promptly do, and the storm immediately stops. He is then swallowed by a "great fish"—usually interpreted as being a whale or, as some scholars suggest, a great white shark, though sharks don't usually swallow people whole.

A Jonah can be someone with red hair, or someone with flat feet, or even an act, such as stepping onto a ship with your left foot first or throwing stones at the sea. Some thought that having a priest aboard could bring catastrophe. And while some believed having a woman onboard was very bad because it would anger the sea, having a *naked* woman onboard was very good because it would calm the sea, hence the nude figureheads on many ships. Even a vessel can be considered a Jonah.

Seafarers have long believed that ships have their own personalities. After a while a crew gets to know a ship's quirks and peculiarities. They can tell whether she's a good ship or a bad ship. Superstitious sailors believe some ships are unlucky or cursed—"jinx ships" they're called. Some of the worst jinx ships are considered to be downright evil. It's believed these ships actively try to murder people.

According to legend, the god of the sea, Neptune (also known as Poseidon), keeps a list of all the world's ships in his "Ledger of the Deep". He also records which ships have offended him and which ships he has cursed—these are jinx ships.

S.S. *Great Eastern*

The S.S. *Great Eastern* was the largest ship in the world when she was built in 1857 and would remain so for the next thirty years. A huge vessel weighing 19,000 tons and featuring six masts, four funnels, a steam-powered paddle wheel on each side, and a single screw, she was intended to be the first ship that could sail from Europe to Australia without having to stop to take on coal. Despite being an engineering marvel of her time, she was considered jinxed.

When being launched, the *Great Eastern* became stuck on the runway and it took three months to slowly move her down into the water, killing one man in the process. The launch ended up costing one-third the total projected cost of building the ship. Then, on one of her first sea trials, part of a water heating system at the base of one of the funnels exploded, shooting the funnel into the air. Four stokers in the engine room were scalded to death by a shrieking blast of steam, while a fifth who jumped overboard to relieve his burns was killed when he became entangled in one of the paddlewheels. A second explosion was barely averted. The problem was that two valves that should have been open, were closed. During the inquiry, a ship's officer and two engineers insisted they checked the valves before sailing and the valves were open, while the boxes preventing access to the valves were locked. After the accident, it was discovered the valves were closed and the boxes they were in were unlocked, even though access to the keys was restricted.

This unlucky ship was involved in many other fatal accidents. Fires broke out in the engine room and in the cabins, along with several dockside fires, some resulted in deaths. Crewmen were killed in mechanical accidents and both crew and passengers disappeared overboard. The captain, the coxswain and the purser's son drowned when a boat taking them to shore flipped over. The S.S. *Great Eastern* crashed into several vessels, badly damaging or sinking them. She also suffered damage similar to the *Titanic* after running aground, tearing an eighty-foot-long gash in her side, though she was able to remain afloat. While the ship could hold 4,000 passengers, the most she ever carried was 1,530, and on several voyages had less then 200 passengers. It's said that she forced many of the companies that owned her into bankruptcy.

The *Great Eastern* was also rumored to be haunted. A number of ghosts were reported and strange banging sounds were heard, that some thought sounded like a hammer banging against the outside of the hull. Rumors circulated that when the ship was being built, one or two riveters were accidentally sealed up between the ship's two hulls. It is still widely reported that when the ship was finally torn apart for scrap, two skeletons were found in the hull, but this is not true.

Mary Celeste

The *Mary Celeste* was widely considered to be another jinx ship. Built in 1861, this 103-foot brigantine was originally christened the *Amazon*. Her first captain became sick and died before setting sail. On her maiden voyage she collided with a fishing weir and was badly damaged. While undergoing repairs, she caught fire. On her first transatlantic voyage, she collided with a brig, which promptly sank. On the return trip, she ran aground. After undergoing extensive repairs, she was renamed.

On November 7, 1872, the *Mary Celeste* sailed out of New York harbor, bound for Genoa with a cargo of 1,701 barrels of alcohol that would be used to fortify wine. On December 5th, the ship was discovered about half way between the Azores and Portugal without a single person on board. The captain, his wife, their baby daughter and a crew of seven had simply vanished forever and for seemingly no good reason.

The vessel was in good condition. There was enough food and all belongings were there. Only navigational items and the ship's papers were missing. The clock was upside-down and the compass water-damaged. It was as though everyone aboard had abandoned ship very quickly. Two of the hatches were off and there was about three feet of water in the hold. The skylight in the main cabin was open and everything, including the captain's bed, was wet. In the galley, the stove had shifted and utensils were strewn about. It appeared a boat was missing and the ship was trailing a frayed rope. Also, nine barrels of alcohol in the hold were damaged and empty. The last entry on the *Mary Celeste*'s slate was on November 25th—ten days before she was found adrift. At that time she had just reached the Azores. Before she was found, she had passed through a gale with heavy seas.

The mysterious disappearance of those onboard the *Mary Celeste* has led to various speculations, including that they were involved in an insurance scam, there was a mutiny, they suffered hallucinations from food poisoning, they were captured by pirates, attacked by a sea monster, hit a "ghost island," passed through a time warp, or were abducted by extraterrestrials.

One of the more logical explanations floating about is that alcohol leaked into the hold and, fearing the ship was about to explode, the captain loaded everyone in the boat attached to the rope behind the ship. Perhaps they left the hatches off, hoping the fumes would air out without igniting. The under jib and foremast headsails were set. The weather was calm on the 25th until the storm hit in late afternoon. If the wind caught the sails, they could have jerked the ship forward, either making the small boat capsize or causing the rope to part, leaving the boat alone on the open ocean. They likely would not have survived the approaching gale, which lasted from November 25th to December 4th.

After this, many were wary of the *Mary Celeste*, considering her to be a jinx ship. She continued to lose cargo, sails and crew members, changing hands seventeen times over the next twelve years, until she was purposely wrecked off the coast of Haiti in an insurance scam. She failed to sink fast enough and insurance examiners arrived in time to expose the fraud. Her wreck was discovered in 2001 by a team of divers (funded by novelist Clive Cussler) off the coast of Haiti, almost completely covered with coral.

DERELICTS AND ABANDONED SHIPS

Derelicts were once a real hazard to shipping. In fact, one of the jobs of the early Coast Guard was to seek them out and sink them. Many were abandoned because they were too old or decrepit, others because they became icebound or because the crew feared their ship was about to sink or explode. Then there are those ships that were abandoned under mysterious circumstances.

Today's best-known mystery ship is, of course, the *Mary Celeste*, which was virtually unknown until made famous in 1884 by a Sir Arthur Conan Doyle short story, which appears later in this book. He named the ship in his story the *Mary Celeste*. Despite her fame, the *Mary Celeste*'s case is not that unusual. Actually, quite a few ships have been found under similar circumstances, even in modern times. Most of their stories are just as interesting as that of the *Mary Celeste*.

A short, and far from complete, list would include the *Seabird* (1750), the *Rosalie* (1840) the *Hermania* (1849), the *Marathon* (1855), the *James B. Chester* (1857), the *Jenny* (1860), the *Freya* (1902), the *Carroll A. Dearing* (1921), the *John and Mary* (1932), the *Gloria Colite* (1940), the *Rubicon* (1944), the *City Belle* (1946), the *Holchu* (1953), the M.V. *Joyita* (1955), the *Connemara IV* (1955), the *Taignmouth Electron* (1969), the *Ortac* (1976), the *Hawarden Bridge* (1978), the *Sea Lure* (1983), the freighter *Fisah Ketsi* (1990), the M.V. *Hemingway* (2000), the *Tropic Bird* (2001), the *Robert Croll* (2001), the *Sea Life* (2005), and the *Bel Amica* (2006).

High Aim 6

On January 9, 2003, a Taiwanese-registered fishing vessel was found adrift 150 nautical miles off Western Australia. The *High Aim 6*'s two officers and crew of about ten had vanished, while an extensive rescue search turned up nothing. Weather had been fair, the ship was in good condition, and the crew's personal effects were untouched. Hundreds of thousands of dollars worth of fish were rotting in the ship's hold. The tear-off calendar was on January 3rd. The throttle was set to full, but the main fuel tank had run dry so the engine had stopped. The auxiliary tank contained plenty of fuel. There was no sign of foul play, and piracy or mutiny were unlikely since very valuable equipment was still on board. A few reports said there were signs a life raft had been launched, while one news story claimed Indonesian police had captured a man who confessed to being one of the crew, this apparently turned out to be false. No explanation for the mystery was ever found and the *High Aim 6* ended up in a landfill.

Jian Seng

Another derelict was found off Northern Australia in March 24, 2006. The 260-foot tanker *Jian Seng* had been inoperable for some time, though there was no sign the vessel was abandoned in distress. She contained large quantities of rice, leading authorities to believe she was a supply vessel, delivering food and fuel to fishing ships. A tow rope was hanging from the bow and the ship's name and other identifying features had been painted over. The rusted hulk was in poor shape and looked like she had been abandoned for quite some time. The owners and country of origin were never located, so this mystery ship was scuttled in deep water.

S.S. *Baychimo*

The S.S. *Baychimo* is the queen of the derelicts. Built to withstand the treacherous Arctic waters, she was a Hudson's Bay Company cargo steamer used to supply remote outposts in Canada's Northwest Territories and to transport furs purchased from Eskimos. She began her final voyage on July 6, 1931, departing from Vancouver, British Columbia. After sailing for a couple months under the never-setting sun, the crew began the return trip with twenty-one bales of furs in the cargo hold. Then, winter came early.

The *Baychimo* crew's Arctic voyages were always treacherous, with the ship often getting stuck in ice or on shoals, lost in dense fog, or having to retrace their route in the hopes of finding an open passage. Sometimes they even had to use dynamite to blast their way through. They always tried to complete their voyage by the onset of winter, but the winter of 1931 was particularly ferocious. By September, they were trapped by the ice about seventy miles south of Point Barrow, Alaska, and it looked like the ship was going to have to spend the winter there. The Hudson's Bay Company sent two airplanes from Nome 600 miles to retrieve 22 of the office staff and passengers. The planes had to make two trips to get all those who were going.

Captain John Cornwall and sixteen crew members stayed behind to wait for the ship to be released from the ice. Since the ship was under threat of being crushed, they built a wooden shelter on the pack-ice nearby so they wouldn't be forced to suddenly abandon ship in the middle of the night. It was also very cold on the ship. The temperature was around ten degrees below zero and the days were getting short. Soon the sun would disappear altogether and they would begin the endless night of Arctic winter.

On November 24th, they were hit by a blizzard, trapping the men in their hut for three days. When they finally able to emerge, the *Baychimo* was gone. They searched fifteen miles up the coast, but couldn't find her. They thought ice had piled up on her, causing her to sink, but they couldn't find any sign of wreckage. The Baychimo did not sink. On December 3rd, they received a report that an Eskimo seal-hunter had seen their ship about eighteen miles south of Point Barrow and five miles off shore. She had sailed fifty miles north during the gale.

Dog teams were sent and the undamaged furs—along with most everything else of value—were salvaged, but the *Baychimo* was found to have a hole in her side and seemed destined to sink once the ice began to brake up. By the middle of January 1932, the ship had disappeared again. A search by aircraft in February was unable to spot her, so it was assumed she had sunk. The remaining crew headed for home.

It wasn't long before the Vancouver office of the Hudson's Bay Company received reports that the *Baychimo* was still afloat. Eskimos saw the ship hundreds of miles to the east. On March 12, 1932, an explorer/trapper named Leslie Melvin was traveling with his dog team from Herschel Island to Nome when he came across and apparently boarded her. Several months later the ship was boarded again, this time by a group of prospectors.

By March 1933, the *Baychimo* had drifted back to the same area where she was abandoned. Reaching her by kayak, about thirty Eskimos got onboard just as a fierce storm hit, sweeping their boats away and trapping them without food for ten days. Seven died while trying to get ashore. In August, the Hudson's Bay Company heard the ship was moving northward, and the following year in July, a group of explorers boarded her, but were chased off by a storm. These incidents prompted marine historian Ron Armstrong to write, "Some sentimental observers claim these storms to be *Baychimo*'s way of ridding herself of humans and regaining her icy freedom."

Reports continued to come in, and during both September 1935 and November 1939 the *Baychimo* was spotted near Wainwright, Alaska. By March 1962 she was seen drifting northward on pack ice in the Beaufort Sea. Then in 1969, a group of Eskimos found her stuck in pack ice on the Chukchi Sea between Icy Cape and Point Barrow, Alaska. Thirty-eight years after the derelict was abandoned, she was still afloat. Chances are, she now rests under the icy waters of the Arctic Ocean, though she might be stuck on floating pack ice, hidden under snow. It's remotely possible the *Baychimo* is still out there continuing her final voyage, drifting alone on the tides of time.

DEATH SHIPS

Not all derelicts are abandoned or had their crews vanish under mysterious circumstances. A few have been found with their crews still aboard—though everyone was dead.

Ourang Medan

The story of the *Ourang Medan* appears in several books on nautical mysteries, but so far no documentation has been produced. Since part of the story involves a government cover-up, that's not surprising. If the story is true, one would not really expect to find much in the way of documentation. So, perhaps we'll never know whether this really happened.

It's said that in either June 1947 or February 1948 (depending on the source), two ships in the Straits of Malacca between Sumatra and Indonesia (or the eastern edge of the Bay of Bengal in some sources) picked up distress signals from the Dutch cargo ship *Ourang Medan*. One of the signals said, "All officers including captain, dead, lying in chartroom in bridge. Possibly entire crew dead or dying." Then another one said, "I die." Then silence. (The wording of the signals varies, depending on the source.)

It was a windless, calm day. When the ships arrived on the scene, a few hours after the first SOS, they found the *Ourang Medan* in fine condition. But on boarding, they found the entire crew dead (a complete number has never been verified). It was as if they suddenly died in the middle of whatever they were doing. Their eyes were wide open, some had expressions of terror, and some were said to be pointing at the sky. Even the face of the ship's dog was supposedly frozen in a snarl. All were stiff with rigor mortis, except for the radio operator, who may have been the last to die. He was still at his desk with his hand on the radio transmitting key. No one showed any signs of injury or violence. A full investigation could not be conducted because, while being towed back to port, the ship was lifted from the water by a tremendous explosion and then sank.

Some have suggested the ship, which was bound for Djakarta, Indonesia, was secretly and illegally transporting nitroglycerine and potassium cyanide for the Dutch government. If seawater somehow got into the hold, it could create cyanide gas, poisoning the crew, and generate enough heat to cause the nitroglycerine to explode. Since it would be a violation of international law for the Dutch government to be involved with chemical weapons, the incident had to be covered up and all evidence of the *Ourang Medan* erased.

There are others who claim, of course, that the crew was frightened to death by extraterrestrials.

Marlborough

The story of the *Marlborough* is difficult to track down. It has been said that the story was originally reported in Wellington, New Zealand's *Evening Post* on November 13, 1913, and then picked up on November 26, 1913, by the French news agency Agence Havas. However, even though a careful read of that issue of the Wellington *Evening Post* shows no signs of that report, it remains a fascinating tale and one well worth taking a look at.

In October 1913, the *Johnson* was making her way through the Straits of Magellan—the narrow passage between the southern tip of mainland of Chile and the island of Tierra del Fuego—when the crew spied an odd-looking ship. According to the captain, who was supposedly quoted in a 1919 article in the *Glasgow Evening Post*:

> We were off the rocky coves near Punta Arenas, keeping near the land for shelter. The coves are deep and silent, the sailing is difficult and dangerous. It was a weirdly wild evening, with the red orb of the sun setting on the horizon. The stillness was uncanny. There was a shining green light reflected on the jagged rocks on our right. We rounded a point into a deep cleft rock. Before us, a mile or more across the water, stood a vessel, with the barest shreds of canvas fluttering in the breeze.
>
> We signalled and hove to. No answer came. We searched the "stranger" with our glasses. Not a soul could we see; not a movement of any sort. Masts and yards were picked out in green—the green of decay. The vessel lay as if in a cradle. It recalled the *Frozen Pirate*, a novel that I read years ago. I conjured up the vessel of the novel, with her rakish masts and the outline of her six small cannon traced with snow. At last we came up. There was no sign of life on board. After an interval our first mate, with a number of the crew, boarded her. The sight that met their gaze was thrilling. Below the wheel lay the skeleton of a man. Treading warily on the rotten decks, which cracked and broke in places as they walked, they encountered three skeletons in the hatchway. In the mess-room were the remains of ten bodies, and six others were found, one alone, possibly the captain, on the bridge. There was an uncanny stillness around, and a dank smell of mould, which made the flesh creep. A few remnants of books were discovered in the captain's cabin, and a rusty cutlass. Nothing more weird in the history of the sea can ever have been seen. The first mate examined the still faint letters on the bow and after much trouble read 'Marlborough, Glasgow.'

The Phantom Ship 'The Marlborough' *discovered near Cape Horn.*

Finding a ship with a dead crew was not, however, even the most interesting part of this incident. What was truly amazing was that this ship had disappeared without a trace in 1890—she had been drifting around the South Pacific with her crew of skeletons for nearly 24 years!

The *Marlborough* originally set out for England from New Zealand in January of 1890 with a cargo of frozen meat and wool. She had previously made this voyage fourteen times between 1878 and 1889. What happened on her final voyage remains a mystery.

It's thought the *Marlborough* had not long been in the cove when she was discovered. Since her wood was soft with rot, she probably wouldn't have survived the violent storms of Straits of Magellan for long without being dashed upon the rocks. Somehow she had made her way more than a hundred miles into the Straits—a narrow route that is difficult to navigate.

Another part of this story comes from survivors of a shipwreck. On July 23, 1890, the bark *Cordova* wrecked on Tierra del Fuego near Cape Horn. All survived, but they struggled to fight off exposure and starvation. Two of the survivors set off for Good Success Bay, where whaling ships were known to put in. First they found the wreck of a bark named *Godiva*. A few miles farther they came across a ship's boat that read "*Marlborough*, London" across the stern. Nearby was the remains of a tent that had been made from a sail and inside were seven skeletons. The two men moved on and never returned to the spot. They and the other survivors were rescued by the German bark *Banca Mobilirio* and were later questioned by the *Marlborough*'s owners, who concluded, "There is no doubt the gig came from the *Marlborough*."

The *Marlborough* had a crew of 29, plus one passenger. Perhaps seven bodies were found on that shore, and the skeletons of twenty more were found by the *Johnson*'s boarding party, leaving some still unaccounted for. As the captain stated, ten were in the mess-room, three were in a hatchway, five in unspecified locations, Captain W. Herd's skeleton apparently still on the bridge, and finally there was the skeleton they found at the ship's wheel.

All of this ultimately begs the question, did the *Marlborough* really sail the South Seas for almost 24 years with a skeleton at her helm?

The Police Officer's Tale

by Henry Fielding

"I have seen a good many things in my time," said the Police Officer. "Before I came to Burma I was a shoeblack in Auckland, and before that I herded sheep in New South Wales; but the only real adventure that ever happened to me occurred when I was an apprentice on a sailing ship."

"A wreck?" asked the Major.

"No," said the Policeman, "there was no wreck; but we abandoned our ship in mid-ocean and had rather a bad time in open boats till we were picked up. It is not pleasant work navigating the Atlantic in an open boat."

"What made you abandon your ship?" asked the Naval Lieutenant. "Had she sprung a leak, or was it a fire?"

"She was as tight and as firm when we abandoned her as any ship could be," said the Police Officer emphatically. "There was nothing the matter with her alow or aloft, except that which obliged us to leave her."

"I do not understand," said the Lieutenant looking puzzled. "I never heard of a crew abandoning a ship in mid-ocean if she was still tight. Was it mutiny?"

"The captain was a favourite with the crew," said the Police Officer.

The Lieutenant stared. "Was it disease, plague, cholera, yellow fever?"

"No," said the Police Officer, "it was none of those things. In fact it may be said to have been rather an exceptional case. She was a barque belonging to

29

Aberdeen, the *Mary Down*, a wooden ship, one of the last of the old clippers and she had gone to the Mediterranean ports with a cargo of metal and hardware. The last place we touched at was Alexandria and there we filled up with bones for New York."

"Bones?" ejaculated the Cavalry Officer.

"Yes, bones," answered the Police Officer; "they are a very valuable manure, you know. Bones to be ground up into manure, and rags to make paper, these composed a good deal of our cargo. We had a wearisome voyage out of the Mediterranean which is always a tricky place to sail about in. Sometimes we were becalmed, and sometimes we had to take in sail in a desperate hurry when the Levanter came up, so that we were not sorry to pass the Strait and get out into the Atlantic. Two days from Gib we found the Trades and went comfortably bowling along on our course making a good ten knots an hour all day.

"It was the second day out from Gib when I noticed that something was wrong. I was in the second mate's watch, and that night we happened to have the middle watch. The ship was sailing easily upon her course, and there was nothing to do. Presently finding that I had used up my matches I went forward to the forecastle to get a box from my bunk. Coming out I noticed three or four hands clustered together by the shrouds talking earnestly. They stopped, and looked at me rather strangely as I passed. I did not pay much attention and was walking aft lighting my pipe when I felt a touch on the arm: it was Jackson the carpenter, one of the men who had been talking. 'We would like to speak to you a minute, Flisher,' he said.

" 'What's the matter, Jackson?' I asked.

"He did not answer at once and we went back to where the other two men were standing by the shrouds. 'Well?' I asked.

"The three men moved uneasily looking to each other to speak first, but each seeming afraid to do so.

" 'Come,' I said, 'what is it? Have it up.' They looked so serious that I knew it was no little joke that was on.

"Then Jackson, seeing that he was expected to do the talking, took the plug out of his mouth and spitting deliberately over the side, said: 'There's something wrong with this 'ere ship.'

" 'What's wrong?'

"'She ain't no ship for decent Christian men to sail in,' he said sulkily. 'If I'd ha' known when we was at Alexandry I'm damned if I wouldn't have left there. Skippers has no right to ask men to sail in ships with such a cargo as this.'

"I was considerably surprised at this as the ship was a good one. The forecastle was roomy and dry, and the provisions sound and good. The old man, too, was a capital sailor and, though strict, was not a man to worry his crew; neither were the mates. I had been two voyages already on her and never heard a serious complaint, at least one founded on reason. 'I suppose she's too slow for you, Jackson,' I said. 'You ought to sail on a mail-boat.'

"Jackson shook his head. 'It ain't that she's a bit slow,' he replied. 'She's fast enough for me. Nor 'ave we any complaint against the grog or the old man or the mates. They ain't so bad as times go. No,' and he shook his head still more decidedly; 'it ain't that at all.'

"'What is it, then?' I asked, a bit angry. 'You aren't afraid to speak of it, are you?'

"'No,' said Jackson slowly; 'I aren't afraid.' Then he paused and spat again meditatively over the bulwark. 'You aren't seen anythink unusual on this ship, 'ave you, Flisher?'

"I hadn't the faintest idea what the man was driving at. 'Unusual,' I answered, 'no, bar a rat or two, and they can't be unusual, I think.'

"'Ah,' he said with a tone of conviction; 'well, we 'ave.'

"His tone roused my curiosity. 'What is it, Jackson? What's wrong? Better tell me.'

"'Ghosts,' said Jackson thickly and glancing apprehensively round, 'ghosts;' and the other men nodded.

"I laughed. The idea of ghosts appeared to me mere childishness. Here were four great hulking men looking as fearful as children.

"'Oh yes,' growled Jackson, 'you laughs. They don't come aft likely.'

"He spoke so savagely that I stopped. 'What are the ghosts like, Jackson?' I asked. 'Do you mean to say that you've seen them?'

"Jackson nodded. 'Aye, I've seen 'em; we've all seen 'em. Tell him what like they are, Christiansen.'

"The man spoken to was a Dane, a tall, scrambling fair-haired Dane with a weak and wandering blue eye. He was usually the butt of the crew, and it surprised me to hear him appealed to.

"'Dead men,' answered Christiansen sepulchrally, 'dead men's ghosts. Dere bones are down dere,' and he tapped his feet on the deck, 'but dere spirits, dey are here.' He stopped and looked up into the great mass of white sails that swelled above us. 'De men of all the nations that have fought and died—ah!'

"He gave a nod forward with his head and even in the dusk I saw his eyes distend. We all started and looked across the deck to where Christiansen was looking. It was a clear starlight night and the outline of everything was plain to see; I could even make out from where I stood the break of the poop and the outline of the rail against the sky. I could see nothing unusual and turned again to my companions. They were all bent forward with fearful faces, glaring over the forehatch to the weather-side opposite us. I followed their glances, and again at first I saw nothing, but suddenly I thought that something was moving there. I could not make it out, but there seemed to me two or more figures moving down under the shadow of the bulwarks.

"I ran forward at once to that side but when I came to where they had been they were gone. Near by was the caboose and the carpenter's shop, but the doors of both were closed. I looked up and down but could see nothing.

"'It's one of the boys fooling,' I said coming back to Jackson, who had not moved.

"'No it ain't,' said Jackson. 'That ain't no boy; it's a ghost. This place and the fo'ksel is just full of 'em.'

"I confess that it gave me a bit of a turn this sudden disappearance of the figures, but I pretended to laugh. 'They are harmless enough anyhow,' I said. 'Your great lump of flesh isn't afraid of the shadows like that, Jackson? I wouldn't tell the old man, if I were you, that you funked the shadow of the main staysail.'

"'Look 'ere, Flisher,' said Jackson; 'we've just told you about this because you, being better eddycated than us, we thought you might have some explanation. We did not tell it for you young shaver to laugh at us and say we're afraid. Never you mind if we're afraid or no. These figures, and more figures than them, has been going up and down the decks ever since we left Alexandry. Christiansen seed 'em first, but now we've all seen 'em. We ax you, as one who's been to school and brought up as a gentleman, if you can explain 'em.'

"I was impressed with the earnestness of the men, and perhaps a little flattered at their consulting me. 'No, I can't,' I said. 'I do not believe in ghosts.'

"'Ah,' said Jackson, 'that's wot they teaches you boys now, is it? Not to believe in ghosts? Well, we sailor-men believe in 'em because we sees 'em. Ay, and we knows the reason too, don't we?'

"Christiansen and the other men grunted an assent. 'It's de bones,' said Christiansen again pointing down the deck.

"'Bones,' I exclaimed. 'Yes, you said that before. What the devil do you mean?'

"'Ay, bones,' said Jackson; 'them bones as we took aboard at Alexandry. They was in bags, but we knew well enough. Some of the bags bust as they came aboard and we seed the bones. They was men's bones, skulls and things; we seed 'em.'

"'Ah, we seed 'em,' said Christiansen grimly. 'It was gut to put dem in de bags, but ven de bag broke, den ve see.'

"My blood ran cold at the idea. I had seen the bags loaded, and had in fact helped to tally them, but none broke that I saw. 'Are you sure?' I asked. 'Were they really men's bones?' None of the four sailors condescended to reply and there was a pause. We stood there and looked at each other.

"'Dere's been a many battle dere in Egypt,' explained Christiansen presently, 'ever since ole Pharaoh's time. Dere's been a many men killed. Dese are de bones. Dere are de skulls and arm and leg bones and all de oder bones down dere. And de spirits, dey are here.'

"He spoke funereally. Overhead the cordage creaked softly as the ship swayed to the breeze, and there came from forward the soft crash of the bows into the seas. 'Look here, I must be off,' I said suddenly, 'or the mate will curse me. Damn your ghosts!' and with that I turned and went aft.

"I crept softly up the gangway to the poop and looked round to see if the mate had missed me. For a moment I did not see him, then as I came past the cabin skylight I suddenly discovered that the skipper was on deck. He and the mate were talking abaft the wheel.

"When the mate saw me he called out to me, 'Flisher.'

"'Yes, sir,' I answered.

"'Come here.'

"'Look here, Flisher,' said the skipper, 'what's all this damned nonsense the hands have got hold of about ghosts? The steward is scared out of his senses.'

"'I do not know, sir,' I answered. 'The men have just been telling me that there are some ghosts about.'

"'You haven't seen any, Flisher?' and he looked at me curiously.

"I thought for a moment of the shadows, and then answered, 'No, sir.'

"The skipper nodded and went forward with the mate, and I to leeward again. The steersman was motionless at the wheel and the ship surged steadily forward on her way. There came a rustle and a mutter from aloft as the wind pressed into the sails and the stars danced between the ropes.

"The next day there was no more concealment about it. It was known all over the ship that the forecastle was haunted by ghosts who passed to and fro all the night. It was Hans Christiansen who had first seen them, but by this time there was no one of the crew who had not encountered at least a dozen ghosts. All sorts of tales were current as to their appearance and shape and the stories grew in horror as the day went on. At six bells, as the sun was sinking into a gorgeous sunset far ahead, the crew came aft in a body and complained to the skipper.

"'Ghosts,' said the old man scornfully when he heard what they had to say, 'ghosts! Who's seen the ghosts?'

"There was a moment's pause among the men and then a sort of grumble. 'We've all seen 'em,' said Jackson who was acting as spokesman for the crew.

"'Ah,' said the skipper, 'you've all seen 'em? And what like are these ghosts that you've all seen? Spirits more like,' he sneered. 'You all drunk enough at Alexandry; a touch of D. T., my men. Now, Jackson, what like was the ghosts you seed?'

"Jackson rubbed his head a little confusedly. 'Well, sir,' he said at length, 'I dunno as I seed much. There was something ghost-like I seed pass the deck at night once or twice; but what like it was I don't know. It made me skeered though,' he added reflectively.

"'They's the spirits of the dead men whose bones are below,' drawled a voice from the crowd, and there followed a hoarse murmur of 'Ay, ay.'

"'Dead men below?' asked the skipper in surprise.

"'Them bones, sir, as was loaded at Alexandry,' explained Jackson. 'They say as how they're no bones of beasts but just bones of dead men, skulls and things.'

"'Say!' roared the skipper. 'Who says that? Who says I've made my ship a damned dead-house? Where's the man? I'd like to see him.'

"The crew looked at each other questioningly. Who was it who had seen them? No one came forward.

"'Now,' shouted the skipper, 'I'm a waiting. Where's the lubber?'

"Still no one moved.

"'Where are the mates?' said the skipper, turning furiously to find them both at his elbow. 'You loaded these 'ere bones; did you see anything?'

"The mates shook their heads. 'A bag broke,' said the second mate, 'but there weren't any men's bones in that. I don't believe there are any at all. It's just a lie, sir, a lie to scare the men from their work.'

"'Ay,' roared the skipper, 'and I'll find the blackguard too! I'll ghost him! I'll teach him to say I've got a damned old graveyard on my ship! Ah—'

"He stopped suddenly as Christiansen half walked, was half jostled forward. 'What have you to say, you milk-faced curd-headed son of a Dutchman? Did you see the bones?'

"'Ya,' answered Christiansen, his light blue eyes wandering nervously from the skipper to the mates and from the mates to the topsail. 'I did the skulls see. Ya, dey are dere,' and he pointed forward. 'Mein Gott, yes! I have seed dem.'

"The skipper's rage cooled before this vacillating light-haired Dane with the expressionless face. He stared at him a moment in contempt. 'Oh,' he sneered, 'it was you, was it, who saw the skulls?' Christiansen did not answer. 'Perhaps it was you too who saw the ghosts?'

"Christiansen looked about as if meditating a retreat, but the men behind would not let him pass. 'Speak up, Christiansen,' they said. 'You saw 'em; tell the skipper.'

"'You were afraid to be alone in the dark, I suppose,' said the skipper scathingly, 'you cur-hearted school-miss. What did you see, you damned long-shore loafer? Are you afraid to speak?'

"'I saw the ghosts,' explained Christiansen briefly, 'de ghosts of de men that is dead. Dey haf all seen dem,' and he waved his hand to the crew, 'but I seed dem de first. I was alvays gut at seeing the ghosts.'

"A sort of half-concealed pride could be seen in his face, which roused the skipper's rage again to red-heat.

"'And you believe this Dutchman and his damned lies, you men? You chicken-hearted fools. I'll—' then he suddenly stopped. 'Open the fore-hatch,' he said to the mate.

"The men went forward in a body headed by the mate, and the tarpaulins were removed from the hatch. In a few minutes, the men working very unwillingly, the hatch was open. Down below in the obscurity could be seen the bags in tiers and layers as they had been loaded by the stevedores. Here and there in the dark gleamed a white bone and a strange charnel-house smell came up from below. The men stood round and looked suspi-ciously and timorously into the hatch.

"'Fetch up a bag,' said the skipper to the mate. But none of the men would go, and finally with a curse I was ordered to go down. I went and slung six bags into a noose, which were drawn up.

"'Now,' said the skipper as the bags dropped on deck with a rattle, 'open them bags and let's see Christiansen's skulls.'

"With a draw of his knife the second mate cut the lashing of a bag; he held up the end and the bones fell out. There was a skurry as the men fell back in terror towards the forecastle, their faces blanched and their eyes starting; for out of the bag amid a quantity of bones bleached with age rolled a human skull. Slowly it rolled along the deck turning its eye-sockets this way and that while we all regarded it with horror. Then as the ship lurched it gave a quick movement and stopped just at the feet of Christiansen.

"There was a dead silence. Then Christiansen, who of all present seemed the only one neither frightened nor astonished, stooped and picked up the skull. He raised it carefully in his hands and peered into the empty eyeholes, turning it round and round almost as if with pleasure at seeing a friend. 'Ya,' he said meditating; 'see de large skull of de dead man.' With his finger he traced a mark upon the forehead regretfully. 'Dey cut him dere and he died. Poor fellow!' Then lifting up his eyes he went on in his curious singsong. 'He is de tall soldier dat I seed last night with the great cut upon his face where de blood poured out. He was near the cuddy door; he was cursing dem dat brought his bones out over de sea.'

"To say that the men listened to him in horror would hardly express their state. They were paralysed with fear. I felt afraid myself when I heard the man talking thus to the poor white nameless skull, and even the captain had remained motionless, but as the Dane stopped he suddenly recovered command of himself and stepping forward he struck Christiansen down. The skull rolled out of his hands, and the skipper picked it up and chucked it overboard contemptuously. Then with an oath he turned to his bewildered crew. 'You white-livered lot of curs, you,' he snarled; 'you let a Dane funk you with an old skull. Suppose there is a skull or two aboard, what does it signify? I ain't afraid o' any man alive nor dead either. As to ghosts, that's all his woman's folly,' and he kicked contemptuously the recumbent form of the ghost-seer. 'There ain't no such things. The next man as sees a ghost goes into irons; you know me.' Then he turned on his heel and went aft.

"For a day or two nothing more happened. The crew went about their work all day with sullen faces and during the night watches they clustered together by the forecastle-head and cursed. Christiansen was in his bunk, for the skipper was a strongish chap and he had let Christiansen have it for all he was worth. The skipper was cheerful. 'Ghosts,' he said to the mate with a laugh; 'you try a hand-spike on the next man who sees a ghost. A bishop with bell and candle don't come up to a marlin-spike in ghost-driving.'

"But the mate was not so happy; he was superstitious as are all seamen. 'Flisher,' he said to me, 'have you seen any of these ghosts?' I told him about the shadows under the forecastle and he shook his head. 'What were they like?' he asked. I could not say; indeed I doubted if I had really seen anything at all. It was that fellow Christiansen; to hear him talk gave one the creeps, and when he said 'Look,' I was ready to believe anything. But I did not really believe in ghosts, I said.

"'Ah,' said the mate, 'but there is ghosts of course, Flisher. I don't say that I've ever seen them, but lots of my people have. My mother saw a ghost once, a little man in white. Then there's Bible warrant for it too. You remember that witch of Endor? You don't deny the Bible?'

"I could not do that, I said, but may be there was good religious reason for those ghosts; that time's past now.

"'And don't you call it reason for these ghosts that we're taking their bones across sea to be manure to tobacco-gardens?' he answered. 'No, no, Flisher, my boy, there's ghosts right enough.'

"I could see that the mate thoroughly believed in the ghosts. As to the men their nerves were stretched to breaking. You could not drop a marlin-spike behind a man without his jumping round with a scared white face on you. And one night, when we were taking in the main-top-gallant sail, the man next me nearly fell off the yard swearing a ghost had touched his face; I had to help him back to the top. When they had nothing to do on deck they collected in little groups and told ghost-stories. All the old ghosts of the sea were resurrected and told of with fear and trembling. The men became possessed, as it were, with ghost-mania.

"On the third or fourth night the breeze suddenly fell. The sky had been overcast all day, and the sun set behind a great purple bank of cloud that hung low upon the horizon. The breeze fell till the sea was one glassy sheet that rolled in league-long undulations from horizon to horizon. The night was hot and close like a crowded room. Now and then a great drop of rain fell heavily upon the deck, and far down in the south the lightning played fitfully, lighting up the broken masses of cloud with sudden vividness. It was a night that unstrung your nerves and made you unhappy and afraid.

"I could hear a man (Williams the cook, I think) telling a ghost story in low and stricken tones to the men. I did not listen much because my nerves were already as tense as I could bear, but in the deadly stillness of the night his words drifted every now and then across to me. He was telling again the old story of the saving of the great ship's company.

"'*Steer Nor'-Nor'-West.* Who had written it upon the slate? The mate rubbed it out but when he came back an hour later to enter upon his log, it was there again: *Steer Nor'-Nor'-West.* The mate rubbed it out a second time and sat down in the dark cuddy to catch the man who wrote it, the man who was playing a joke upon him. As he sat waiting, suddenly a shadowy figure appeared. Whence he came or how the mate could not say, but he was there, writing on the slate; the mate heard the chalk creak. With a bound he was up catching at the man, and finding—nothing! Before him was the empty companion and behind him the empty cuddy, and on the slate were the words again, *Steer Nor'-Nor'-West.*'

"I had heard the story before, and did not care to hear it again. I turned away and looked out at the sea, black as death save where the fitful lightning broke. It was coming nearer and nearer; in the darkness between the flashes the heavens

seemed to press right down upon the ship; faint moans, as of dying men came
from far away.

"The lad had finished his story and the men sat silently brooding upon it.
No one spoke. The creaking of the cordage, as the ship rolled, made the silence
even more notice-able. Suddenly I heard a voice low and dreamy come out of the
dark close by me. 'Spirits of de dead men,' it moaned, 'spirits of de dead men.'
It brought the heart into my mouth, and I turned abruptly. Very dimly I could
make out a figure lying on the break of the forecastle peering over into the main
deck. It seemed to be gazing at something.

"'I see dem, the dead men,' it moaned on. 'Dey come up in tens and twenties;
dey are dere below. Dey have red coats and blue coats, dose dead soldiers of the
wars. Deir faces are bloody with sword-cuts, and dere are holes in dere bodies
whence the blood oozes out. Dey look at me mit deir dead eyes.' A cold horror
had fallen upon us as Christiansen spoke. My limbs were numbed, and in my ears
were strange throbbings. From some inexplicable attraction I crept nearer to the
Dane and I found the crew doing the same. No one spoke, or looked except at
Christiansen. We became packed as a flock of sheep.

"'Dere are more and more,' he went on, still in that strange moaning voice.
'De deck is full of dem. Dere are men with black faces and white eyeballs which
glare at me. De deck is full of dem; dey throng upon each other.'

"In the pause I heard two bells strike from aft, the sound coming to me as
out of a dream. The man next me had caught my arm in a grip that numbed it,
but I hardly noticed. The lightning flashed nearer, and in the glare the men's
faces, tense and agonised, shone out with a deadly paleness. My temples were
bursting.

"'Dey come up and up; dere are many thousands of dem now. Dey cluster in
de rigging. Dere are many dead sailors of de great wars there.'

"He now raised himself from his recumbent position and half stood up leaning
upon the rail.

'Dey come more and more.' He looked away out to sea. 'Dey are passing
upon de waters. Dey drive their chariots upon de sea.'

"He rose to his feet, and there was a movement among the men. It was evident
their nerves were strung to breaking-point; now and then one gasped as if in agony.

"'Dey gallop upon the sea. Dey are all dere, de old Pharaoh and his men that died so long ago. Dey look at us with angry eyes as they pass.'

"There was a flicker of phosphorus in a passing wave, glinting as if struck up by horses' hoofs. Here and there across that dark deadly plain there suddenly flashed other phosphorescent gleams. It seemed as if dim forms passed to and fro; I could see them. 'My God!' muttered a man next to me. I would have given worlds to have shouted, to have screamed, but I was held as in a spell.

"Christiansen was standing now leaning over the rail. His arms waved as he spoke, and his voice had become faster and more guttural. 'Dey shake deir heads at me; dey threaten!' he cried. 'Dey say, "why have you taken our bones from deir graves?" Dere is hatred in deir eyes.'

"He was holding now by a foretop-stay; a flash of lightning showed him clearly, glaring down at the sea. 'Do not look so at me,' he cried; 'it was not me! What have I done, den? Mein Gott, to see deir eyes!' He began to gesticulate wildly to the sea. 'Go,' he shrieked, 'go! Dey tear me down!' He planted his feet against the butts in fierce resistance, while the lightning played more and more brightly. His shrieks became wilder and more horrible. 'De dead men take me! Ah, ah, ah!' he screamed, his voice passing far across the sea in unutterable agony. The darkness came down now dense as a veil and we could see no more. We were frozen to stone, while within a hand's grasp of us Christiansen fought with unseen foes. He stamped upon the deck; we heard the groans and panting of the fight. And then the darkness was suddenly lifted again. From the vault above a violet light, ghastly and cold, shone out in unendurable brilliance repeated in throbbing waves of radiance. It showed the ship clear to the trucks, every rope and spar cut in black against the fire; it showed the decks below us, and the sea black and smooth as though cast in black marble, and the stricken faces of the men. And by the rail stood Christiansen, every nerve and muscle strained, his feet braced, his hands gripping fiercely at the stays. He was the central figure, and ere the light had failed, in a moment of time, we saw him drawn from his hold. His feet slipped, his hands were forced from their grip. With one piercing cry of agony he fell before our eyes into the sea.

"Then the night shut down once more, and there burst a roar of thunder as if the universe had broken up. The spell had passed. With inarticulate cries of fear we leapt to our feet and fled. Hither and thither we ran, blinded in a paroxysm of maddening fear. We fell, and picked ourselves up, and fell again. Men met and wrestled and parted; their faces streamed with blood, their breath came hot and quick; till at last in an excess of frenzy they burst suddenly down upon the main-deck and rushed aft for the quarter-boats.

"The first mate, who was on watch, and the skipper hearing the rush of men tried to face them. They were overborne and flung senseless to the deck. With feverish haste the quarter-boats were dropped from the davits and the men fell in. Then without food or water, without compass or chart, they set to work to row away from the ship, bending to their oars like demons.

"All night they rowed. The lightning flashed and the rain poured down, but the men never stopped. They did not look anywhere; their eyes were held to their labouring hands, and thus they did not notice behind them a red glare that rose gradually upon the sky, a glare that was not of the lightning for it was steady. But as the boats increased their distance it fell and fell, until at last the horizon hid it.

"We were picked up two days later, the men exhausted and almost dead. The skipper and the mates were also picked up by another ship. That last flash of lightning had set the *Mary Down* on fire, and the skipper and first mate being disabled the second mate could not put it out single-handed; but they had managed somehow between them to launch the remaining boat in time.

"The *Mary Down* was burnt to the water's edge and then sank. She lies now a thousand fathoms deep beneath the Atlantic and let us hope that the bones have peace at last. They deserve it."

THE SPECTER SHIP

BY JOHN GREENLEAF WHITTIER

The Legend of the Spectre Ship of Salem is still preserved among some of the old descendants of the Puritans. A particular description of the pretenatural visitation is given in Magnalia Christi Americana**. The story is that a ship, which left Salem sometime during the 17th century for "old England," contained, among other passengers, a young man of a strange and wild appearance, and a girl, still younger, and of surpassing beauty. She was deadly pale, and trembled, even while she leaned on the arm of her companion. No one knew them— they spoke not—they paid no regard to anything around them. This excited the alarm of some of the credulous people of the place, who supposed them to be demons: and who, in consequence, endeavored to dissuade their friends from entering the ship—notwithstanding which, a goodly number went on board. The remainder of the story is told in the following lines.*

*—*AUTHOR

*By Cotton Mather, published in 1702.

The morning light is breaking forth
  All over the dark blue sea—
And the waves are changed—they are rich with gold
  As the morning waves should be,
And the rising winds are wandering out
  On their seaward pinions free.
The bark is ready—the sails are set,
  And the boat rocks on the shore—
Say why do the passengers linger yet?—
  Is not the farewell o'er?
Do those who enter that gallant ship
  Go forth to return no more?"

A wailing rose by the water-side,
  A young, fair girl was there—
With a face as pale as the face of Death
  When its coffin-lid is bare;—
And an eye as strangely beautiful
  As a star in the upper air.
She leaned on a youthful stranger's arm,
  A tall and silent one—
Who stood in the very midst of the crowd,
  Yet uttered a word to none;
He gazed on the sea and the waiting ship—
  But he gazed on them alone!
The fair girl leaned on the stranger's arm,
  And she wept as one in fear,
But he heeded not the plaintive moan
  And the dropping of the tear;—
His eye was fixed on the stirring sea,
  Cold, darkly and severe!
The boat was filled—the shore was left—
  The farewell word was said—

But the vast crowd lingered still behind
    With an over-powering dread;

They feared that stranger and his bride,
    So pale and like the dead.
And many said that an evil pair
    Among their friends had gone,—
A demon with his human prey,
    From the quiet grave-yard drawn;
And a prayer was heard that the innocent
    Might escape the Evil One.
Away—the good ship sped away,
    Out on the broad high seas—
The sun upon her path before—
    Behind, the steady breeze—
And there was naught in sea or sky
    Of fearful auguries.
The day passed on—the sunlight fell
    All slantwise from the west,
And then the heavy clouds of storm
    Sat on the ocean's breast;
And every swelling billow mourn'd
    Like a living thing distressed.
The sun went down among the clouds,
    Tinging with sudden gold,

The pall-like shadow of the storm,
    On every mighty fold—
And then the lightning's eye look'd forth,
    And the red thunder rolled.
The storm came down upon the sea,
    In its surpassing dread,

Rousing the white and broken surge
    Above its rocky bed,
As if the deep was stirred beneath
    A giant's viewless tread.
All night the hurricane went on.
    And all along the shore,
The smothered cry of shipwreck'd men
    Blent with the ocean's roar;—
The grey-haired man had scarcely known
    So wild a night before.
Morn rose upon a tossing sea,
    The tempest's work was done,
And freely over land and wave,
    Shone out the blessed sun—
But where was she—that merchant-bark—
    Where had the good ship gone?

Men gathered on the shore to watch
    The billow's heavy swell,
Hoping, yet fearing much, some frail
    Memorial might tell
The fate of that disastrous ship,—
    Of friends they loved so well.
None came—the billows smoothed away—
    And all was strangely calm,
As if the very sea had felt
    A necromancer's charm;
And not a trace was left behind,
    Of violence and harm.
The twilight came with sky of gold—
    And curtaining of night—
And then a sudden cry rang out,
    "A ship—the ship in sight!"

And lo!—tall masts grew visible
    Within the fading light.
Near and more near the ship came on,
    With all her broad sails spread—
The night grew thick, but a phantom light
    Around her path was shed,

And the gazers shuddered as on she came,
    For against the wind she sped.
They saw by the dim and baleful glare
    Around that voyager thrown,
The upright forms of the well known crew,
    As pale and fixed as stone—
And they called to them, but no sound came back,
    Save the echoed cry alone.
The fearful stranger-youth was there,
    And clasped in his embrace,
The pale and passing sorrowful
    Gazed wildly in his face;—
Like one who had been wakened from
    The silent burial-place.
A shudder ran along the crowd—
    And a holy man knelt there,
On the wet sea-sand, and offered up
    A faint and trembling prayer,
That God would shield his people from
    The Spirits of the air!
And lo!—the vision passed away—
    The Spectre Ship—the crew—

The stranger and his pallid bride,
    Departed from their view;
And nought was left upon the waves
    Beneath the arching blue.
It passed away—that vision strange—
    Forever from their sight,—
Yet, long shall Naumkeag's annals tell
    The story of that night—
The phantom-bark—the ghostly crew—
    The pale, encircling light.

The Ship Seen on the Ice

by W. Clark Russell

In the middle of April, in the year 1855, the three-masted schooner *Lightning* sailed from the Mersey for Boston with a small general cargo of English manufactured goods. She was commanded by a man named Thomas Funnel. The mate, Salamon Sweers, was of Dutch extraction, and his broad-beamed face was as Dutch to the eye as was the sound of his name to the ear. Yet he spoke English with as good an accent as ever one could hear in the mouth of an Englishman; and, indeed, I pay Salamon Sweers no compliment by saying this, for he employed his *h*'s correctly, and the grammar of his sentences was fairly good, albeit salt: and how many Englishmen are there who correctly employ the letter *h*, and whose grammar is fairly good, salt or no salt?

We carried four forecastle hands and three apprentices. There was Charles Petersen, a Swede, who had once been "fancy man" in a toy shop; there was David Burton, who had been a hairdresser and proved unfortunate as a gold-digger in Australia; there was James Lussoni, an Italian, who claimed to be a descendant of the old Genoese merchants; and there was John Jones, a runaway man-of-warsman, pretty nearly worn out, and subject to apoplexy.

Four sailors and three apprentices make seven men, a cook and a boy are nine, and a mate and a captain make eleven; and eleven of a crew were we, all told, men and boy, aboard the three-masted schooner *Lightning* when we sailed away one April morning out of the river Mersey, bound to Boston, North America.

My name was then as it still is—for during the many years I have used the sea, never had I occasion to ship with a "purser's name"—my name, I say, is David Kerry, and in that year of God 1855 I was a strapping young fellow, seventeen years old, making a second voyage with Captain Funnel, having been bound apprentice to that most excellent but long-departed mariner by my parents, who, finding me resolved to go to sea had determined that my probation should be thorough: no half-laughs and pursers' grins would satisfy them; my arm was to plunge deep into the tar bucket straight away; and certainly there was no man then hailing from the port of Liverpool better able to qualify a young chap for the profession of the sea—but a young chap, mind you, who liked his calling, who meant to be a man and not a "sojer" in it—than Captain Funnel of the schooner *Lightning*.

The four sailors slept in a bit of a forecastle forward; we three apprentices slung our hammocks in a bulkheaded part of the run or steerage, a gloomy hole, the obscurity of which was defined rather than illuminated by the dim twilight sifting down aslant from the hatch. Here we stowed our chests, and here we took our meals, and here we slept and smoked and yarned in our watch below. I very well remember my two fellow apprentices. One was named Corbin, and the other Halsted. They were both of them smart, honest, bright lads, coming well equipped and well educated from respectable homes, in love with the calling of the sea, and resolved in time not only to command ships, but to own them.

Well, nothing in any way noteworthy happened for many days. Though the schooner was called the *Lightning*, she was by no means a clipper. She was built on lines which were fashionable forty years before, when the shipwright held that a ship's stability must be risked if she was one inch longer than five times her beam. She was an old vessel, but dry as a stale cheese; wallowed rather than rolled, yet was stiff; would sit upright with erect spars, like the cocked ears of a horse, in breezes which bowed passing vessels down to their wash-streaks. Her round bows bruised the sea, and when it entered her head to take to her heels, she would wash through it like a "gallied whale," all smothered to the hawse-pipes, and a big round polished hump of brine on either quarter.

We ambled, and wallowed, and blew, and in divers fashions drove along till we were deep in the heart of the North Atlantic. It was then a morning that brought the first of May within a biscuit-toss of our reckoning of time: a very cold morning, the sea flat, green, and greasy, with a streaking of white about it, as though it were a flooring of marble; there was wind but no lift in the water; and Salamon Sweers, in whose watch I was, said to me, when the day broke and showed us the look of the ocean:

"Blowed," said he, "if a man mightn't swear that we were under the lee of a range of high land."

It was very cold, the wind about north-west, the sky a pale grey, with patches of weak hazy blue in it here and there; and here and there again lay some darker shadow of cloud curled clean as though painted. There was nothing in sight saving the topmost cloths of a little barque heading eastwards away down to leeward. Quiet as the morning was, not once during the passage had I found the temperature so cold. I was glad when the job of washing down was over, and not a little grateful for the hook-pot of steam tea which I took from the galley to my quarters in the steerage.

I breakfasted in true ocean fashion, off ship's biscuit, a piece of pork, the remains of yesterday's dinner, and a potful of black liquor called tea, sweetened by molasses and thickened with sodden leaves and fragments of twigs; and then, cutting a pipeful of tobacco from a stick of cavendish, I climbed into my hammock, and lay there smoking and trying to read in Norie's *Epitome* until my pipe went out, on which I fell asleep.

I was awakened by young Halsted, whose hand was upon the edge of my hammock.

"Not time to turn out yet, I hope?" I exclaimed. "I don't feel to have been below ten minutes."

"There's the finest sight to see on deck," said he, "that you're likely to turn up this side of Boston. Tumble up and have a look if only for five minutes"; and without another word he hastened up the ladder.

I dropped out of my hammock, pulled on my boots and monkey-jacket, and went on deck, noting the hour by the cabin clock to be twenty minutes before eleven. The captain stood at the mizzen-rigging with a telescope at his eye, and beside him stood Mr. Sweers, likewise holding a glass, and both men pointed their telescopes towards the sea on the lee bow, where—never having before beheld an iceberg—I perceived what I imagined to be an island covered with snow.

An iceberg it was—not a very large one. It was about five miles distant; it had a ragged sky line which made it resemble a piece of cliff gone adrift—such a fragment of cliff as, let me say, a quarter of a mile of the chalk of the South Foreland would make, if you can imagine a mass of the stuff detaching itself from under the verdure at the top and floating off jagged and precipitous. There was nothing to be seen but that iceberg. No others. The sea ran smooth as oil, and of a hard green, piebald foam lines as in the earlier morning, with but a light swell out of the west, which came lifting stealthily to the side of the schooner. There was a small breeze; the sky had a somewhat gloomy look; the schooner was at this hour crawling along at the rate of about four and a half knots.

I said to Halsted: "There was nothing in sight when I went below at eight bells. Where's that berg come from?"

"From behind the horizon," he answered. "The breeze freshened soon after you left the deck, and only slackened a little while since."

"What can they see to keep them staring so hard?" said I, referring to the captain and Mr. Sweers, who kept their glasses steadily levelled at the iceberg.

"They've made out a ship upon the ice," he answered; "a ship high and dry upon a slope of foreshore. I believe I can see her now—the gleam of the snow is confusing; there's a black spot at the base almost amidships of the berg."

I had a good sight in those days. I peered awhile and made out the object, but with the naked eye I could never have distinguished it as a ship at that distance.

"She's a barque," I heard Mr. Sweers say.

"I see that," said the captain.

"She's got a pretty strong list," continued the mate, talking with the glass at his eye; "her topgallantmasts are struck, but her topmasts are standing."

"I tell you what it is," said the captain, after a pause, likewise speaking whilst he gazed through his telescope, "that ship's come down somewhere from out of the North Pole. She never could have struck the ice and gone ashore as we see her there. She's been locked up; then the piece she's on broke away and made sail to the south. I've fallen in with bergs with live polar bears on them in my time."

"What is she—a whaler?" said Mr. Sweers. "She's got a lumbersome look about the bulwarks, as though she wasn't short of cranes; but I can't make out any boats, and there's no appearance of life aboard her."

"Let her go off a point," said the captain to the fellow at the wheel. "Mr. Sweers, she'll be worth looking at," he continued, slowly directing his gaze round the sea-line, as though considering the weather. "You've heard of Sir John Franklin?"

"Have I heard?" said the mate, with a Dutch shrug.

"It's the duty of every English sailor," said the captain, "to keep his weather eye lifting whenever he smells ice north of the equator; for who's to tell what relics of the Franklin expedition he may not light on? And how are we to know," continued he, again directing his glass at the berg, "that yonder vessel may not have taken part in that expedition?"

"There's a reward going," said Mr. Sweers, "for the man who can discover anything about Sir John Franklin and his party."

The captain grinned and quickly grew grave.

We drew slowly towards the iceberg, at which I gazed with some degree of disappointment; for, never before having beheld ice in a great mass like the heap that was yonder, I had expected to see something admirable and magnificent, an island of glass, full of fiery sparklings and ruby and emerald beams, a shape of crystal cut by the hand of King Frost into a hundred inimitable devices. Instead of which, the island of ice, on which lay the hull of the ship, was of a dead, unpolished whiteness, abrupt at the extremities, about a hundred and twenty feet tall at its loftiest point, not more picturesque than a rock covered with snow, and interesting only to my mind because of the distance it had measured, and because of the fancies it raised in one of the white, silent, and stirless principalities from which it had floated into these parts.

"Get the jolly-boat over, Mr. Sweers," said the captain, "and take a hand with you, and go and have a look at that craft there; and if you can board her, do so, and bring away her log-book, if you come across it. The newspapers sha'n't say that I fell in with such an object as that and passed on without taking any notice."

I caught Mr. Sweers' eye. "You'll do," said he, and in a few minutes he and I were pulling away in the direction of the ice, I in the bow and he aft, rowing fisherman fashion, face forward. The schooner had backed her yards on the fore when she was within a mile of the berg, and we had not far to row. Our four arms made the fat little jolly-boat buzz over the wrinkled surface of the green, cold water. The wreck—if a wreck she could be called—lay with her decks sloping seawards upon an inclined shelf or beach of ice, with a mass of rugged, abrupt stuff behind her, and vast coagulated lumps heaped like a Stonehenge at her bows and at her stern. When we approached the beach, as I may term it, Salamon Sweers said:

"I'll tell you what: I am not going to board that craft alone, Kerry. Who's to tell what's inside of her? She may have been lying twenty years, for all we know, frozen up where it's always day or always night—where everything's out of the order of nature, in fact; and rat me if I'm going to be the first man to enter her cabin."

"I'm along with you," said I.

"So you are, David," said he, "and we'll overhaul her together, and the best way to secure the boat'll be to drag her high and dry"; and as he said this, the stem of the boat touched the ice, and we both of us jumped out, and, catching hold of her by the gunwale, walked her up the slope by some five times her own length, where she lay as snug as though chocked aboard her own mother, the schooner.

Sweers and I stood, first of all, to take a view of the barque—for a barque she was: her topgallantmasts down, but her topsail and lower yards across, sails bent, all gear rove, and everything right so far as we could see, saving that her flying jib-boom was gone. There was no need to look long at her to know that she hadn't been one of Franklin's ships. Her name and the place she hailed from were on her stern: the *President*, New Bedford. And now it was easy to see that she was a Yankee whaler. Her sides bristled with cranes or davits for boats, but every boat was gone. The tackles were overhauled, and the blocks of two of them lay upon the ice. She was a stout, massive, round-bowed structure, to all appearances as sound as on the day when she was launched. She was coppered; not a sheet of metal was off, not a rent anywhere visible through the length and breadth of the dingy green surface of it.

We first of all walked round her, not knowing but that on the other side, concealed from the landing-place by the interposition of the hull, some remains of her people might be lying; but there was nothing in that way to see. We united our voices in a loud "Hallo!" and the rocks re-echoed us; but all was still, frozen, lifeless.

"Let's get aboard," said Mr. Sweers, gazing, nevertheless, up at the ship's side with a flat face of reluctance and doubt.

I grasped a boat's fall and went up hand over hand, and Sweers followed me. The angle of the deck was considerable, but owing to the flat bilge of the whaler's bottom, not greater than the inclination of the deck of a ship under a heavy press of canvas. It was possible to walk. We put our legs over the rail and came to a stand, and took a view of the decks of the ship. Nothing, saving the boats, seemed to be missing. Every detail of deck furniture was as complete as though the ship were ready for getting under way, with a full hold, for a final start home. Caboose, scuttle-butts, harness-cask, wheel, binnacle, companion-cover, skylight, winch, pumps, capstan—nothing was wanting; nothing but boats and men.

"Is it possible that all hands can be below?" said Sweers, straining his ear.

I looked aloft and about me, wondering that the body of the vessel and her masts and rigging should not be sheathed with ice; but if ever the structure had been glazed in her time, when she lay hard and fast far to the north of Spitzbergen, for all one could tell, nothing was now frozen; there was not so much as an icicle anywhere visible about her. The decks were dry, and on my kicking a coil of rope that was near my feet the stuff did not crackle, as one could have expected, as though frosted to the core.

"The vessel seems to have been thawed through," said I, "and I expect that this berg is only a fragment of the mass that broke adrift with her."

"Likely enough," said Sweers. "Hark! what is that?"

"What do you hear?" I exclaimed.

"Why, that!" cried he, pointing to a shallow fissure in the icy rocks which towered above the ship: and down the fissure I spied a cascade of water falling like smoke, with a harsh, hissing noise, which I had mistaken for the seething of the sea. I ran my eye over the face of the heights and witnessed many similar falls of water.

"There'll not be much of this iceberg left soon," said I, "if the drift is to the southward."

"What d'ye think,—that the drift's northerly?" exclaimed Sweers. "I'll tell you what it is; it's these icebergs drifting in masses down south into the Atlantic which cause the sudden spells of cold weather you get in England during seasons when it ought to be hot."

As he said this he walked to the companion-hatch, the cover of which was closed, and the door shut. The cover yielded to a thrust of his hand. He then pulled open the doors and put his head in, and I heard him spit.

"There's foul air here," said he; "but where a match will burn a man can breathe, I've learnt."

He struck a match, and descended two or three steps of the ladder, and then called out to me to follow. The air was not foul, but it was close, and there was a dampish smell upon it, and it was charged with a fishy odour like that of decaying spawn and dead marine vegetation. Light fell through the companion-way, and a sort of blurred dimness drained through the grimy skylight.

We thoroughly overhauled this interior, spending some time in looking about us, for Sweers' fear of beholding something affrighting vanished when he found himself in a plain ship's cabin, with nothing more terrible to behold than the ship's furniture of a whaleman's living-room of near half a century old. There were three sleeping-berths, and these we explored, but met with nothing that in any way hinted at the story of the ship. It was impossible to tell, indeed, which had been the captain's cabin. All three berths were filled alike with lockers, hammocks, wash-stands, and so forth; and two of them were lighted by dirty little scuttles in the ship's side; but the third lay athwartships, and all the light that it received came from the cabin through its open door.

I don't know how long we were occupied in hunting these cabins for any sort of papers which would enable Captain Funnel to make out the story of the barque. We were too eager and curious and interested to heed the passage of time. There were harpoons and muskets racked in the state cabin, some wearing apparel in the berths, a few books on nautical subjects, but without the owners' names in them, and there was a bundle of what proved to be bear's skins stowed away in the corner of the berth that was without a scuttle. A door led to a couple of bulkheaded compartments in the fore part of the state cabin, and Sweers was in the act of advancing to it when he cried out:

"By the tunder of heaven, what is dot?" losing his customary hold of the English tongue in the excitement of the moment.

"The ice is melting and discharging in Niagara Falls upon the whaler's deck!" I cried, after listening a moment to the noise of a downpour that rang through the cabin in a hollow thunder.

We rushed on deck. A furious squall was blowing, but the air was becalmed where the vessel lay by the high cliffs of ice, and the rain of the squall fell almost up and down in a very sheet of water, intermingled with hailstones as big as the eggs of a thrush. The whole scene of the ocean was a swirling, revolving smother, as though the sky was full of steam, and the screech of the wind, as it fled off the edge of the dead white heights which sheltered us, pierced the ear like the whistlings of a thousand locomotives.

There was nothing to be seen of the schooner: but *that* was trifling for the moment compared to this: *there was nothing to be seen of the boat!* The furious discharge of the squall would increase her weight by half filling her with water; the slashing wet of the rain would also render the icy slope up which we had hauled her as slippery as a sheet for skaters; a single shock or blast of wind might suffice to start her. Be this as it will, she had launched herself—she was gone! We strained our sight, but no faintest blotch of shadow could we distinguish amid the white water rushing smoothly off from the base of the berg, and streaming into the pallid shadow of the squall where you saw the sea clear of the ice beginning to work with true Atlantic spite.

"Crate Cott!" cried Sweers, "what's to be done? There was no appearance of a squall when we landed here. It drove up abaft this berg, and it may have been hidden from the schooner herself by the ice."

We crouched in the companion-way for shelter, not doubting that the squall would speedily pass, and that the schooner, which we naturally supposed lay close to the berg hove-to, would, the instant the weather cleared, send a boat to take us off. But the squall, instead of abating, gradually rose into half a gale of wind—a wet dark gale that shrouded the sea with flying spume and rain to within a musket-shot of the iceberg, whilst the sky was no more than a weeping, pouring shadow coming and going as it were with a lightening and darkening of it by masses of headlong torn vapour. Some of the ragged pinnacles of the cliffs of ice seemed to pierce that wild dark, flying sky of storm as it swept before the gale close down over our heads.

We could not bring our minds to realise that we were to be left aboard this ice-stranded whaler all night, and perhaps all next day, and for heaven alone knows how much longer for the matter of that; and it was not until the darkness of the evening had drawn down, coming along early with the howling gloom of the storm-shrouded ocean, without so much as a rusty tinge of hectic to tell us where the West lay, that we abandoned our idle task of staring at the sea, and made up our minds to go through with the night as best we could.

And first of all we entered the galley, and by the aid of such dim light as still lived we contrived to catch sight of a tin lamp with a spout to it dangling over the coppers. There was a wick in the spout, but one might swear that the lamp hadn't been used for months and months.

"We must have a light anyhow," said Sweers, "and if this *President* be a whaler, there should be no lack of oil aboard."

After groping awhile in some shelves stocked with black-handled knives and forks, tin dishes, pannikins, and the like, I put my hand upon a stump of candle-end. This we lighted, Sweers luckily having a box of lucifers in his pocket, and with the aid of the candle-flame, we discovered in the corner of the galley a lime-juice jar half-full of oil. With this we trimmed the lamp, and then stepped on deck to grope our way to the cabin, meaning to light the lamp down there, for no unsheltered flame would have lived an instant in the fierce draughts which rushed and eddied about the decks.

We stayed a moment to look seawards, but all was black night out there, touched in places with a sudden flash of foam. The voice of the gale was awful with the warring noise of the waters, and with the restless thunder of seas smiting the ice on the weather side, and with the wild and often terrific crackling sounds which arose out of the heart of the solid mass of the berg itself, as though earth-quakes in endless processions were trembling through it, and as though, at any moment, the whole vast bulk would be rent into a thousand crystal splinters. Sweers was silent until we had gained the cabin and lighted the lamp. He then looked at me with an ashen face, and groaned.

"This gale's going to blow the schooner away," said he. "We're lost men, David. I'd give my right eye to be aboard the *Lightning*. D'ye understand the trick of these blooming icebergs? They wash away underneath, grow topheavy, and then over goes the show. And to think of the jolly-boat making off, as if two sailormen like you and me couldn't have provided for *that*!"

He groaned again, and then seated himself, and appeared wholly deprived of energy and spirit.

However, now that I was below, under shelter, out of the noise of the weather, and therefore able to collect my thoughts, I began to feel very hungry and thirsty; in fact, neither Sweers nor I had tasted food since breakfast at eight o'clock that morning. A lamp hung aslant from the cabin ceiling. It was a small lamp of brass, glazed. I unhooked it, and brought it to the light, but it was without a wick, and there was no oil in it, and to save time I stuck the lighted candle in the lamp, and leaving the other lamp burning to enable Sweers to rummage also, I passed through the door that was in the forepart of the cabin; and here I found three berths, one of which was furnished as a pantry, whilst the other two were sleeping-places, with bunks in them, and I observed also a sheaf or two of harpoons, together with spades and implements used in dealing with the whale after the monster has been killed and towed alongside.

The atmosphere was horribly close and fishy in this place, reeking of oil, yet cold as ice, as though the ship lay drowned a thousand fathoms deep. I called to Sweers to bring his lamp, for my candle gave so poor a light I could scarce see by it; and in the berth that looked to have been used as a pantry we found half a barrel of pork, a bag of ship's biscuit, and a quantity of Indian meal, beans, and rice, a canister of coffee, and a few jars of pickles. But we could find nothing to drink.

I was now exceedingly thirsty; so I took a pannikin—a number of vessels of the sort were on the shelf in the pantry—and carried it with the lamp on deck. I had taken notice during the day of four or five buckets in a row abaft the main-mast, and, approaching them, I held the light close, and found each bucket full. I tasted the water; it was rain and without the least flavour of salt: and, after drinking heartily, I filled the pannikin afresh and carried it down to Sweers.

There was a spiritlessness in this man that surprised me. I had not thought to find the faculties of Salamon Sweers so quickly benumbed by what was indeed a wild and dangerous confrontment, yet not so formidable and hopeless as to weaken the nerves of a seaman. I yearned for a bottle of rum, for any sort of strong waters indeed, guessing that a dram would help us both; and after I had made a meal off some raw pork and molasses spread upon the ship's biscuit, which was mouldy and astir with weevils, I took my lantern and again went on deck, and made my way to the galley where the oil jar stood, and here in a drawer I found what now I most needed, but what before I had overlooked; I mean a parcel; of braided lamp wicks. I trimmed the lamp and got a brilliant light. The glass protected the flame from the rush of the wind about the deck. I guessed there would be nothing worth finding in the barque's forecastle, and not doubting that there was a lazarette in which would be stored such ship provisions as the crew had left behind them, I returned to the cabin, looked for the lazarette hatch, and found it under the table.

Well, to cut this part of the story short, Sweers and I dropped into the lazarette, and after spending an hour or two in examining what we met with, we discovered enough provisions, along with some casks of rum and bottled beer, to last a ship's company of twenty men a whole six months. This was Sweers' reckoning. We carried some of the bottled beer into the cabin, and having pipes and tobacco with us in our pockets, we filled and smoked, and sat listening to the wet storming down the decks overhead, and to the roaring of the wind on high, and to the crackling noises of the ice.

That first night with us on board the whaler was a fearful time. Sometimes we dozed as we sat confronting each other on the lockers, but again and again would we start up and go on deck, but only to look into the blindness of the night, and only to hearken to the appalling noises of the weather and the ice. When day broke there was nothing in sight. It was blowing strong, a high sea was running, and the ocean lay shrouded as though with vapour.

During the course of the morning we entered the forepeak, where we found a quantity of coal. This enabled us to light the galley fire, to cook a piece of pork, and to boil some coffee. Towards noon Sweers proposed to inspect the hold, and to see what was inside the ship. Accordingly we opened the main hatch and found the vessel loaded with casks, some of which we examined and found them full of oil.

"By tunder!" cried Sweers; "if we could only carry this vessel home there'd be a fortune for both of us, David. Shall I tell you what this sort of oil's worth? Well, it's worth about thirty pounds a ton. And how much d'ye think there's aboard?

Not less than a hundred ton, if I don't see double. There's no man can teach me the capacity of a cask, and there are casks below varying from forty-two to two hundred and seventy-five gallons, with no lack of whalebone stored dry somewhere, I don't doubt, if those casks would let us look for it."

But this was no better than idle and ironical chatter in the mouths of men so hideously situated as we were. For my part I had no thought of saving the ship; indeed, I had scarce any hope of saving my own life. We found an American ensign in a small flag-locker that was lashed near the wheel, and we sent it half-mast high, with the stars inverted. Then we searched for fresh water, and found three iron tanks nearly full in the after-hold. The water stunk with keeping, as though it had grown rank in the bilge, but after it had stood a little while exposed to air it became sweet enough to use. There was no fear then of our perishing from hunger and thirst whilst the whaler kept together. Our main and imminent danger lay in the sudden dissolution of the ice, or in the capsizal of the berg. It was our unhappy fortune that, numerous as were the cranes overhanging the whaler's side, we should not have found a boat left in one of them. Our only chance lay in a raft; but both Sweers and I, as sailors, shrank from the thought of such a means of escape. We might well guess that a raft would but prolong our lives in the midst of so wide a sea, by a few days, and perhaps by a few hours only, after subjecting us to every agony of despair and of expectation, and torturing us with God alone would know what privations.

We thoroughly overhauled the forecastle of the vessel, but found nothing of interest. There were a few seamen's chests, some odds and ends of wearing apparel, and here and there a blanket in a bunk; but the crew in clearing out appeared to have carried off most of their effects with them. Of course we could only conjecture what they had done and how they had managed; but it was to be guessed that all the boats being gone the sailors had taken advantage of a split in the ice to get away from their hard and fast ship, employing all their boats that they might carry with them a plentiful store of water and provisions.

I should but weary you to dwell day by day upon the passage of time that Sweers and I passed upon this ship that we had seen upon the ice. We kept an eager look-out for craft, crawling to the mastheads so as to obtain a view over the blocks of ice which lay in masses at the stem and stern of the whaler. But though we often caught sight of a distant sail, nothing ever approached us close enough to observe our signal. Once, indeed, a large steamer passed within a couple of miles of the iceberg, and we watched her with devouring eyes, forever imagining that she was slowing down and about to stop, until she vanished out of our sight past the north end of the berg. Yet, we had no other hope of rescue than that of being taken off by a passing ship.

I never recollect meeting at sea with such a variety of weather as we encountered. There would be clear sunshine and bright blue skies for a day, followed by dark and bellowing nights of storm. Then would come periods of thick fogs, followed by squalls, variable winds, and so on. We guessed, however, that our trend was steadily southwards, by the steady cascading of the ice, by the frequent falls of large blocks, and by the increasing noises of sudden, tremendous disruptions, loud and heart-subduing as thundershocks heard close to.

"If we aren't taken off," said Sweers to me one day, "there's just this one chance for us. The ice is bound to melt. All these bergs, as I reckon, disappear somewhere to the nor'ard of the verge of the Gulf Stream. Well, now the Lord may be good to us, and it may happen that this berg'll melt away and leave the whaler afloat; and float she must if she isn't crushed by the ice. Let her leak like a sieve—there's oil enough in her to keep her standing upright as though she were a line-of-battle ship."

Well, we had been a little more than a fortnight upon this ship hard and fast upon the ice. Many a vessel had we sighted, but never a one of them, saving the steamer I have mentioned, had approached within eyeshot of our distress signal. Yet our health was good, and our spirits tolerably easy; we had fared well, there was no lack of food and drink, and we were beginning to feel some confidence in the iceberg—by which I mean to say that the rapid thawing of its upper parts, where all the weight was, filled us with the hope that the mass wouldn't capsize as we had feared; that it would hold together so as to keep the ship on end as she now was until we were rescued, or, failing our being rescued, that it would dissolve in such a way as to leave the whaler afloat.

It was somewhere about the end of a fortnight, as I have said. My bed was a cabin locker, on which I had placed a mattress and a bear-skin. Both Sweers and I turned in of a night, unless it was clear weather; though if I awoke I'd sometimes steal on deck to take a peep, for nothing could come of our keeping a look-out if it was blowing hard, and if it was black and thick.

This night it was a bit muddy and dark, with a moderate breeze out of the south-west, as far as we could guess at the bearings of the wind. I was awakened from a deep slumber by an extraordinary convulsion in the ship. I was half-stupefied with sleep, and can therefore but imperfectly recall my sensations and the character of what I may term the throes and spasms of the vessel. I was thrown from the locker and lay for some moments incapable of rising by the shock of the fall. But one thing my senses, even when they were scarce yet awake, took note of, and that was a prodigious roaring noise, similar in effect to what might be produced by a cannon-ball rolling along a hollow wooden floor, only that the noise was thousands of times greater than ever could have been produced by a cannon-ball. The lamp was out, and the cabin in pitch blackness. I heard Sweers from some corner of the cabin, bawling out my name; but before I could answer, and even whilst I was staggering to my feet, a second convulsion threw me down again; the next instant there was a sensation as of the vessel being hove up into the air, attended by an extraordinary grinding noise, that thrilled through every beam of her; next, in the space of a few beats of the heart, she plunged into the sea, raising such a boiling and roaring of waters, as, spite of the sounds being dulled to our ears by our being in the cabin, persuaded us that the vessel was foundering.

But even whilst I thus thought, holding my breath and waiting for the death that was to come with the pouring of the water down the open companion-way, I felt the ship right; she lifted buoyant under foot, and I sprang to the steps which conducted on deck, with Sweers—as I might know by his voice—close at my heels, roaring out, "By tunder, we're adrift and afloat!"

The stars were shining, there was a red moon low in the west, the weather had cleared, and a quiet wind was blowing. At the distance of some hundred yards from the ship stood a few pallid masses—the remains of the berg. It was just possible to make out that the water in the neighbourhood of those dim heaps was covered with fragments of ice. How the liberation of the ship had come about neither Sweers nor I did then pause to consider. We were sailors, and our first business was to act as sailors, and as quickly as might be we loosed and hoisted the jib and foretopmast staysail, so that the vessel might blow away from the neighbourhood of the dangerous remains of her jail of ice. We then sounded the well, and, finding no water, went to work to loose the foresail and foretopsail, which canvas we made shift to set with the aid of the capstan. I then lighted the binnacle lamp whilst Sweers held the wheel; and having sounded the well afresh, to make sure of the hull, we headed away to the eastwards, the wind being about W.S.W.

Before the dawn broke we had run the ice out of sight. Sweers and I managed, as I have no doubt, to arrive at the theory of the liberation of the ship by comparing our sensations and experiences. There can be no question that the berg had split in twain almost amidships. This was the cause of the tremendous noise of thunder which I heard. The splitting of the ice had hoisted the shelf or beach on which the barque lay, and occasioned that sensation of flying into the air which I had noticed. But the lifting of the beach of ice had also violently and sharply sloped it, and the barque, freeing herself, had fled down it broadside on, taking the water with a mighty souse and crash, then rising buoyant, and lifting and falling upon the seas as we had both of us felt her do.

And now to bring this queer yarn to a close, for I have no space to dwell upon our thankfulness and our proceedings until we obtained the help we stood in need of. We managed to handle the barque without assistance for three days, then fell in with an American ship bound to Liverpool, who lent us three of her men, and within three weeks of the date of our release from the iceberg we were in soundings in the Chops of the Channel, and a few days later had safely brought the barque to an anchor in the river Thames.

The adventure yielded Sweers and I a thousand pounds apiece as salvage money, but we were kept waiting a long time before receiving our just reward. It was necessary to communicate with the owners of the barque in America, and then the lawyers got hold of the job, and I grew so weary of interviews, so vexed and sickened by needless correspondence, that I should have been thankful to have taken two hundred pounds for my share merely to have made an end.

It seems that the *President* had been abandoned two years and five months by her crew before the *Lightning* sighted her on the ice. Her people had stuck to her for eight months, then made off in a body with the boats, carrying their captain and mates along with them. They regarded the situation of their ship as hopeless, and indeed, as it turned out, they were not very wrong, so far as their notions of reasonable detention went; for they never could have liberated the vessel by their own efforts; they must have waited, as we had, for the ice to free her; and this would have signified to them an imprisonment of two years and a half over and above the eight months they had already spent in her whilst ice-bound.

Sweers gave up the sea, started in business, and died, about ten years since, a fairly well-to-do man. And shall I tell you what I did with my thousand pounds?... But my story has already run to greater length than I had intended when sitting down to write it.

SHIPWRECK

BY ANN RADCLIFFE

'Tis solemn midnight! On this lonely steep,
Beneath this watch-tow'r's desolated wall,
Where mystic shapes the wanderer appal,
I rest; and view below the desert deep.
As through tempestuous clouds the moon's cold light
Gleams on the wave. Viewless, the winds of night
With loud mysterious force the billows sweep,
And sullen roar the surges far below.
In the still pauses of the gust I hear
The voice of spirits, rising sweet and slow,
And oft among the clouds their forms appear.
But hark! what shriek of death comes in the gale
And in the distant ray what glimmering sail
Bends to the storm?—Now sinks the note of fear!
Ah! wretched mariners! no more shall day
Unclose his cheering eye to light you on your way!"

THE DERELICT

BY WILLIAM HOPE HODGSON

"It's the *material*," said the old ship's doctor—"the *material* plus the conditions—and, maybe," he added slowly, "a third factor—yes, a third factor; but there, there—" He broke off his half-meditative sentence and began to charge his pipe.

"Go on, doctor," we said encouragingly, and with more than a little expectancy. We were in the smoke-room of the *Sand-a-lea*, running across the North Atlantic; and the doctor was a character. He concluded the charging of his pipe, and lit it; then settled himself, and began to express himself more fully.

"The *material*," he said with conviction, "is inevitably the medium of expression of the life-force—the fulcrum, as it were; lacking which it is unable to exert itself, or, indeed, to express itself in any form or fashion that would be intelligible or evident to us. So potent is the share of the material in the production of that thing which we name life, and so eager the life-force to express itself, that I am convinced it would, if given the right conditions, make itself manifest even through so hopeless seeming a medium as a simple block of sawn wood; for I tell you, gentlemen, the life-force is both as fiercely urgent and as indiscriminate as fire—the destructor; yet which some are now growing to consider the very essence of life rampant. There is a quaint seeming paradox there," he concluded, nodding his old grey head.

"Yes, doctor," I said. "In brief, your argument is that life is a thing, state, fact, or element, call it what you like, which requires the *material* through which to manifest itself, and that given the *material*, plus the conditions, the result is life. In other words, that life is an evolved product, manifested through matter and bred of conditions—eh?"

"As we understand the word," said the old doctor. "Though, mind you, there may be a third factor. But, in my heart, I believe that it is a matter of chemistry— conditions and a suitable medium; but given the conditions, the brute is so almighty that it will seize upon anything through which to manifest itself. It is a force gener- ated by conditions; but, nevertheless, this does not bring us one iota nearer to its explanation, any more than to the explanation of electricity or fire. They are, all three, of the outer forces—monsters of the void. Nothing we can do will *create* any one of them, our power is merely to be able, by providing the conditions, to make each one of them manifest to our physical senses. Am I clear?"

"Yes, doctor, in a way, you are," I said. "But I don't agree with you, though I think I understand you. Electricity and fire are both what I might call natural things, but life is an abstract something—a kind of all-permeating wakefulness. Oh, I can't explain it! Who could? But it's spiritual, not just a thing bred out of a condition, like fire, as you say, or electricity. It's a horrible thought of yours. Life's a kind of spiritual mystery—"

"Easy, my boy!" said the old doctor, laughing gently to himself. "Or else I may be asking you to demonstrate the spiritual mystery of life of the limpet, or the crab, shall we say." He grinned at me with ineffable perverseness. "Anyway," he continued, "as I suppose you've all guessed, I've a yarn to tell you in support of my impression that life is no more a mystery or a miracle than fire or electricity. But, please to remember, gentlemen, that because we've succeeded in naming and making good use of these two forces, they're just as much mysteries, fundamentally as ever. And, anyway, the thing I'm going to tell you won't explain the mystery of life, but only give you one of my pegs on which I hang my feeling that life is as I have said, a force made manifest through conditions—that is to say, natural chemistry—and that it can take for its purpose and need, the most incredible and unlikely matter; for without matter it cannot come into existence—it cannot become manifest—"

"I don't agree with you, doctor," I interrupted. "Your theory would destroy all belief in life after death. It would—"

"Hush, sonny," said the old man, with a quiet little smile of comprehension. "Hark to what I've to say first; and, anyway, what objection have you to material life after death? And if you object to a material framework, I would still have you remember that I am speaking of life, as we understand the word in this our life. Now do be a quiet lad, or I'll never be done:

"It was when I was a young man, and that is a good many years ago, gentlemen. I had passed my examinations, but was so run down with overwork that it was decided that I had better take a trip to sea. I was by no means well off, and very glad in the end to secure a nominal post as doctor in the sailing passenger clipper running out to China.

"The name of the ship was the *Bheospsé*, and soon after I had got all my gear aboard she cast off, and we dropped down the Thames, and next day were well away out in the Channel.

"The captain's name was Gannington, a very decent man, though quite illiterate. The first mate, Mr. Berlies, was a quiet, sternish, reserved man, very well-read. The second mate, Mr. Selvern, was, perhaps, by birth and upbringing, the most socially cultured of the three, but he lacked the stamina and indomitable pluck of the two others. He was more of a sensitive, and emotionally and even mentally, the most alert man of the three.

"On our way out, we called at Madagascar, where we landed some of our passengers; then we ran eastward, meaning to call at North-West Cape; but about a hundred degrees east we encountered very dreadful weather, which carried away all our sails, and sprung the jibboom and foret'gallantmast.

"The storm carried us northward for several hundred miles, and when it dropped us finally, we found ourselves in a very bad state. The ship had been strained, and had taken some three feet of water through her seams; the main-topmast had been sprung, in addition to the jibboom and foret'gallantmast, two of our boats had gone, as also one of the pigstys, with three fine pigs, these latter having been washed overboard but some half-hour before the wind began to ease, which it did very quickly, though a very ugly sea ran for some hours after.

"The wind left us just before dark, and when morning came it brought splendid weather—a calm, mildly undulating sea, and a brilliant sun, with no wind. It showed us also that we were not alone, for about two miles away to the westward was another vessel, which Mr. Selvern, the second mate, pointed out to me.

"'That's a pretty rum-looking packet, doctor,' he said, and handed me his glass.

"I looked through it at the other vessel, and saw what he meant; at least, I thought I did.

"'Yes, Mr. Selvern,' I said. 'She's got a pretty old-fashioned look about her.'

"He laughed at me in his pleasant way.

"'It's easy to see you're not a sailor, doctor,' he remarked. 'There's a dozen rum things about her. She's a derelict, and has been floating round, by the look of her, for many a score of years. Look at the shape of her counter, and the bows and cutwater. She's as old as the hills, as you might say, and ought to have gone down to Davy Jones a good while ago. Look at the growths on her, and the thickness of her standing rigging; that's all salt encrustations, I fancy, if you notice the white colour. She's been a small barque; but, don't you see, she's not a yard left aloft. They've all dropped out of the slings; everything rotted away; wonder the standing rigging hasn't gone, too. I wish the old man would let us take the boat and have a look at her. She'd be well worth it.'

"There seemed little chance, however, of this, for all hands were turned to and kept hard at it all day long repairing the damage to the masts and gear; and this took a long while, as you may think. Part of the time I gave a hand heaving on one of the deck capstans, for the exercise was good for my liver. Old Captain Gannington approved, and I persuaded him to come along and try some of the same medicine, which he did; and we got very chummy over the job.

"We got talking about the derelict, and he remarked how lucky we were not to have run full tilt on to her in the darkness, for she lay right away to leeward of us, according, to the way that we had been drifting in the storm. He also was of the opinion that she had a strange look about her, and that she was pretty old; but on this latter point he plainly had far less knowledge than the second mate, for he was, as I have said, an illiterate man, and knew nothing of seacraft beyond what experience had taught him. He lacked the book knowledge which the second mate had of vessels previous to his day, which it appeared the derelict was.

"'She's an old 'un, doctor,' was the extent of observations in this direction.

"Yet, when I mentioned to him that it would be interesting to go aboard and give her a bit of an overhaul, he nodded his head as if the idea had been already in his mind and accorded with his own inclinations.

"'When the work's over, doctor,' he said. 'Can't spare the men now, ye know. Got to get all shipshape an' ready as smart as we can. But, we'll take my gig, an' go off in the second dog-watch. The glass is steady, an' it'll be a bit of gam for us.'

"That evening, after tea, the captain gave orders to clear the gig and get her overboard. The second mate was to come with us, and the skipper gave him word to see that two or three lamps were put into the boat, as it would soon fall dark. A little later we were pulling across the calmness of the sea with a crew of six at the oars, and making very good speed of it.

"Now, gentlemen, I have detailed to you with great exactness all the facts, both big and little, so that you can follow step by step each incident in this extraordinary affair, and I want you now to pay the closest attention. I was sitting in the stern-sheets with the second mate and the captain, who was steering, and as we drew nearer and nearer to the stranger I studied her with an ever-growing attention, as, indeed, did Captain Gannington and the second mate. She was, as you know, to the westward of us, and the sunset was making a great flame of red light to the back of her, so that she showed a little blurred and indistinct by reason of the halation of the light, which almost defeated the eye in any attempt to see her rotting spars and standing rigging, submerged, as they were, in the fiery glory of the sunset.

"It was because of this effect of the sunset that we had come quite close, comparatively, to the derelict before we saw that she was all surrounded by a sort of curious scum, the colour of which was difficult to decide upon by reason of the red light that was in the atmosphere, but which afterwards we discovered to be brown. This scum spread all about the old vessel for many hundreds of yards in a huge, irregular patch, a great stretch of which reached out to the eastward, upon the starboard side of the boat some score or so fathoms away.

"'Queer stuff,' said Captain Gannington, leaning to the side and looking over. 'Something in the cargo as 'as gone rotten, and worked out through 'er seams.'

"'Look at her bows and stern,' said the second mate. 'Just look at the growth on her!'

"There were, as he said, great clumpings of strange-looking sea-fungi under the bows and the short counter astern. From the stump of her jibboom and her cutwater great beards of rime and marine growths hung downward into the scum that held her in. Her blank starboard side was presented to us—all a dead, dirtyish white, streaked and mottled vaguely with dull masses of heavier colour.

"'There's a steam or haze rising off her,' said the second mate, speaking again. 'You can see it against the light. It keeps coming and going. Look!'

"I saw then what he meant—a faint haze or steam, either suspended above the old vessel or rising from her. And Captain Gannington saw it also.

"'Spontaneous combustion!' he exclaimed. 'We'll 'ave to watch when we lift the 'atches, 'nless it's some poor devil that's got aboard of 'er. But that ain't likely.'

"We were now within a couple of hundred yards of the old derelict, and had entered into the brown scum. As it poured off the lifted oars I heard one of the men mutter to himself, 'Dam' treacle!' And, indeed, it was not something unlike it. As the boat continued to forge nearer and nearer to the old ship the scum grew thicker and thicker, so that, at last, it perceptibly slowed us.

"'Give way, lads! Put some beef to it!' sang out Captain Gannington. And thereafter there was no sound except the panting of the men and the faint, reiterated suck, suck of the sullen brown scum upon the oars as the boat was forced ahead. As we went, I was conscious of a peculiar smell in the evening air, and whilst I had no doubt that the puddling of the scum by the oars made it rise, I could give no name to it; yet, in a way, it was vaguely familiar.

"We were now very close to the old vessel, and presently she was high about us against the dying light. The captain called out then to 'in with the bow oars and stand by with the boat-hook,' which was done.

"'Aboard there! Ahoy! Aboard there! Ahoy!' shouted Captain Gannington; but there came no answer, only the dull sound his voice going lost into the open sea, each time he sung out.

"'Ahoy! Aboard there! Ahoy!' he shouted time after time, but there was only the weary silence of the old hulk that answered us; and, somehow as he shouted, the while that I stared up half expectantly at her, a queer little sense of oppression, that amounted almost to nervousness, came upon me. It passed, but I remember how I was suddenly aware that it was growing dark. Darkness comes fairly rapidly in the tropics, though not so quickly as many fiction writers seem to think; but it was not that the coming dusk had perceptibly deepened in that brief time of only a few moments, but rather that my nerves had made me suddenly a little hyper-sensitive. I mention my state particularly, for I am not a nervy man normally, and my abrupt touch of nerves is significant, in the light of what happened.

"'There's no one on board there!' said Captain Gannington. 'Give way, men!' For the boat's crew had instinctively rested on their oars, as the captain hailed the old craft. The men gave way again; and then the second mate called out excitedly, 'Why, look there, there's our pigsty! See, it's got *Bheospsé* painted on the end. It's drifted down here and the scum's caught it. What a blessed wonder!'

"It was, as he had said, our pigsty that had been washed overboard in the storm; and most extraordinary to come across it there.

"'We'll tow it off with us, when we go,' said the captain, and shouted to the crew to get down to their oars; for they were hardly moving the boat, because the scum was so thick, close in around the old ship, that it literally clogged the boat from moving. I remember that it struck me, in a half-conscious sort of way, as curious that the pigsty, containing our three dead pigs, had managed to drift in so far unaided, whilst we could scarcely manage to force the boat in, now that we had come right into the scum. But the thought passed from my mind, for so many things happened within the next few minutes.

"The men managed to bring the boat in alongside, within a couple of feet of the derelict, and the man with the boat-hook hooked on.

"''Ave ye got 'old there, forrard?' asked Captain Gannington.

"'Yessir!' said the bowman; and as he spoke there came a queer noise of tearing.

"'What's that?' asked the Captain.

"'It's tore, sir. Tore clean away!' said the man, and his tone showed that he had received something of a shock.

"'Get a hold again, then!' said Captain Gannington irritably. 'You don't s'pose this packet was built yesterday! Shove the hook into the main chains.' The man did so gingerly, as you might say, for it seemed to me, in the growing dusk, that he put no strain on to the hook, though, of course there was no need—you see the boat could not go very far of herself, in the stuff in which she was imbedded.

I remember thinking this, also as I looked up at the bulging side of the old vessel. Then I heard Captain Gannington's voice:

"'Lord, but she's old! An' what a colour, doctor! She don't half want paint, do she? Now then, somebody, one of them oars.' An oar was passed to him, and he leant it up against the ancient, bulging side; then he paused, and called to the second mate to light a couple of the lamps, and stand by to pass them up, for darkness had settled down now upon the sea.

"The second mate lit two of the lamps, and told one of the men to light a third, and keep it handy in the boat; then he stepped across, with a lamp in each hand, to where Captain Gannington stood by the oar against the side of the ship.

"'Now, my lad,' said the captain to the man who had pulled stroke, 'up with you, an' we'll pass ye up the lamps.'

"The man jumped to obey, caught the oar, and put his weight upon it; and as he did so, something seemed to give way a little.

"'Look!' cried out the second mate, and pointed, lamp in hand. 'It's sunk in!'

"This was true. The oar had made quite an indentation into the bulging, somewhat slimy side of the old vessel.

"'Mould, I reckon,' said Captain Gannington, bending towards the derelict to look. Then to the man:

"'Up you go, my lad, and be smart! Don't stand there waitin'!'

"At that the man, who had paused a moment as he felt the oar give beneath his weight began to shin' up, and in a few seconds he was aboard, and leant out over the rail for the lamps. These were passed up to him, and the captain called to him to steady the oar. Then Captain Gannington went, calling to me to follow, and after me the second mate.

"As the captain put his face over the rail, he gave a cry of astonishment.

"'Mould, by gum! Mould—tons of it. Good lord!'

"As I heard him shout that I scrambled the more eagerly after him, and in a moment or two I was able to see what he meant—everywhere that the light from the two lamps struck there was nothing but smooth great masses and surfaces of a dirty white coloured mould. I climbed over the rail, with the second mate close behind, and stood upon the mould covered decks. There might have been no planking beneath the mould, for all that our feet could feel. It gave under our tread with a spongy, puddingy feel. It covered the deck furniture of the old ship, so that the shape of each article and fitment was often no more than suggested through it.

"Captain Gannington snatched a lamp from the man and the second mate reached for the other. They held the lamps high, and we all stared. It was most extraordinary, and somehow most abominable. I can think of no other word, gentlemen, that so much describes the predominant feeling that affected me at the moment.

"'Good lord!' said Captain Gannington several times. 'Good lord!' But neither the second mate nor the man said anything, and, for my part I just stared, and at the same time began to smell a little at the air, for there was a vague odour of something half familiar, that somehow brought to me a sense of half-known fright.

"I turned this way and that, staring, as I have said. Here and there the mould was so heavy as to entirely disguise what lay beneath, converting the deck-fittings into indistinguishable mounds of mould all dirty-white and blotched and veined with irregular, dull, purplish markings.

"There was a strange thing about the mould which Captain Gannington drew attention to—it was that our feet did not crush into it and break the surface, as might have been expected, but merely indented it.

"'Never seen nothin' like it before! Never!' said the captain after having stooped with his lamp to examine the mould under our feet. He stamped with his heel, and the mould gave out a dull, puddingy sound. He stooped again, with a quick movement, and stared, holding the lamp close to the deck. 'Blest if it ain't a reg'lar skin to it!'

"The second mate and the man and I all stooped and looked at it. The second mate progged it with his forefinger, and I remember I rapped it several times with my knuckles, listening to the dead sound it gave out, and noticing the close, firm texture of the mould.

"'Dough!' the second mate. 'It's just like blessed dough! Pouf!' He stood up with a quick movement. 'I could fancy it stinks a bit,' he said.

"As he said this I knew, suddenly, what the familiar thing was in the vague odour that hung about us—it was that the smell had something animal-like in it; something of the same smell, only *heavier*, that you would smell in any place that is infested with mice. I began to look about with a sudden very real uneasiness. There might be vast numbers of hungry rats aboard. They might prove exceedingly dangerous, if in a starving condition; yet, as you will understand, somehow I hesitated to put forward my idea as a reason for caution, it was too fanciful.

"Captain Gannington had begun to go aft along the mould-covered main-deck with the second mate, each of them holding their lamps high up, so as to cast a good light about the vessel. I turned quickly and followed them, the man with me keeping close to my heels, and plainly uneasy. As we went, I became aware that there was a feeling of moisture in the air, and I remembered the slight mist, or smoke, above the hulk, which had made Captain Gannington suggest spontaneous combustion in explanation.

"And always, as we went, there was that vague, animal smell; suddenly I found myself wishing we were well away from the old vessel.

"Abruptly, after a few paces, the captain stopped and pointed at a row of mould-hidden shapes on each side of the maindeck. 'Guns,' he said. 'Been a privateer in the old days, I guess—maybe worse! We'll 'ave a look below, doctor; there may be something worth touchin'. She's older than I thought. Mr. Selvern thinks she's about two hundred years old; but I scarce think it.'

"We continued our way aft, and I remember that I found myself walking as lightly and gingerly as possible, as if I were subconsciously afraid of treading through the rotten, mould-hid decks. I think the others had a touch of the same feeling, from the way that they walked. Occasionally the soft stuff would grip our heels, releasing them with a little sullen suck.

"The captain forged somewhat ahead of the second mate; and I know that the suggestion he had made himself, that perhaps there might be something below worth carrying away, had stimulated his imagination. The second mate was, however, beginning to feel somewhat the same way that I did; at least I have that impression. I think, if it had not been for what I might truly describe as Captain Gannington's sturdy courage, we should all of us have just gone back over the side very soon, for there was most certainly an unwholesome feeling abroad that made one feel queerly lacking in pluck; and you will soon see that this feeling was justified.

"Just as the captain reached the few mould-covered steps leading up on to the short half-poop, I was suddenly aware that the feeling of moisture in the air had grown very much more definite. It was perceptible now, intermittently, as a sort of thin, moist, fog-like vapour, that came and went oddly, and seemed to make the decks a little indistinct to the view, this time and that. Once an odd puff of it beat up suddenly from somewhere, and caught me in the face, carrying a queer, sickly, heavy odour with it that somehow frightened me strangely with a suggestion of a waiting and half-comprehended danger.

"We had followed Captain Gannington up the three mould covered steps, and now went slowly along the raised after-deck. By the mizzenmast Captain Gannington paused, and held his lantern near to it. 'My word, mister,' he said to the second mate, 'it's fair thickened up with mould! Why, I'll g'antee it's close on four foot thick.' He shone the light down to where it met the deck. 'Good lord!' he said. 'Look at the sea-lice on it!' I stepped up, and it was as he had said; the sea-lice were thick upon it, some of them huge, not less than the size of large beetles, and all a clear, colourless shade, like water, except where there were little spots of grey on them.

"'I've never seen the like of them, 'cept on a live cod,' said Captain Gannington, in an extremely puzzled voice. 'My word! But they're whoppers!' Then he passed on; but a few paces farther aft he stopped again, and held his lamp near to the mould-hidden deck.

"'Lord bless me, doctor,' he called out, in a low voice, 'did ye ever see the like of that? Why, it's a foot long, if it's a hinch!'

"I stooped over his shoulder, and saw what he meant; it was a clear, colourless creature about a foot long, and about eight inches high, with a curved back that was extraordinarily narrow. As we stared, all in a group, it gave a queer little flick, and was gone.

"'Jumped!' said the captain. 'Well, if that ain't a giant of all the sea-lice that ever I've seen. I guess it's jumped twenty foot clear.' He straightened his back, and scratched his head a moment, swinging the lantern this way and that with the other hand, and staring about us. 'Wot are they doin' aboard 'ere?' he said. 'You'll see 'em—little things—on fat cod an' such-like. I'm blowed, doctor, if I understand.'

"He held his lamp towards a big mound of the mould that occupied part of the after portion of the low poop-deck, a little foreside of where there came a two-foot high 'break' to a kind of second and loftier poop, that ran away aft to the taffrail. The mound was pretty big, several feet across, and more than a yard high. Captain Gannington walked up to it.

"'I reck'n this's the scuttle,' he remarked, and gave it a heavy kick. The only result was a deep indentation into the huge, whiteish hump of mould, as if he had driven his foot into a mass of some doughy substance. Yet I am not altogether correct in saying that this was the only result, for a certain other thing happened. From the place made by the captain's foot there came a sudden gush of a purplish fluid, accompanied by a peculiar smell, that was, and was not, half familiar. Some of the mould-like substance had stuck to the toe of the captain's boot, and from this likewise there issued a sweat, as it were, of the same colour.

'Well?' said Captain Gannington, in surprise, and drew back his foot to make another kick at the hump of mould. But he paused at an exclamation from the second mate:

"'Don't sir,' said the second mate.

"I glanced at him, and the light from Captain Gannington's lamp showed me that his face had a bewildered, half-frightened look, as if he were suddenly and unexpectedly half afraid of something, and as if his tongue had given away his sudden fright, without any intention on his part to speak. The captain also turned and stared at him.

"'Why, mister?' he asked, in a somewhat puzzled voice, through which there sounded just the vaguest hint of annoyance. 'We've got to shift this muck, if we're to get below.'

"I looked at the second mate, and it seemed to me that, curiously enough he was listening less to the captain than to some other sound. Suddenly he said, in a queer voice, 'Listen, everybody!'

"Yet we heard nothing, beyond the faint murmur of the men talking together in the boat alongside.

"'I don't, hear nothing,' said Captain Gannington, after a short pause. 'Do you, doctor?'

"'No,' I said.

"'Wot was it you thought you heard?' the captain, turning again to the second mate. But the second mate shook his head in a curious, almost irritable way, as if the captain's question interrupted his listening. Captain Gannington stared a moment at him, then held his lantern up and glanced about him almost uneasily. I know I felt a queer sense of strain. But the light showed nothing beyond the greyish dirty-white of the mould in all directions.

"'Mister Selvern,' said the captain, at last, looking at him, 'don't get fancying, things. Get hold of your bloomin' self. Ye know ye heard nothin'?'

"'I'm quite sure I heard something, sir,' said the second mate. 'I seemed to hear—' He broke off sharply, and appeared to listen with an almost painful intensity.

"'What did it sound like?' I asked.

"'It's all right, doctor,' said Captain Gannington, laughing gently. 'Ye can give him a tonic when we get back. I'm goin' to shift this stuff.' He drew back, and kicked for the second time at the ugly mass which he took to hide the companion-way. The result of his kick was startling, for the whole thing wobbled sloppily, like a mound of unhealthy-looking jelly.

"He drew his foot out of it quickly, and took a step backward, staring, and holding his lamp towards it. 'By gum,' he said, and it was plain that he was generally startled, 'the blessed thing's gone soft!'

"The man had run back several steps from the suddenly flaccid mound, and looking horribly frightened. Though of what, I am sure he had not the least idea. The second mate stood where he was, and stared. For my part, I know I had a most hideous uneasiness upon me. The captain continued to hold his light towards the wobbling mound and stare.

"'It's gone squashy all through,' he said. 'There's no scuttle there. There's no bally woodwork inside that lot! Phoo! What a rum smell!'

"He walked round to the after side of the strange mound, to see whether there might be some signs of an opening, into the hull at the back of the great heap of mould-stuff. And then:

"'Listen!' said the second mate again, in the strangest sort of voice.

"Captain Gannington straightened himself upright, and there succeeded a pause of the most intense quietness, in which there was not even the hum of talk from the men alongside in the boat. We all heard it—a kind of dull, soft thud, thud, thud, thud, somewhere in the hull under us, yet so vague as to make me half doubtful I heard it, only that the others did so, too.

"Captain Gannington turned suddenly to where the man stood.

"'Tell them—' he began. But the fellow cried out something, and pointed. There had come a strange intensity into his somewhat unemotional face, so that the captain's glance followed his action instantly. I stared also as you may think. It was the great mound at which the man was pointing. I saw what he meant. From the two gapes made in the mould-like stuff by Captain Gannington's boot, the purple fluid was jetting out in a queerly regular fashion, almost as if it were being forced out by a pump. My word! But I stared! And even as I stared a larger jet squirted out, and splashed as far as the man, spattering his boots and trouser legs.

"The fellow had been pretty nervous before, in a stolid, ignorant sort of way, and his funk had been growing steadily; but at this he simply let out a yell, and turned about to run. He paused an instant, as if a sudden fear of the darkness that held the decks, between him and the boat, had taken him. He snatched at the second mate's lantern, tore it out of his hand, and plunged heavily away over the vile stretch of mould.

"Mr. Selvern, the second mate, said not a word; he was just staring, staring at the strange-smelling twin-streams of dull purple that were jetting out from the wobbling mound. Captain Gannington, however, roared an order to the man to come back, but the man plunged on and on across the mould, his feet seeming to be clogged by the stuff, as if it had grown suddenly soft. He zigzagged as he ran, the lantern swaying, in wild circles as he wrenched his feet free with a constant plop, plop; and I could hear his frightened gasps even from where I stood.

"'Come back with that lamp!' roared the captain again; but still the man took no notice.

"And Captain Gannington was silent an instant, his lips working in a queer, inarticulate fashion, as if he were stunned momentarily by the very violence of his anger at the man's insubordination. And in the silence I heard the sounds again—thud, thud, thud, thud! Quite distinctly now, beating, it seemed suddenly to me, right down under my feet, but deep.

"I stared down at the mould on which I was standing, with a quick, disgusting sense of the terrible all about me; then I looked at the captain, and tried to say something, without appearing frightened. I saw that he had turned again to the mound, and all the anger had gone out of his face. He had his lamp out towards the mound, and was listening. There was another moment of absolute silence, at least, I knew that I was not conscious of any sound at all in all the world, except that extraordinary thud, thud, thud, thud, down somewhere in the huge bulk under us.

"The captain shifted his feet with a sudden, nervous movement, and as he lifted them the mould went plop, plop! He looked quickly at me, trying to smile, as if he were not thinking anything very much about it.

"'What do you make of it, doctor?' he said.

"'I think—' I began. But the second mate interrupted with a single word, his voice pitched a little high, in a tone that made us both stare instantly at him.

"'Look!' he said, and pointed at the mound. The thing was all of a slow quiver. A strange ripple ran outward from it, along the deck, like you will see a ripple run inshore out of a calm sea. It reached a mound a little foreside of us, which I had supposed to be the cabin skylight, and in a moment the second mound sank nearly level with the surrounding decks, quivering floppily in a most extraordinary fashion. A sudden quick tremor took the mould right under the second mate, and he gave out a hoarse little cry, and held his arms out on each side of him, to keep his balance. The tremor in the mould spread, and Captain Gannington swayed, and spread out his feet with a sudden curse of fright. The second mate jumped across to him, and caught him by the wrist.

"'The boat, sir!' he said, saying the very thing that I had lacked the pluck to say. 'For God's sake—'

"But he never finished, for a tremendous hoarse scream cut off his words. They hove themselves round and looked. I could see without turning. The man who had run from us was standing in the waist of the ship, about a fathom from the starboard bulwarks. He was swaying from side to side, and screaming, in a dreadful fashion. He appeared to be trying to lift his feet, and the light from his swaying lantern showed an almost incredible sight. All about him the mould was in active movement. His feet had sunk out of sight. The stuff appeared to be *lapping* at his legs and abruptly his bare flesh showed. The hideous stuff had rent his trouser-leg away as if it were paper. He gave out a simply sickening scream, and, with a vast effort, wrenched one leg free. It was partly destroyed. The next instant he pitched face downward, and the stuff heaped itself upon him, as if it were actually alive, with a dreadful, severe life. It was simply infernal. The man had gone from sight. Where he had fallen was now a writhing, elongated mound, in constant and horrible increase, as the mould appeared to move towards it in strange ripples from all sides.

"Captain Gannington and the second mate were stone silent in amazed and incredulous horror, but I had begun to reach towards a grotesque and terrific conclusion, both helped and hindered by my professional training.

"From the men in the boat alongside there was a loud shouting. and I saw two of their faces appear suddenly above the rail. They showed clearly a moment in the light from the lamp which the man had snatched from Mr. Selvern; for, strangely enough, this lamp was standing upright and unharmed on the deck, a little way foreside of that dreadful, elongated, growing mound, that still swayed and writhed with an incredible horror. The lamp rose and fell on the passing ripples of the mould, just—for all the world—as you will see a boat rise and fall on little swells. It is of some interest to me now, psychologically, to remember how that rising and falling lantern brought home to me more than anything the incomprehensible dreadful strangeness of it all.

"The men's faces disappeared with sudden yells, as if they had slipped, or been suddenly hurt; and there was a fresh uproar of shouting from the boat. The men were calling to us to come away—to come away. In the same instant I felt my left boot drawn suddenly and forcibly downward, with a horrible, painful grip. I wrenched it free, with a yell of angry fear. Forrard of us, I saw that the vile surface was all amove, and abruptly I found myself shouting in a queer, frightened voice, 'The boat, captain! The boat, captain!'

"Captain Gannington stared round at me, over his right shoulder, in a peculiar, dull way, that told me he was utterly dazed with bewilderment and the incomprehensibleness of it all. I took a quick, clogged, nervous step towards him, and gripped his arm, and shook it fiercely. 'The boat!' I shouted at him. 'The boat! For God's sake, tell the men to bring the boat aft!'

"Then the mound must have drawn his feet down, for abruptly he bellowed fiercely with terror, his momentary apathy giving place to furious energy. His thickset, vastly muscular body doubled and writhed with his enormous effort, and he struck out madly dropping the lantern. He tore his feet free, something ripping as he did so. The *reality* and necessity of the situation had come upon him brutishly real, and he was roaring to the men in the boat, 'Bring the boat aft! Bring 'er aft! Bring 'er aft!' The second mate and I were shouting the same thing madly.

"'For God's sake, be smart, lads!' roared the captain, and stooped quickly for his lamp, which still burned. His feet were gripped again, and he hove them out, blaspheming breathlessly, and leaping a yard high with his effort. Then he made a run for the side, wrenching his feet free at each step. In the same instant the second mate cried out something, and grabbed at the captain.

"'It's got hold of my feet! It's got hold of my feet!' he screamed. His feet, had disappeared up to his boot-tops, and Captain Gannington caught him round the waist with his powerful left arm, gave a mighty heave, and the next instant had him free; but both his boot-soles had gone. For my part, I jumped madly from foot to foot, to avoid the plucking of the mould; and suddenly I made a run for the ship's side. But before I could get there, a queer gape came in the mould between us and the side, at least a couple of feet wide, and how deep I don't know. It closed up in an instant, and all the mould where the gape had been went into a sort of flurry of horrible ripplings, so that I ran back from it; for I did not dare to put my foot upon it. Then the captain was shouting to me:

"'Aft, doctor! Aft, doctor! This way, doctor! Run!' I saw then that he had passed me, and was up on the after raised portion of the poop. He had the second mate, thrown like a sack, all loose and quiet, over his left shoulder; for Mr. Selvern had fainted, and his long legs flogged limp and helpless against the captain's massive knees as he ran. I saw, with a queer, unconscious noting of minor details, how the torn soles of the second mate's boots flapped and jigged as the captain staggered aft.

"'Boat ahoy! Boat ahoy! Boat ahoy!' shouted the captain; and then I was beside him, shouting also. The men were answering with loud yells of encouragement, and it was plain they were working desperately to force the boat aft through the thick scum about the ship.

"We reached the ancient, mould-hid taffrail, and slewed about breathlessly in the half-darkness to see what was happening. Captain Gannington had left his lantern by the big mound when he picked up the second mate; and as we stood, gasping we discovered suddenly that all the mould between us and the light was full of movement. Yet, the part on which we stood, for about six or eight feet forrard of us, was still firm.

"Every couple of seconds we shouted to the men to hasten, and they kept on calling to us that they would be with us in an instant. And all the time we watched the deck of that dreadful hulk, feeling, for my part, literally sick with mad suspense, and ready to jump overboard into that filthy scum all about us.

"Down somewhere in the huge bulk of the ship there was all the time that extraordinary dull, ponderous thud, thud, thud, thud growing ever louder. I seemed to feel the whole hull of the derelict, beginning to quiver and thrill with each dull beat. And to me, with the grotesque and hideous suspicion of what made that noise, it was at once the most dreadful and incredible sound I have ever heard.

"As we waited desperately for the boat, I scanned incessantly so much of the grey white bulk as the lamp showed. The whole of the decks seemed to be in strange movement. Forrard of the lamp, I could see indistinctly the moundings of the mould swaying and nodding hideously beyond the circle of the brightest rays. Nearer, and full in the glow of the lamp, the mound which should have indicated the skylight, was swelling steadily. There were ugly, purple veinings on it, and as it swelled, it seemed to me that the veinings and mottlings on it were becoming plainer, rising as though embossed upon it, like you will see the veins stand out on the body of a powerful, full-blooded horse. It was most extraordinary. The mound that we had supposed to cover the companionway had sunk flat with the surrounding mould, and I could not see that it jetted out any more of the purplish fluid.

"A quaking movement of the mound began away forrard of the lamp, and came flurrying away aft towards us, and at the sight of that I climbed up on to the spongy-feeling taffrail, and yelled afresh for the boat. The men answered with a shout, which told me they were nearer, but the beastly scum was so thick that it was evidently a fight to move the boat at all. Beside me, Captain Gannington was shaking the second mate furiously, and the man stirred and began to moan. The captain shook him again, 'Wake up! Wake up, mister!' he shouted.

"The second mate staggered out of the captain's arms, and collapsed suddenly, shrieking: 'My feet! Oh, God! My feet!' The captain and I lugged him off the mound, and got him into a sitting position upon the taffrail, where he kept up a continual moaning.

'Hold 'im, doctor,' said the captain. And whilst I did so, he ran forrard a few yards, and peered down over the starboard quarter rail. 'For God's sake, be smart, lads! Be smart! Be smart!' he shouted down to the men, and they answered him, breathless, from close at hand, yet still too far away for the boat to be any use to us on the instant.

"I was holding the moaning, half-unconscious officer, and staring forrard along the poop decks. The flurrying of the mould was coming aft, slowly and noiselessly. And then, suddenly, I saw something closer:

"'Look out, captain!' I shouted. And even as I shouted, the mould near to him gave a sudden, peculiar slobber. I had seen a ripple stealing towards him through the mould. He gave an enormous, clumsy leap, and landed near to us on the sound part of the mould, but the movement followed him. He turned and faced it, swearing fiercely. All about his feet there came abruptly little gapings, which made horrid sucking noises. 'Come back, captain!' I yelled. 'Come back, *quick!*' As I shouted, a ripple came at his feet—lipping at them; and he stamped insanely at it, and leaped back, his boot torn half off his foot. He swore madly with pain and anger, and jumped swiftly for the taffrail.

"'Come on, doctor! Over we go!' he called. Then he remembered the filthy scum, and hesitated, and roared out desperately to the men to hurry. I stared down, also.

'The second mate?' I said.

"'I'll take charge doctor,' said Captain Gannington, and caught hold of Mr. Selvern. As he spoke, I thought I saw something beneath us, outlined against the scum. I leaned out over the stern, and peered. There was something under the port-quarter.

"'There's something down there, captain!' I called, and pointed in the darkness. He stooped far over, and stared.

"'A boat, by gum! A boat!' he yelled, and began to wriggle swiftly along the taffrail, dragging the second mate after him. I followed. 'A boat it is, sure!' he exclaimed a few moments later, and, picking up the second mate clear of the rail, he hove him down into the boat, where he fell with a crash into the bottom.

"'Over ye go, doctor!' he yelled at me, and pulled me bodily off the rail and dropped me after the officer. As he did so, I felt the whole of the ancient, spongy rail give a peculiar, sickening quiver, and begin to wobble. I fell on to the second mate, and the captain came after, almost in the same instant, but, fortunately, he landed clear of us, on to the fore thwart, which broke under his weight, with a loud crack and splintering of wood.

"'Thank God!' I heard him mutter. 'Thank God! I guess that was a mighty near thing to going to Hades.'

"He struck a match, just as I got to my feet, and between us we got the second mate straightened out on one of the after fore-and-aft thwarts. We shouted to the men in the boat, telling them where we were, and saw the light of their lantern shining round the starboard counter of the derelict. They called back to us to tell us they were doing their best, and then, whilst we waited, Captain Gannington struck another match, and began to overhaul the boat we had dropped into. She was a modern, two-bowed boat, and on the stern there was painted 'Cyclone, Glasgow.' She was in pretty fair condition, and had evidently drifted into the scum and been held by it.

"Captain Gannington struck several matches, and went forrard towards the derelict. Suddenly he called to me, and I jumped over the thwarts to him. 'Look, doctor,' he said, and I saw what he meant—a mass of bones up in the bows of the boat. I stooped over them, and looked; there were the bones of at least three people, all mixed together in an extraordinary fashion, and quite clean and dry. I had a sudden thought concerning the bones, but I said nothing, for my thought was vague in some ways, and concerned the grotesque and incredible suggestion that had come to me as to the cause of that ponderous, dull thud, thud, thud thud, that beat on so infernally within the hull, and was plain to hear even now that we had got off the vessel herself. And all the while, you know, I had a sick, horrible mental picture of that frightful, wriggling mound aboard the hulk.

"As Captain Gannington struck a final match, I saw something that sickened me and the captain saw it in the same instant. The match went out, and he fumbled clumsily for another, and struck it. We saw the thing again. We had not been mistaken. A great lip of grey-white was protruding in over the edge of the boat— a great lappet of the mould was coming stealthily towards us—a live mass of *the very hull itself!* And suddenly Captain Gannington yelled out in so many words the grotesque and incredible thing I was thinking: *'She's alive!'*

"I never heard such a sound of comprehension and terror in a man's voice. The very horrified assurance of it made actual to me the thing that before had only lurked in my subconscious mind. I knew he was right; I knew that the explanation my reason and my training both repelled and reached towards was the true one. Oh, I wonder whether anyone can possibly understand our feelings in that moment? The unmitigated horror of it and the incredibleness!

"As the light of the match burned up fully, I saw that the mass of living matter coming towards us was streaked and veined with purple, the veins standing out, enormously distended. The whole thing quivered continuously to each ponderous thud, thud, thud, thud, of that gargantuan organ that pulsed within the huge grey-white bulk. The flame of the match reached the captain's fingers, and there came to me a little sickly whiff of burned flesh, but he seemed unconscious of any pain. Then the flame went out in a brief sizzle, yet at the last moment I had seen an extraordinary raw look become visible upon the end of that monstrous, protruding lappet. It had become dewed with a hideous, purplish sweat. And with the darkness there came a sudden charnel-like stench.

"I heard the matchbox split in Captain Gannington's hands as he wrenched it open. Then he swore, in a queer frightened voice, for he had come to the end of his matches. He turned clumsily in the darkness, and tumbled over the nearest thwart, in his eagerness to get to the stern of the boat; and I after him. For we knew that thing was coming towards us through the darkness, reaching over that piteous mingled heap of human bones all jumbled together in the bows. We shouted madly to the men, and for answer saw the bows of the boat emerge dimly into view round the starboard counter of the derelict.

"'Thank God!' I gasped out. But Captain Gannington roared to them to show a light. Yet this they could not do, for the lamp had just been stepped on in their desperate efforts to force the boat round to us.

"'Quick! Quick!' I shouted.

"'For God's sake, be smart, men!' roared the captain.

"And both of us faced the darkness under the port-counter, out of which we knew—but could not see—the thing was coming to us.

"'An oar! Smart, now—pass me an oar!' shouted the captain; and reached out his hands through the gloom towards the on-coming boat. I saw a figure stand up in the bows, and hold something out to us across the intervening yards of scum. Captain Gannington swept his hands through the darkness, and encountered it.

"'I've got it! Let go there!' he said, in a quick, tense voice.

"In the same instant the boat we were in was pressed over suddenly to starboard by some tremendous weight. Then I heard the captain shout, 'Duck y'r head, doctor!' And directly afterwards he swung the heavy, fourteen-foot oar round his head, and struck into the darkness. There came a sudden squelch, and he struck again, with a savage grunt of fierce energy. At the second blow the boat righted with a slow movement, and directly afterwards the other boat bumped gently into ours.

"Captain Gannington dropped the oar, and, springing across to the second mate, hove him up off the thwart, and pitched him with knee and arms clear in over the bows among the men; then he shouted to me to follow, which I did, and he came after me, bringing the oar with him. We carried the second mate aft, and the captain shouted to the men to back the boat a little; then they got her bows clear of the boat we had just left, and so headed out through the scum for the open sea.

"'Where's Tom 'Arrison?" gasped one of the men, in the midst of his exertions. He happened to be Tom Harrison's particular chum, and Captain Gannington answered him briefly enough:

"'Dead! Pull! Don't talk!'

"Now, difficult as it had been to force the boat through the scum to our rescue, the difficulty to get clear seemed tenfold. After some five minutes pulling, the boat seemed hardly to have moved a fathom, if so much, and a quite dreadful fear took me afresh, which one of the panting men put suddenly into words, 'It's got us!' he gasped out. 'Same as poor Tom!' It was the man who had inquired where Harrison was.

"'Shut y'r mouth an' *pull!*' roared the captain. And so another few minutes passed. Abruptly, it seemed to me that the dull, ponderous thud, thud, thud, thud came more plainly through the dark, and I stared intently over the stern. I sickened a little, for I could almost swear that the dark mass of the monster was actually nearer—that it was coming *nearer* to us through the darkness. Captain Gannington must have had the same thought, for, after a brief look into the darkness, he jumped forrard, and began to double-bank the stroke-oar.

"'Get forrid under the oars, doctor,' he said to me rather breathlessly. 'Get in the bows, an' see if you can't free the stuff a bit round the bows.'

"I did as he told me, and a minute later I was in the bows of the boat, puddling the scum from side to side, and trying to break up the viscid, clinging muck. A heavy almost animal-like smell rose off it, and all the air seemed full of the deadening, heavy smell. I shall never find words to tell anyone on earth the whole horror of it all—the threat that seemed to hang in the very air around us, and but a little astern that incredible thing, coming, as I firmly believed, nearer, and scum holding us, like half-melted glue.

"The minutes passed in a deadly, eternal fashion, and I kept staring back astern into the darkness but never ceasing to puddle that filthy scum, striking at it and switching it from side to side until I sweated.

"Abruptly Captain Gannington sang out: 'We're gaining, lads. Pull!' And I felt the boat forge ahead perceptibly, as they gave way with renewed hope and energy. There was soon no doubt of it, for presently that hideous thud, thud, thud, thud had grown quite dim and vague somewhere astern and I could no longer see the derelict, for the night had come down tremendously dark and all the sky was thick, overset with heavy clouds. As we drew nearer and nearer to the edge of the scum, the boat moved more and more perceptibly, until suddenly we emerged with a clean, sweet, fresh sound into the open sea.

"'Thank God!' I said aloud, and drew in the boathook, and made my way aft again to where Captain Gannington now sat once more at the tiller. I saw him looking anxiously up at the sky and across to where the lights of our vessel burned, and again he would seem to listen intently, so that I found myself listening also.

"'What's that, Captain?' I said sharply; for it seemed to me that I heard a sound far astern, something, between a queer whine and a low whistling. 'What's that?'

"'It's wind, doctor,' he said in a low voice. 'I wish to God we were aboard.' Then to the men: 'Pull! Put y'r backs into it, or ye'll never put y'r teeth through good bread again!' The men obeyed nobly, and we reached the vessel safely, and had the boat safely stowed before the storm came, which it did in a furious white smother out of the west. I could see it for some minutes beforehand, tearing the sea in the gloom into a wall of phosphorescent foam; and as it came nearer, that peculiar whining, piping sound grew louder and louder, until it was like a vast steam whistle rushing towards us. And when it did come, we got it very heavy indeed, so that the morning showed us nothing but a welter of white seas, with that grim derelict many a score of miles away in the smother, lost as utterly as our hearts could wish to lose her.

"When I came to examine the second mate's feet, I found them in a very extraordinary condition. The soles of them had the appearance of having been partly digested. I know of no other word that so exactly describes their condition, and the agony the man suffered must have been dreadful.

"Now," concluded the doctor, "that is what I call a case in point. If we could know exactly what the old vessel had originally been loaded with, and the juxtaposition of the various articles of her cargo, plus the heat and time she had endured, plus one or two other only guessable quantities, we should have solved the chemistry of the life-force, gentlemen. Not necessarily the *origin*, mind you; but, at least, we should have taken a big step on the way. I've often regretted that gale, you know— in a way, that is, in a way. It was a most amazing discovery, but at the same time I had nothing but thankfulness to be rid of it. A most amazing chance. I often think of the way the monster woke out of its torpor. And that scum! The dead pigs caught in it! I fancy that was a grim kind of a net, gentlemen. It caught many things. It—"

The old doctor sighed and nodded.

"If I could have had her bill of lading," he said, his eyes full of regret. "If— It might have told me something to help. But, anyway—" He began to fill his pipe again. "I suppose," he ended, looking round at us gravely, "I s'pose we humans are an ungrateful lot of beggars at the best! But—but, what a chance? What a, chance, eh?"

The Murdered Lady

by John Greenleaf Whittier

In the 17th century, when the sea-robbers were ravaging the commerce of Spain, a vessel of that nation was brought into the port of Marblehead, by a pirate brig. For the better security of its rich cargo, the unfortunate crew were barbarously massacred. A lady was brought on shore by the pirates, and murdered, and afterwards buried in a deep glen or valley, at a little distance from the village. The few inhabitants of the place, at that early period of its history, were unable to offer any resistance to the fierce and well-armed buccaneers. They heard the shrieks of the unfortunate lady, mingled with the savage shouts of her murderers, but could afford her no succor. There is a tradition among some of the old inhabitants of Marblehead, that these same sounds have been heard ever since, at intervals of two or three years, in the valley where the lady was buried.

—Author

A dark-hulled brig at anchor rides,
    Within the still and moonlight bay,
And round its black, portentous sides
    The waves like living creatures play!—
And close at hand a tall ship lies—
A voyager from the Spanish Main,
Laden with gold and merchandize—
She'll ne'er return again!
The fisher in his seaward skiff,
    Creeps stealthily along the shore,
Within the shadow of the cliff,
    Where keel had never ploughed before;

He turns him from that stranger bark,
    And hurries down the silver bay,
Where, like a demon still and dark,
    She watches o'er her prey.
The midnight came.—A dash of oars
    Broke on the ocean-stillness then,
And swept towards the rocky shores,
    The fierce wild forms of outlawed men;—
The tenants of that fearful ship,
    Grouped strangely in the pale moon-light—
Dark, iron brow and bearded lip,
    Ghastly with storm and fight.
They reach the shore,—but who is she—
The white-robed one they bear along?
She shrieks—she struggles to be free—
God shield that gentle one from wrong;
It may not be,—those pirate men,
    Along the hushed, deserted street,
Have borne her to a narrow glen,
    Scarce trod by human feet.

And there the ruffians murdered her,
    When not an eye, save Heaven's beheld,

Ask of the shuddering villager,
    What sounds upon the night air swelled
Woman's long shriek of mortal fear—
Her wild appeal to hearts of stone,
The oath—the taunt—the brutal jeer—
The pistol-shot—the groan!
With shout and jest and losel song,
    From savage tongues which knew no rein,
The stained with murder passed along,
    And sought their ocean-home again;—
And all the night their revel came
    In hoarse and sullen murmurs on,—
A yell rang up—a burst of flame—
The Spanish Ship was gone!
The morning light came red and fast
    Along the still and blushing sea;
The phantoms of the night had passed—
That ocean-robber—where was she?—
Her sails were reaching from the wind,
    Her crimson banner-folds were stirred;
And ever and anon behind,
    Her shouting crew were heard.

Then came the village-dwellers forth,
    And sought with fear the fatal glen;—
The stain of blood—the trampled earth
    Told where the deed of death had been.
They found a grave—a new-made one—
With bloody sabres hollowed out,

And shadowed from the searching sun,
    By tall trees round about.
They left the hapless stranger there;
    They knew her sleep would be as well,
As if the priest had poured his prayer
    Above her—with the funeral-bell.
The few poor rites which man can pay,
    Are felt not by the lonely sleeper;
The deaf, unconscious ear of clay
    Heeds not the living weeper.
They tell a tale—those sea-worn men,
    Who dwell along that rocky coast,
Of sights and sounds within the glen,
    Of midnight shriek and gliding ghost.
And oh! if ever from their chill
    And dreamless sleep, the dead arise,
That victim of unhallowed ill
    Might wake to human eyes!

They say that often when the morn,
    Is struggling with the gloomy even;
And over moon and star is drawn
    The curtain of a clouded heaven—
Strange sounds swell up the narrow glen,
As if that robber-crew were there—
The hellish laugh—the shouts of men—
    And woman's dying prayer!

Phantom Ships and the Sargasso Sea

by Elliott O'Donnell

I very often sound sailors as to whether they have ever come across this ominous vessel, and sometimes hear very enthralling accounts of it. An old sea captain whom I met on the pier at Southampton, in reply to my inquiry, said: "Yes! I have seen the phantom ship, or at any rate a phantom ship, once—but only once. It was one night in the fifties, and we were becalmed in the South Pacific about three hundred miles due west of Callao. It had been terrifically hot all day, and, only too thankful that it was now a little cooler, I was lolling over the bulwarks to get a few mouthfuls of fresh air before turning into my berth, when one of the crew touched me on the shoulder, and ejaculating, 'For God's sake—' abruptly left off. Following the direction of his glaring eyes, I saw to my amazement a large black brig bearing directly down on us. She was about a mile off, and, despite the intense calmness of the sea, was pitching and tossing as if in the roughest water. As she drew nearer I was able to make her out better, and from her build—she carried two masts and was square-rigged forward and schooner-rigged aft—as well as from her tawdry gilt figurehead, concluded she was a hermaphrodite brig of, very possibly, Dutch nationality. She had evidently seen a great deal of rough weather, for her foretop-mast and part of her starboard bulwarks were gone, and what added to my astonishment and filled me with fears and doubts was, that in spite of the pace at which she was approaching us and the dead calmness of the air, she had no other sails than her foresail and mainsail, and flying-jib.

"By this time all of our crew were on deck, and the skipper and the second mate took up their positions one on either side of me, the man who had first called my attention to the strange ship, joining some other seamen near the fore-castle. No one spoke, but, from the expression in their eyes and ghastly pallor of their cheeks, it was very easy to see that one and all were dominated by the same feelings of terror and suspicion. Nearer and nearer drew the brig, until she was at last so close that we could perceive her crew—all of whom, save the helmsman, were leaning over the bulwarks—grinning at us. Never shall I forget the horror of those grins. They were hideous, meaningless, hellish grins, the grins of corpses in the last stage of putrefaction. And that is just what they were—all of them—corpses, but corpses possessed by spirits of the most devilish sort, for as we stared, too petrified with fear to remove our gaze, they nodded their ulcerated heads and gesticulated vehemently. The brig then gave a sudden yaw, and with that motion there was wafted a stink—a stink too damnably foul and rotten to originate from anywhere, save from some cesspool in hell. Choking, retching, and all but fainting, I buried my face in the skipper's coat, and did not venture to raise it, till the far-away sounds of plunging and tossing assured me the cursed ship had passed. I then looked up, and was just in time to catch a final glimpse of the brig, a few hundred yards to leeward (she had passed close under our stern) before her lofty stern rose out of the water, and, bows foremost, she plunged into the stilly depths and we saw her no more. There was no need for the skipper to tell us that she was the phantom ship, nor did she belie her sinister reputation, for within a week of seeing her, yellow fever broke out on board, and when we arrived at port, there were only three of us left."

THE SARGASSO SEA

Of all the seas in the world, none bear a greater reputation for being haunted than the Sargasso. Within this impenetrable waste of rank, stinking seaweed, in places many feet deep, are collected wreckages of all ages and all climes, grim and permanent records of the world's maritime history, unsinkable and undestroyable. It has ever been my ambition to explore the margins of this unsightly yet fascinating marine wilderness, but, so far, I have been unable to extend my peregrinations further south than the thirty-fifth degree of latitude.

Among the many stories I have heard in connection with this sea, the following will, I think, bear repeating:—

"A brig with twelve hands aboard, bound from Boston to the Cape Verde Islands, was caught in a storm, and, being blown out of her course, drifted on to the northern extremities of the Sargasso. The wind then sinking, and an absolute calm taking its place, there seemed every prospect that the brig would remain where it was for an indefinite period. A most horrible fate now stared the crew in the face, for although they had food enough to last them for many weeks, they only had a very limited supply of water, and the intense heat and terrific stench from the weeds made them abnormally thirsty.

"After a long and earnest consultation, in which the skipper acted as chairman, it was decided that on the consumption of the last drop of water they should all commit suicide, anything rather than to perish of thirst, and it would be far less harrowing to die in a body and face the awful possibilities of the next world in company than alone.

"As there was only one firearm on board, and the idea of throat-cutting was disapproved of by several of the more timid, rat poison, of which there was just enough to go all round, was chosen. Meanwhile, in consideration of the short time left to them on earth, the crew insisted that they should be allowed to enjoy themselves to the utmost. To this the captain, knowing only too well what that would mean, reluctantly gave his consent. A general pandemonium at once ensued, one of the men producing a mouth accordion and another a concertina, whilst the rest, selecting partners with much mock gallantry, danced to the air of a popular Vaudeville song till they could dance no longer.

"The next item on the programme was dinner. The best of everything on board was served up, and they all ate and drank till they could hold no more. They were then so sleepy that they tumbled off their seats, and, lying on the floor, soon snored like hogs. The cool of the evening restoring them, they played pitch and toss, and poker, till tea-time, and then fooled away the remainder of the evening in more cards and more drink. In this manner the best part of a week was beguiled. Then the skipper announced the fact that the last drop of liquor on board had gone, and that, according to the compact, the hour had arrived to commit suicide. Had a bombshell fallen in their midst, it could not have caused a greater consternation than this announcement. The men had, by this time, become so enamoured with their easy and irresponsible mode of living, that the idea of quitting it in so abrupt a manner was by no means to their liking, and they evinced their displeasure in the roughest and most forcible of language. The skipper could damned well put an end to himself if he had a mind to, but they would see themselves somewhere else before they did any such thing—it would be time enough to talk of dying when the victuals were all eaten up. Then they thoroughly overhauled the ship, and on discovering half a dozen bottles of rum and a small cask of water stowed away in the skipper's cabin, they threw him overboard and pelted him with empty bottles till he sank; after which they cleared the deck and danced till sunset.

"Two nights later, when they were all lying on the deck near the companion way, licking their parched lips and commiserating with themselves on the prospect of their gradually approaching end—for they had abandoned all idea of the rat poison—they suddenly saw a hideous, sea-weedy object rise up over the bulwarks on the leeward side of the ship. In breathless expectation they all sat up and watched. Inch by inch it rose, until they saw before them a tall form enveloped from head to foot in green slime, and horribly suggestive of the well-known figure of the murdered captain. Gliding noiselessly over the deck, it shook its hands menacingly at each of the sailors, until it came to the cabin-boy—the only one among them who had not participated in the skipper's death—when it touched him gently on the forehead, and, stooping down, appeared to whisper something in his ears. It then re-crossed the deck, and, mounting the bulwarks, leaped into the sea.

"For some seconds no one stirred; and then, as if under the influence of some hypnotic spell, one by one, each of the crew, with the exception of the cabin-boy, got up, and, marching in Indian file to the spot where the apparition had vanished, flung themselves overboard. The last of the procession had barely disappeared from view, when the cabin-boy, whose agony of mind during this infernal tragedy cannot be described, fell into a heavy stupor, from which he did not awake till morning. In the meanwhile the brig, owing to a stiff breeze that had arisen in the night, was freed from its environment, and was drifting away from the seaweed. It went on and on, day after day, and day after day, till it was eventually sighted by a steamer and taken in tow. The cabin-boy, by this time barely alive, was nursed with the tenderest care, and, owing to the assiduous attention bestowed on him, he completely recovered."

I think this story, though naturally ridiculed and discredited by some, may be unreservedly accepted by those whose knowledge and experience of the occult warrant their belief in it.

The Sailor's Grave

by Eliza Cook

Our bark was far, far from the land
When the bravest of our gallant band
Went deadly pale, an' pined away
Like the twilight of an autumn day.

We watched him through long hours of pain
Our hopes were great, our task in vain.
His end was near, we felt sad qualms
But he smiled and died in his shipmates' arms.

He had no costly winding sheet
We placed two round shot at his feet,
And we sewed him up, he was canvas-bound
Like a king he lay in his hammock sound.

We proudly decked his broken chest
With the "Blood'n'Guts"* across his breast
The flag we gave as a mark o' the brave
And he was ready for a sailor's grave.

Our voices broke, our hearts were weak
And wet was seen on the toughest cheek
We lowered him down o'er the ship's dark side
And he was received by the rollin' tide.

With a splash and a plunge and our task was o'er
And the billows rolled as they rolled before,
And many a wild prayer hallowed the wave
As he sank deep to a sailor's grave.

*Sailor's name for the red ensign of Britain.

A Descent into the Maelström

by Edgar Allan Poe

The ways of God in Nature, as in Providence, are not as our ways; nor are the models that we frame any way commensurate to the vastness, profundity, and unsearchableness of His works, which have a depth in them greater than the well of Democritus.

—Joseph Glanville

We had now reached the summit of the loftiest crag. For some minutes the old man seemed too much exhausted to speak.

"Not long ago," said he at length, "and I could have guided you on this route as well as the youngest of my sons; but, about three years past, there happened to me an event such as never happened before to mortal man—or at least such as no man ever survived to tell of—and the six hours of deadly terror which I then endured have broken me up body and soul. You suppose me a *very* old man—but I am not. It took less than a single day to change these hairs from a jetty black to white, to weaken my limbs, and to unstring my nerves, so that I tremble at the least exertion, and am frightened at a shadow. Do you know I can scarcely look over this little cliff without getting giddy?"

The "little cliff," upon whose edge he had so carelessly thrown himself down to rest that the weightier portion of his body hung over it, while he was only kept from falling by the tenure of his elbow on its extreme and slippery edge—this "little cliff" arose, a sheer unobstructed precipice of black shining rock, some fifteen or sixteen hundred feet from the world of crags beneath us. Nothing would have tempted me to within half a dozen yards of its brink. In truth so deeply was I excited by the perilous position of my companion, that I fell at full length upon the ground, clung to the shrubs around me, and dared not even glance upward at the sky—while I struggled in vain to divest myself of the idea that the very foundations of the mountain were in danger from the fury of the winds. It was long before I could reason myself into sufficient courage to sit up and look out into the distance.

"You must get over these fancies," said the guide, "for I have brought you here that you might have the best possible view of the scene of that event I mentioned—and to tell you the whole story with the spot just under your eye.

"We are now," he continued, in that particularizing manner which distinguished him—"we are now close upon the Norwegian coast—in the sixty-eighth degree of latitude—in the great province of Nordland—and in the dreary district of Lofoden. The mountain upon whose top we sit is Helseggen, the Cloudy. Now raise yourself up a little higher—hold on to the grass if you feel giddy—so—and look out beyond the belt of vapor beneath us, into the sea."

I looked dizzily, and beheld a wide expanse of ocean, whose waters wore so inky a hue as to bring at once to my mind the Nubian geographer's account of the *Mare Tenebrarum*. A panorama more deplorably desolate no human imagination can conceive. To the right and left, as far as the eye could reach, there lay outstretched, like ramparts of the world, lines of horridly black and beetling cliff, whose character of gloom was but the more forcibly illustrated by the surf which reared high up against it its white and ghastly crest, howling and shrieking for ever. Just opposite the promontory upon whose apex we were placed, and at a distance of some five or six miles out at sea, there was visible a small, bleak-looking island; or, more properly, its position was discernible through the wilderness of surge in which it was enveloped. About two miles nearer the land, arose another of smaller size, hideously craggy and barren, and encompassed at various intervals by a cluster of dark rocks.

The appearance of the ocean, in the space between the more distant island and the shore, had something very unusual about it. Although, at the time, so strong a gale was blowing landward that a brig in the remote offing lay to under a double-reefed trysail, and constantly plunged her whole hull out of sight, still there was here nothing like a regular swell, but only a short, quick, angry cross dashing of water in every direction—as well in the teeth of the wind as otherwise. Of foam there was little except in the immediate vicinity of the rocks.

"The island in the distance," resumed the old man, "is called by the Norwegians Vurrgh. The one midway is Moskoe. That a mile to the northward is Ambaaren. Yonder are Iflesen, Hoeyholm, Kieldholm, Suarven, and Buckholm. Farther off— between Moskoe and Vurrgh—are Otterholm, Flimen, Sandflesen, and Skarholm. These are the true names of the places—but why it has been thought necessary to name them at all, is more than either you or I can understand. Do you hear any thing? Do you see any change in the water?"

We had now been about ten minutes upon the top of Helseggen, to which we had ascended from the interior of Lofoden, so that we had caught no glimpse of the sea until it had burst upon us from the summit. As the old man spoke, I became aware of a loud and gradually increasing sound, like the moaning of a vast herd of buffaloes upon an American prairie; and at the same moment I perceived that what seamen term the *chopping* character of the ocean beneath us, was rapidly changing into a current which set to the eastward. Even while I gazed, this current acquired a monstrous velocity. Each moment added to its speed—to its headlong impetuosity. In five minutes the whole sea, as far as Vurrgh, was lashed into ungovernable fury; but it was between Moskoe and the coast that the main uproar held its sway. Here the vast bed of the waters, seamed and scarred into a thousand conflicting channels, burst suddenly into phrensied convulsion—heaving, boiling, hissing—gyrating in gigantic and innumerable vortices, and all whirling and plunging on to the eastward with a rapidity which water never elsewhere assumes except in precipitous descents.

In a few minutes more, there came over the scene another radical alteration. The general surface grew somewhat more smooth, and the whirlpools, one by one, disappeared, while prodigious streaks of foam became apparent where none had been seen before. These streaks, at length, spreading out to a great distance, and entering into combination, took unto themselves the gyratory motion of the sub- sided vortices, and seemed to form the germ of another more vast. Suddenly—very suddenly—this assumed a distinct and definite existence, in a circle of more than half a mile in diameter. The edge of the whirl was represented by a broad belt of gleaming spray; but no particle of this slipped into the mouth of the terrific funnel, whose interior, as far as the eye could fathom it, was a smooth, shining, and jet-black wall of water, inclined to the horizon at an angle of some forty-five degrees, speeding dizzily round and round with a swaying and sweltering motion, and sending forth to the winds an appalling voice, half shriek, half roar, such as not even the mighty cataract of Niagara ever lifts up in its agony to Heaven.

The mountain trembled to its very base, and the rock rocked. I threw myself upon my face, and clung to the scant herbage in an excess of nervous agitation.

"This," said I at length, to the old man—"this *can* be nothing else than the great whirlpool of the Maelström."

"So it is sometimes termed," said he. "We Norwegians call it the Moskoe-ström, from the island of Moskoe in the midway."

The ordinary accounts of this vortex had by no means prepared me for what I saw. That of Jonas Ramus, which is perhaps the most circumstantial of any, cannot impart the faintest conception either of the magnificence, or of the horror of the scene—or of the wild bewildering sense of *the novel* which confounds the beholder. I am not sure from what point of view the writer in question surveyed it, nor at what time; but it could neither have been from the summit of Helseggen, nor during a storm. There are some passages of his description, nevertheless, which may be quoted for their details, although their effect is exceedingly feeble in conveying an impression of the spectacle.

"Between Lofoden and Moskoe," he says, "the depth of the water is between thirty-six and forty fathoms; but on the other side, toward Ver (Vurrgh) this depth decreases so as not to afford a convenient passage for a vessel, without the risk of splitting on the rocks, which happens even in the calmest weather. When it is flood, the stream runs up the country between Lofoden and Moskoe with a boisterous rapidity; but the roar of its impetuous ebb to the sea is scarce equalled by the loudest and most dreadful cataracts; the noise being heard several leagues off, and the vortices or pits are of such an extent and depth, that if a ship comes within its attraction, it is inevitably absorbed and carried down to the bottom, and there beat to pieces against the rocks; and when the water relaxes, the fragments thereof are thrown up again. But these intervals of tranquillity are only at the turn of the ebb and flood, and in calm weather, and last but a quarter of an hour, its violence gradually returning. When the stream is most boisterous, and its fury heightened by a storm, it is dangerous to come within a Norway mile of it. Boats, yachts, and ships have been carried away by not guarding against it before they were within its reach. It likewise happens frequently, that whales come too near the stream, and are overpowered by its violence; and then it is impossible to describe their howlings and bellowings in their fruitless struggles to disengage themselves. A bear once, attempting to swim from Lofoden to Moskoe, was caught by the stream and borne down, while he roared terribly, so as to be heard on shore. Large stocks of firs and pine trees, after being absorbed by the current, rise again broken and torn to such a degree as if bristles grew upon them. This plainly shows the bottom to consist of craggy rocks, among which they are whirled to and fro. This stream is regulated by the flux and reflux of the sea—it being constantly high and low water every six hours. In the year 1645, early in the morning of Sexagesima Sunday, it raged with such noise and impetuosity that the very stones of the houses on the coast fell to the ground."

In regard to the depth of the water, I could not see how this could have been ascertained at all in the immediate vicinity of the vortex. The "forty fathoms" must have reference only to portions of the channel close upon the shore either of Moskoe or Lofoden. The depth in the centre of the Moskoe-ström must be immeasurably greater; and no better proof of this fact is necessary than can be obtained from even the sidelong glance into the abyss of the whirl which may be had from the highest crag of Helseggen. Looking down from this pinnacle upon the howling Phlegethon below, I could not help smiling at the simplicity with which the honest Jonas Ramus records, as a matter difficult of belief, the anecdotes of the whales and the bears; for it appeared to me, in fact, a self-evident thing, that the largest ships of the line in existence, coming within the influence of that deadly attraction, could resist it as little as a feather the hurricane, and must disappear bodily and at once.

The attempts to account for the phenomenon—some of which, I remember, seemed to me sufficiently plausible in perusal—now wore a very different and unsatisfactory aspect. The idea generally received is that this, as well as three smaller vortices among the Feroe islands, "have no other cause than the collision of waves rising and falling, at flux and reflux, against a ridge of rocks and shelves, which confines the water so that it precipitates itself like a cataract; and thus the higher the flood rises, the deeper must the fall be, and the natural result of all is a whirlpool or vortex, the prodigious suction of which is sufficiently known by lesser experiments."—These are the words of the *Encyclopædia Britannica*. Kircher and others imagine that in the centre of the channel of the Maelström is an abyss penetrating the globe, and issuing in some very remote part—the Gulf of Bothnia being somewhat decidedly named in one instance. This opinion, idle in itself, was the one to which, as I gazed, my imagination most readily assented; and, mentioning it to the guide, I was rather surprised to hear him say that, although it was the view almost universally entertained of the subject by the Norwegians, it nevertheless was not his own. As to the former notion he con-fessed his inability to comprehend it; and here I agreed with him—for, however conclusive on paper, it becomes altogether unintelligible, and even absurd, amid the thunder of the abyss.

"You have had a good look at the whirl now," said the old man, "and if you will creep round this crag, so as to get in its lee, and deaden the roar of the water, I will tell you a story that will convince you I ought to know something of the Moskoe-ström."

I placed myself as desired, and he proceeded.

"Myself and my two brothers once owned a schooner-rigged smack of about seventy tons burthen, with which we were in the habit of fishing among the islands beyond Moskoe, nearly to Vurrgh. In all violent eddies at sea there is good fishing, at proper opportunities, if one has only the courage to attempt it; but among the whole of the Lofoden coastmen, we three were the only ones who made a regular business of going out to the islands, as I tell you. The usual grounds are a great way lower down to the southward. There fish can be got at all hours, without much risk, and therefore these places are preferred. The choice spots over here among the rocks, however, not only yield the finest variety, but in far greater abundance; so that we often got in a single day, what the more timid of the craft could not scrape together in a week. In fact, we made it a matter of desperate speculation—the risk of life standing instead of labor, and courage answering for capital.

"We kept the smack in a cove about five miles higher up the coast than this; and it was our practice, in fine weather, to take advantage of the fifteen minutes' slack to push across the main channel of the Moskoe-ström, far above the pool, and then drop down upon anchorage somewhere near Otterholm, or Sandflesen, where the eddies are not so violent as elsewhere. Here we used to remain until nearly time for slack-water again, when we weighed and made for home. We never set out upon this expedition without a steady side wind for going and coming— one that we felt sure would not fall us before our return—and we seldom made a miscalculation upon this point. Twice, during six years, we were forced to stay all night at anchor on account of a dead calm, which is a rare thing indeed just about here; and once we had to remain on the grounds nearly a week, starving to death, owing to a gale which blew up shortly after our arrival, and made the channel too boisterous to be thought of. Upon this occasion we should have been driven out to sea in spite of everything, (for the whirlpools threw us round and round so violently that, at length, we fouled our anchor and dragged it) if it had not been that we drifted into one of the innumerable cross currents—here to-day and gone to-morrow—which drove us under the lee of Flimen, where, by good luck, we brought up.

"I could not tell you the twentieth part of the difficulties we encountered 'on the ground'—it is a bad spot to be in, even in good weather—but we made shift always to run the gauntlet of the Moskoe-ström itself without accident; although at times my heart has been in my mouth when we happened to be a minute or so behind or before the slack. The wind sometimes was not as strong as we thought it at starting, and then we made rather less way than we could wish, while the current rendered the smack unmanageable. My eldest brother had a son eighteen years old, and I had two stout boys of my own. These would have been of great assistance at such times, in using the sweeps, as well as afterward in fishing—but, somehow, although we ran the risk ourselves, we had not the heart to let the young ones get into the danger—for, after all said and done, it was a horrible danger, and that is the truth.

"It is now within a few days of three years since what I am going to tell you occurred. It was on the tenth of July, 18—, a day which the people of this part of the world will never forget—for it was one in which blew the most terrible hurricane that ever came out of the heavens. And yet all the morning, and indeed until late in the afternoon, there was a gentle and steady breeze from the south-west, while the sun shone brightly, so that the oldest seaman among us could not have foreseen what was to follow.

"The three of us—my two brothers and myself—had crossed over to the islands about two o'clock P.M., and soon nearly loaded the smack with fine fish, which, we all remarked, were more plenty that day than we had ever known them. It was just seven, *by my watch*, when we weighed and started for home, so as to make the worst of the Ström at slack water, which we knew would be at eight.

"We set out with a fresh wind on our starboard quarter, and for some time spanked along at a great rate, never dreaming of danger, for indeed we saw not the slightest reason to apprehend it. All at once we were taken aback by a breeze from over Helseggen. This was most unusual—something that had never happened to us before—and I began to feel a little uneasy, without exactly knowing why. We put the boat on the wind, but could make no headway at all for the eddies, and I was upon the point of proposing to return to the anchorage, when, looking astern, we saw the whole horizon covered with a singular copper-colored cloud that rose with the most amazing velocity.

"In the meantime the breeze that had headed us off fell away, and we were dead becalmed, drifting about in every direction. This state of things, however, did not last long enough to give us time to think about it. In less than a minute the storm was upon us—in less than two the sky was entirely overcast—and what with this and the driving spray, it became suddenly so dark that we could not see each other in the smack.

"Such a hurricane as then blew it is folly to attempt describing. The oldest seaman in Norway never experienced any thing like it. We had let our sails go by the run before it cleverly took us; but, at the first puff, both our masts went by the board if they had been sawed off—the mainmast taking with it my as I youngest brother, who had lashed himself to it for safety.

"Our boat was the lightest feather of a thing that ever sat upon water. It had a complete flush deck, with only a small hatch near the bow, and this hatch it had always been our custom to batten down when about to cross the Ström, by way of precaution against the chopping seas. But for this circumstance we should have

foundered at once—for we lay entirely buried for some moments. How my elder brother escaped destruction I cannot say, for I never had an opportunity of ascertaining. For my part, as soon as I had let the foresail run, I threw myself flat on deck, with my feet against the narrow gunwale of the bow, and with my hands grasping a ring-bolt near the foot of the foremast. It was mere instinct that prompted me to do this—which was undoubtedly the very best thing I could have done—for I was too much flurried to think.

"For some moments we were completely deluged, as I say, and all this time I held my breath, and clung to the bolt. When I could stand it no longer I raised myself upon my knees, still keeping hold with my hands, and thus got my head clear. Presently our little boat gave herself a shake, just as a dog does in coming out of the water, and thus rid herself, in some measure, of the seas. I was now trying to get the better of the stupor that had come over me, and to collect my senses so as to see what was to be done, when I felt somebody grasp my arm. It was my elder brother, and my heart leaped for joy, for I had made sure that he was overboard—but the next moment all this joy was turned into horror—for he put his mouth close to my ear, and screamed out the word '*Moskoe-ström!*'

"No one ever will know what my feelings were at that moment. I shook from head to foot as if I had had the most violent fit of the ague. I knew what he meant by that one word well enough—I knew what he wished to make me understand. With the wind that now drove us on, we were bound for the whirl of the Ström, and nothing could save us.

"You perceive that in crossing the Ström *channel*, we always went a long way up above the whirl, even in the calmest weather, and then had to wait and watch carefully for the slack—but now we were driving right upon the pool itself, and in such a hurricane as this! 'To be sure,' I thought, 'we shall get there just about the slack—there is some little hope in that'—but in the next moment I cursed myself for being so great a fool as to dream of hope at all. I knew very well that we were doomed, had we been ten times a ninety-gun ship.

"By this time the first fury of the tempest had spent itself, or perhaps we did not feel it so much, as we scudded before it, but at all events the seas, which at first had been kept down by the wind, and lay flat and frothing, now got up into absolute mountains. A singular change, too, had come over the heavens. Around in every direction it was still as black as pitch, but nearly overhead there burst out, all at once, a circular rift of clear sky—as clear as I ever saw—and of a deep bright blue—and through it there blazed forth the full moon with a lustre that I never before knew her to wear. She lit up every thing about us with the greatest distinctness—but, oh God, what a scene it was to light up!

"I now made one or two attempts to speak to my brother—but in some manner which I could not understand, the din had so increased that I could not make him hear a single word, although I screamed at the top of my voice in his ear. Presently he shook his head, looking as pale as death, and held up one of his fingers, as to say '*listen!*'

"At first I could not make out what he meant—but soon a hideous thought flashed upon me. I dragged my watch from its fob. It was not going. I glanced as its face by the moonlight, and then burst into tears as I flung it far away into the ocean. *It had run down at seven o'clock! We were behind the time of the slack, and the whirl of the Ström was in full fury!*

"When a boat is well built, properly trimmed, and not deep laden, the waves in a strong gale, when she is going large, seem always to slip from beneath her—which appears very strange to a landsman—and this is what is called '*riding*', in sea phrase.

"Well, so far we had ridden the swells very cleverly; but presently a gigantic sea happened to take us right under the counter, and bore us with it as it rose—up—up—as if into the sky. I would not have believed that any wave could rise so high. And then down we came with a sweep, a slide, and a plunge, that made me feel sick and dizzy, as if I was falling from some lofty mountain-top in a dream. But while we were up I had thrown a quick glance around—and that one glance was all sufficient. I saw our exact position in an instant. The Moskoe-ström whirlpool was about a quarter of a mile dead ahead—but no more like the every-day Moskoe-ström, than the whirl as you now see it, is like a mill-race. If I had not known where we were, and what we had to expect, I should not have recognised the place at all. As it was, I involuntarily closed my eyes in horror. The lids clenched themselves together as if in a spasm.

"It could not have been more than two minutes afterwards until we suddenly felt the waves subside, and were enveloped in foam. The boat made a sharp half turn to larboard, and then shot off in its new direction like a thunderbolt. At the same moment the roaring noise of the water was completely drowned in a kind of shrill shriek—such a sound as you might imagine given out by the waste-pipes of many thousand steam-vessels, letting off their steam all together. We were now in the belt of surf that always surrounds the whirl; and I thought, of course, that another moment would plunge us into the abyss—down which we could only see indistinctly on account of the amazing velocity with which we were borne along. The boat did not seem to sink into the water at all, but to skim like an air-bubble upon the surface of the surge. Her starboard side was next the whirl, and on the larboard arose the world of ocean we had left. It stood like a huge writhing wall between us and the horizon.

"It may appear strange, but now, when we were in the very jaws of the gulf, I felt more composed than when we were only approaching it. Having made up my mind to hope no more, I got rid of a great deal of that terror which unmanned me at first. I suppose it was despair that strung my nerves.

"It may look like boasting—but what I tell you is the truth—I began to reflect how magnificent a thing it was to die in such a manner, and how foolish it was in me to think of so paltry a consideration as my own individual life, in view of so wonderful a manifestation of God's power. I do believe that I blushed with shame when this idea crossed my mind. After a little while I became possessed with the keenest curiosity about the whirl itself. I positively felt a *wish* to explore its depths, even at the sacrifice I was going to make; and my principal grief was that I should never be able to tell my old companions on shore about the mysteries I should see. These, no doubt, were singular fancies to occupy a man's mind in such extremity— and I have often thought since, that the revolutions of the boat around the pool might have rendered me a little light-headed.

"There was another circumstance which tended to restore my self-possession; and this was the cessation of the wind, which could not reach us in our present situation—for, as you saw yourself, the belt of surf is considerably lower than the general bed of the ocean, and this latter now towered above us, a high, black, mountainous ridge. If you have never been at sea in a heavy gale, you can form no idea of the confusion of mind occasioned by the wind and the spray together. They blind, deafen and strangle you, and take away all power of action or reflection.

But we were now, in a great measure, rid of these annoyances—just as death-condemned felons in prison are allowed petty indulgences, forbidden them while their doom is yet uncertain.

"How often we made the circuit of the belt it is impossible to say. We careered round and round for perhaps an hour, flying rather than floating, getting gradually more and more into the middle of the surge, and then nearer and nearer to its horrible inner edge. All this time I had never let go of the ring-bolt. My brother was at the stern, holding on to a large empty water-cask which had been securely lashed under the coop of the counter, and was the only thing on deck that had not been swept overboard when the gale first took us. As we approached the brink of the pit he let go his hold upon this, and made for the ring, from which, in the agony of his terror, he endeavored to force my hands, as it was not large enough to afford us both a secure grasp. I never felt deeper grief than when I saw him attempt this act—although I knew he was a madman when he did it—a raving maniac through sheer fright. I did not care, however, to contest the point with him. I thought it could make no difference whether either of us held on at all; so I let him have the bolt, and went astern to the cask. This there was no great difficulty in doing; for the smack flew round steadily enough, and upon an even keel—only swaying to and fro, with the immense sweeps and swelters of the whirl. Scarcely had I secured myself in my new position, when we gave a wild lurch to starboard, and rushed headlong into the abyss. I muttered a hurried prayer to God, and thought all was over.

"As I felt the sickening sweep of the descent, I had instinctively tightened my hold upon the barrel, and closed my eyes. For some seconds I dared not open them—while I expected instant destruction, and wondered that I was not already in my death-struggles with the water. But moment after moment elapsed. I still lived. The sense of falling had ceased; and the motion of the vessel seemed much as it had been before while in the belt of foam, with the exception that she now lay more along. I took courage and looked once again upon the scene.

"Never shall I forget the sensations of awe, horror, and admiration with which I gazed about me. The boat appeared to be hanging, as if by magic, midway down, upon the interior surface of a funnel vast in circumference, prodigious in depth, and whose perfectly smooth sides might have been mistaken for ebony, but for the bewildering rapidity with which they spun around, and for the gleaming and ghastly radiance they shot forth, as the rays of the full moon, from that circular rift amid the clouds which I have already described, streamed in a flood of golden glory along the black walls, and far away down into the inmost recesses of the abyss.

"At first I was too much confused to observe anything accurately. The general burst of terrific grandeur was all that I beheld. When I recovered myself a little, however, my gaze fell instinctively downward. In this direction I was able to obtain an unobstructed view, from the manner in which the smack hung on the inclined surface of the pool. She was quite upon an even keel—that is to say, her deck lay in a plane parallel with that of the water—but this latter sloped at an angle of more than forty-five degrees, so that we seemed to be lying upon our beam-ends. I could not help observing, nevertheless, that I had scarcely more difficulty in maintaining my hold and footing in this situation, than if we had been upon a dead level; and this, I suppose, was owing to the speed at which we revolved.

"The rays of the moon seemed to search the very bottom of the profound gulf; but still I could make out nothing distinctly, on account of a thick mist in which everything there was enveloped, and over which there hung a magnificent rainbow, like that narrow and tottering bridge which Mussulmen say is the only pathway between Time and Eternity. This mist, or spray, was no doubt occasioned by the clashing of the great walls of the funnel, as they all met together at the bottom—but the yell that went up to the Heavens from out of that mist, I dare not attempt to describe.

"Our first slide into the abyss itself, from the belt of foam above, had carried us to a great distance down the slope; but our farther descent was by no means proportionate. Round and round we swept—not with any uniform movement—but in dizzying swings and jerks, that sent us sometimes only a few hundred feet—sometimes nearly the complete circuit of the whirl. Our progress downward, at each revolution, was slow, but very perceptible.

"Looking about me upon the wide waste of liquid ebony on which we were thus borne, I perceived that our boat was not the only object in the embrace of the whirl. Both above and below us were visible fragments of vessels, large masses of building timber and trunks of trees, with many smaller articles, such as pieces of house furniture, broken boxes, barrels and staves. I have already described the unnatural curiosity which had taken the place of my original terrors. It appeared to grow upon me as I drew nearer and nearer to my dreadful doom. I now began to watch, with a strange interest, the numerous things that floated in our company. I *must* have been delirious—for I even sought *amusement* in speculating upon the relative velocities of their several descents toward the foam below. 'This fir tree,' I found myself at one time saying, 'will certainly be the next thing that takes the awful plunge and disappears,'—and then I was disappointed to find that the wreck of a Dutch merchant ship overtook it and went down before. At length, after making several guesses of this nature, and being deceived in all—this fact—the fact of my invariable miscalculation, set me upon a train of reflection that made my limbs again tremble, and my heart beat heavily once more.

"It was not a new terror that thus affected me, but the dawn of a more exciting *hope.* This hope arose partly from memory, and partly from present observation. I called to mind the great variety of buoyant matter that strewed the coast of Lofoden, having been absorbed and then thrown forth by the Moskoe-ström. By far the greater number of the articles were shattered in the most extraordinary way—so chafed and roughened as to have the appearance of being stuck full of splinters— but then I distinctly recollected that there were *some* of them which were not disfigured at all. Now I could not account for this difference except by supposing that the roughened fragments were the only ones which had been *completely absorbed*— that the others had entered the whirl at so late a period of the tide, or, from some reason, had descended so slowly after entering, that they did not reach the bottom before the turn of the flood came, or of the ebb, as the case might be. I conceived it possible, in either instance, that they might thus be whirled up again to the level of the ocean, without undergoing the fate of those which had been drawn in more early or absorbed more rapidly. I made, also, three important observations. The first was, that as a general rule, the larger the bodies were, the more rapid their descent;—the second, that, between two masses of equal extent, the one spherical, and the other *of any other shape*, the superiority in speed of descent was with the sphere;—the third, that, between two masses of equal size, the one cylindrical, and the other of any other shape, the cylinder was absorbed the more slowly.

Since my escape, I have had several conversations on this subject with an old school-master of the district; and it was from him that I learned the use of the words 'cylinder' and 'sphere.' He explained to me—although I have forgotten the explanation—how what I observed was, in fact, the natural consequence of the forms of the floating fragments—and showed me how it happened that a cylinder, swimming in a vortex, offered more resistance to its suction, and was drawn in with greater difficulty than an equally bulky body, of any form whatever.*

"There was one startling circumstance which went a great way in enforcing these observations, and rendering me anxious to turn them to account, and this was that, at every revolution, we passed something like a barrel, or else the broken yard or the mast of a vessel, while many of these things, which had been on our level when I first opened my eyes upon the wonders of the whirlpool, were now high up above us, and seemed to have moved but little from their original station.

"I no longer hesitated what to do. I resolved to lash myself securely to the water cask upon which I now held, to cut it loose from the counter, and to throw myself with it into the water. I attracted my brother's attention by signs, pointed to the floating barrels that came near us, and did everything in my power to make him understand what I was about to do. I thought at length that he comprehended my design—but, whether this was the case or not, he shook his head despairingly, and refused to move from his station by the ring-bolt. It was impossible to force him; the emergency admitted no delay; and so, with a bitter struggle, I resigned him to his fate, fastened myself to the cask by means of the lashings which secured it to the counter, and precipitated myself with it into the sea, without another moment's hesitation.

"The result was precisely what I had hoped it might be. As it is myself who now tell you this tale—as you see that I *did* escape—and as you are already in possession of the mode in which this escape was effected, and must therefore anticipate all that I have farther to say—I will bring my story quickly to conclusion. It might have been an hour, or thereabout, after my quitting the smack, when, having descended to a vast distance beneath me, it made three or four wild gyrations in rapid succession, and, bearing my loved brother with it, plunged headlong, at once and forever, into the chaos of foam below. The barrel to which I was attached sunk very little farther than half the distance between the bottom of the gulf and the spot at

*See Archimedes, *De Incidentibus in Fluido.*—lib.2.

which I leaped overboard, before a great change took place in the character of the whirlpool. The slope of the sides of the vast funnel became momently less and less steep. The gyrations of the whirl grew, gradually, less and less violent. By degrees, the froth and the rainbow disappeared, and the bottom of the gulf seemed slowly to uprise. The sky was clear, the winds had gone down, and the full moon was setting radiantly in the west, when I found myself on the surface of the ocean, in full view of the shores of Lofoden, and above the spot where the pool of the Moskoe-ström *had been.* It was the hour of the slack—but the sea still heaved in mountainous waves from the effects of the hurricane. I was borne violently into the channel of the Ström and in a few minutes, was hurried down the coast into the 'grounds' of the fishermen. A boat picked me up—exhausted from fatigue— and (now that the danger was removed) speechless from the memory of its horror. Those who drew me on board were my old mates and dally companions—but they knew me no more than they would have known a traveller from the spirit-land. My hair, which had been raven-black the day before, was as white as you see it now. They say too that the whole expression of my countenance had changed. I told them my story—they did not believe it. I now tell it to *you*—and I can scarcely expect you to put more faith in it than did the merry fishermen of Lofoden."

DAVY JONES'S GIFT

BY JOHN MASEFIELD

"Once upon a time," said the sailor, "the Devil and Davy Jones came to Cardiff, to a place called Tiger Bay. They put up at Tony Adams's, not far from Pier Head, at the corner of Sunday Lane. And all the time they stayed there they used to be going to the rumshop, where they sat at a table, smoking their cigars, and dicing each other for different persons' souls. Now you must know that the Devil gets landsmen, and Davy Jones gets sailorfolk; and they get tired of having always the same, so then they dice each other for some of another sort.

"One time they were in a place in Mary Street, having some burnt brandy, and playing red and black for the people passing. And while they were looking out on the street and turning the cards, they saw all the people on the pavement breaking their necks to get into the gutter. And they saw all the shop-people running out and kowtowing, and all the carts pulling up, and all the police saluting. 'Here comes a big nob,' said Davy Jones. 'Yes,' said the Devil; 'it's the Bishop that's stopping with the Mayor.' 'Red or black?' said Davy Jones, picking up a card. 'I don't play for bishops,' said the Devil. 'I respect the cloth,' he said. 'Come on, man,' said Davy Jones. 'I'd give an admiral to have a bishop. Come on, now; make your game. Red or black?' 'Well, I say red,' said the Devil. 'It's the ace of clubs,' said Davy Jones; 'I win; and it's the first bishop ever I had in my life.' The Devil was mighty angry at that—at losing a bishop. 'I'll not play any more,' he said; 'I'm off

121

home. Some people gets too good cards for me. There was some queer shuffling when that pack was cut, that's my belief.'

"'Ah, stay and be friends, man,' said Davy Jones. 'Look at what's coming down the street. I'll give you that for nothing.'

"Now, coming down the street there was a reefer—one of those apprentice fellows. And he was brass-bound fit to play music. He stood about six feet, and there were bright brass buttons down his jacket, and on his collar, and on his sleeves. His cap had a big gold badge, with a house-flag in seven different colours in the middle of it, and a gold chain cable of a chinstay twisted round it. He was wearing his cap on three hairs, and he walked on both the pavements and all the road. His trousers were cut like wind-sails round the ankles. He had a fathom of red silk tie rolling out over his chest. He'd a cigarette in a twisted clay holder a foot and a half long. He was chewing tobacco over his shoulders as he walked. He'd a bottle of rum-hot in one hand, a bag of jam tarts in the other, and his pockets were full of love-letters from every port between Rio and Callao, round by the East.

"'You mean to say you'll give me that?' said the Devil. 'I will,' said Davy Jones, 'and a beauty he is. I never see a finer.' 'He is, indeed, a beauty,' said the Devil. 'I take back what I said about the cards. I'm sorry I spoke crusty. What's the matter with some more burnt brandy?' 'Burnt brandy be it,' said Davy Jones. So then they rang the bell, and ordered a new jug and clean glasses.

"Now the Devil was so proud of what Davy had given him, he couldn't keep away from him. He used to hang about the East Bute Docks, under the red-brick clock-tower, looking at the barque the young man worked aboard. Bill Harker his name was. He was in a West Coast barque, the *Coronel*, loading fuel for Hilo. So at last, when the *Coronel* was sailing, the Devil shipped himself aboard her, as one of the crowd in the fo'c'sle, and away they went down the Channel. At first he was very happy, for Bill Harker was in the same watch, and the two would yarn together. And though he was wise when he shipped, Bill Harker taught him a lot. There was a lot of things Bill Harker knew about. But when they were off the River Plate, they got caught in a pampero, and it blew very hard, and a big green sea began to run. The *Coronel* was a wet ship, and for three days you could stand upon her poop, and look forward and see nothing but a smother of foam from the break of the poop to the jib-boom. The crew had to roost on the poop. The fo'c'sle was flooded out. So while they were like this the flying jib worked loose. 'The jib will be gone in half a tick,' said the mate. 'Out there, one of you, and make it fast, before it blows away.' But the boom was dipping under every minute, and the waist was four feet deep, and green water came aboard all along her length. So none of the crowd would go forward. Then Bill Harker shambled out, and away he went forward, with the green seas smashing over him, and he lay out along the jib-boom and made the sail fast, and jolly nearly drowned he was. 'That's a brave lad, that Bill Harker,' said the Devil. 'Ah, come off,' said the sailors. 'Them reefers, they haven't got souls to be saved.' It was that that set the Devil thinking.

"By and by they came up with the Horn; and if it had blown off the Plate, it now blew off the roof. Talk about wind and weather. They got them both for sure aboard the *Coronel*. And it blew all the sails off her, and she rolled all her masts out, and the seas made a breach of her bulwarks, and the ice knocked a hole in her bows. So watch and watch they pumped the old *Coronel*, and the leak gained steadily, and there they were hove to under a weather cloth, five and a half degrees to the south of anything. And while they were like this, just about giving up hope, the old man sent the watch below, and told them they could start prayers. So the Devil crept on to the top of the half-deck, to look through the scuttle, to see what the reefers were doing, and what kind of prayers Bill Harker was putting up. And he saw them all sitting round the table, under the lamp, with Bill Harker at the head. And each of them had a hand of cards, and a length of knotted rope-yarn, and they were playing able-whackets. Each man in turn put down a card, and swore a new blasphemy, and if his swear didn't come as he played the card, then all the others hit him with their teasers. But they never once had a chance to hit Bill Harker. 'I think they were right about his soul,' said the Devil. And he sighed, like he was sad.

"Shortly after that the Coronel went down, and all hands drowned in her, saving only Bill and the Devil. They came up out of the smothering green seas, and saw the stars blinking in the sky, and heard the wind howling like a pack of dogs. They managed to get aboard the *Coronel*'s hen-house, which had come adrift, and floated. The fowls were all drowned inside, so they lived on drowned hens. As for drink, they had to do without, for there was none. When they got thirsty they splashed their faces with salt water; but they were so cold they didn't feel thirsty very bad. They drifted three days and three nights, till their skins were all cracked and salt-caked. And all the Devil thought of was whether Bill Harker had a soul. And Bill kept telling the Devil what a thundering big feed they would have as soon as they fetched to port, and how good a rum-hot would be, with a lump of sugar and a bit of lemon peel.

"And at last the old hen-house came bump on to Tierra Del Fuego, and there were some natives cooking rabbits. So the Devil and Bill made a raid of the whole jing bang, and ate till they were tired. Then they had a drink out of a brook, and a warm by the fire, and a pleasant sleep. 'Now,' said the Devil, 'I will see if he's got a soul. I'll see if he give thanks.' So after an hour or two Bill took a turn up and down and came to the Devil. 'It's mighty dull on this forgotten continent,' he said. 'Have you got a ha'penny?' 'No,' said the Devil. 'What in joy d'ye want with a ha'penny?' 'I might have played you pitch and toss,' said Bill. 'It was better fun on the hen-coop than here.' 'I give you up,' said the Devil; 'you've no more soul than the inner part of an empty barrel.' And with that the Devil vanished in a flame of sulphur.

"Bill stretched himself, and put another shrub on the fire. He picked up a few round shells, and began a game of knucklebones."

The Kraken

by Alfred, Lord Tennyson

Below the thunders of the upper deep;
Far, far beneath in the abysmal sea,
His ancient, dreamless, uninvaded sleep
The Kraken sleepeth: faintest sunlights flee
About his shadowy sides: above him swell
Huge sponges of millennial growth and height;
And far away into the sickly light,
From many a wondrous grot and secret cell
Unnumber'd and enormous polypi
Winnow with giant arms the slumbering green.
There hath he lain for ages and will lie
Battening upon huge seaworms in his sleep,
Until the latter fire shall heat the deep;
Then once by man and angels to be seen,
In roaring he shall rise and on the surface die.

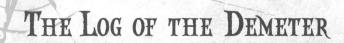

The Log of the Demeter

by Bram Stoker

(Pasted in Mina Murray's Journal)
Cutting from *The Dailygraph*, 8 August

From a correspondent.
Whitby.

One of the greatest and suddenest storms on record has just been experienced here, with results both strange and unique. The weather had been somewhat sultry, but not to any degree uncommon in the month of August. Saturday evening was as fine as was ever known, and the great body of holiday-makers laid out yesterday for visits to Mulgrave Woods, Robin Hood's Bay, Rig Mill, Runswick, Staithes, and the various trips in the neighborhood of Whitby. The steamers *Emma* and *Scarborough* made trips up and down the coast, and there was an unusual amount of "tripping" both to and from Whitby. The day was unusually fine till the afternoon, when some of the gossips who frequent the East Cliff churchyard, and from the commanding eminence watch the wide sweep of sea visible to the north and east, called attention to a sudden show of "mares'-tails" high in the sky to the north-west. The wind was then blowing from the south-west in the mild degree which in barometrical language is ranked "No. 2, light breeze."

The coastguard on duty at once made report, and one old fisherman, who for more than half a century has kept watch on weather signs from the East Cliff, foretold in an emphatic manner the coming of a sudden storm. The approach of sunset was so very beautiful, so grand in its masses of splendidly-coloured clouds, that there was quite an assemblage on the walk along the cliff in the old churchyard to enjoy the beauty. Before the sun dipped below the black mass of Kettleness, standing boldly athwart the western sky, its downward was marked by myriad clouds of every sunset-colour—flame, purple, pink, green, violet, and all the tints of gold; with here and there masses not large, but of seemingly absolute blackness, in all sorts of shapes, as well outlined as colossal silhouettes. The experience was not lost on the painters, and doubtless some of the sketches of the "Prelude to the Great Storm" will grace the R. A and R. I. walls in May next.

More than one captain made up his mind then and there that his "cobble" or his "mule," as they term the different classes of boats, would remain in the harbour till the storm had passed. The wind fell away entirely during the evening, and at midnight there was a dead calm, a sultry heat, and that prevailing intensity which, on the approach of thunder, affects persons of a sensitive nature.

There were but few lights in sight at sea, for even the coasting steamers, which usually "hug" the shore so closely, kept well to seaward, and but few fishing-boats were in sight. The only sail noticeable was a foreign schooner with all sails set, which was seemingly going westwards. The foolhardiness or ignorance of her officers was a prolific theme for comment whilst she remained in sight, and efforts were made to signal her to reduce sail in the face of her danger. Before the night shut down she was seen with sails idly flapping as she gently rolled on the undulating swell of the sea.

> "As idle as a painted ship upon a
> painted ocean."

Shortly before ten o'clock the stillness of the air grew quite oppressive, and the silence was so marked that the bleating of a sheep inland or the barking of a dog in the town was distinctly heard, and the band on the pier, with its lively French air, was like a discord in the great harmony of nature's silence. A little after midnight came a strange sound from over the sea, and high overhead the air began to carry a strange, faint, hollow booming.

Then without warning the tempest broke. With a rapidity which, at the time, seemed incredible, and even afterwards is impossible to realize, the whole aspect of nature at once became convulsed. The waves rose in growing fury, each overtopping its fellow, till in a very few minutes the lately glassy sea was like a roaring and devouring monster. White-crested waves beat madly on the level sands and rushed up the shelving cliffs; others broke over the piers, and with their spume swept the lanthorns of the lighthouses which rise from the end of either pier of Whitby Harbour.

The wind roared like thunder, and blew with such force that it was with difficulty that even strong men kept their feet, or clung with grim clasp to the iron stanchions. It was found necessary to clear the entire pier from the mass of onlookers, or else the fatalities of the night would have increased manifold. To add to the difficulties and dangers of the time, masses of sea-fog came drifting inland—white, wet clouds, which swept by in ghostly fashion, so dank and damp and cold that it needed but little effort of imagination to think that the spirits of those lost at sea were touching their living brethren with the clammy hands of death, and many a one shuddered at the wreaths of sea-mist swept by.

At times the mist cleared, and the sea for some distance could be seen in the glare of the lightning, which came thick and fast, followed by such peals of thunder that the whole sky overhead seemed trembling under the shock of the footsteps of the storm.

Some of the scenes thus revealed were of immeasurable grandeur and of absorbing interest—the sea, running mountains high, threw skywards with each wave mighty masses of white foam, which the tempest seemed to snatch at and whirl away into space. Here and there a fishing boat, with a rag of sail, running madly for shelter before the blast, now and again the white wings of a storm-tossed seabird. On the summit of the East Cliff the new searchlight was ready for experiment, but had not yet been tried. The officers in charge of it got it into working order, and in the pauses of inrushing mist swept with it the surface of the sea. Once or twice its service was most effective, as when a fishing boat, with gunwale under water, rushed into the harbour, able, by the guidance of the sheltering light, to avoid the danger of dashing against the piers. As each boat achieved the safety of the port there was a shout of joy from the mass of people on the shore, a shout which for a moment seemed to cleave the gale and was then swept away in its rush.

Before long the searchlight discovered some distance away a schooner with all sails set, apparently the same vessel which had been noticed earlier in the evening. The wind had by this time backed to the east, and there was a shudder amongst the watchers on the cliff as they realized the terrible danger in which she now was.

Between her and the port lay the great flat reef on which so many good ships have from time to time suffered, and, with the wind blowing from its present quarter, it would be quite impossible that she should fetch the entrance of the harbour.

It was now nearly the hour of high tide, but the waves were so great that in their troughs the shallows of the shore were almost visible, and the schooner, with all sails set, was rushing with such speed that, in the words of one old salt, "she must fetch up somewhere, if it was only in hell." Then came another rush of sea-fog, greater than any hitherto—a mass of dank mist, which seemed to close on all things like a gray pall, and left available to men only the organ of hearing, for the roar of the tempest, and the crash of the thunder, and the booming of the mighty billows came through the damp oblivion even louder than before. The rays of the searchlight were kept fixed on the harbour mouth across the East Pier, where the shock was expected, and men waited breathless.

The wind suddenly shifted to the north-east, and the remnant of the sea-fog melted in the blast; and then, *mirabile dictu*, between the piers, leaping from wave to wave as it rushed at headlong speed, swept the strange schooner before the blast, with all sail set, and gained the safety of the harbour. The searchlight followed her, and a shudder ran through all who saw her, for lashed to the helm was a corpse, with drooping head, which swung horribly to and fro at each motion of the ship. No other form could be seen on the deck at all.

A great awe came on all as they realised that the ship, as if by a miracle, had found the harbour, unsteered save by the hand of a dead man! However, all took place more quickly than it takes to write these words. The schooner paused not, but rushing across the harbour, pitched herself on that accumulation of sand and gravel washed by many tides and many storms into the south-east corner of the pier jutting under the East Cliff, known locally as Tate Hill Pier.

There was of course a considerable concussion as the vessel drove up on the sand heap. Every spar, rope, and stay was strained, and some of the "top-hammer" came crashing down. But, strangest of all, the very instant the shore was touched, an immense dog sprang up on deck from below, as if shot up by the concussion, and running forward, jumped from the bow on the sand.

Making straight for the steep cliff, where the churchyard hangs over the laneway to the East Pier so steeply that some of the flat tombstones—"thruffsteans" or "through-stones," as they call them in Whitby vernacular—actually project over where the sustaining cliff has fallen away, it disappeared in the darkness, which seemed intensified just beyond the focus of the searchlight.

It so happened that there was no one at the moment on Tate Hill Pier, as all those whose houses are in close proximity were either in bed or were out on the heights above. Thus the coastguard on duty on the eastern side of the harbour, who at once ran down to the little pier, was the first to climb aboard. The men working the searchlight, after scouring the entrance of the harbour without seeing anything, then turned the light on the derelict and kept it there. The coastguard ran aft, and when he came beside the wheel, bent over to examine it, and recoiled at once as though under some sudden emotion. This seemed to pique general curiosity, and quite a number of people began to run.

It is a good way round from the West Cliff by the Drawbridge to Tate Hill Pier, but your correspondent is a fairly good runner, and came well ahead of the crowd. When I arrived, however, I found already assembled on the pier a crowd, whom the coastguard and police refused to allow to come on board. By the courtesy of the chief boatman, I was, as your correspondent, permitted to climb on deck, and was one of a small group who saw the dead seaman whilst actually lashed to the wheel.

It was no wonder that the coastguard was surprised, or even awed, for not often can such a sight have been seen. The man was simply fastened by his hands, tied one over the other, to a spoke of the wheel. Between the inner hand and the wood was a crucifix, the set of beads on which it was fastened being around both wrists and wheel, and all kept fast by the binding cords. The poor fellow may have been seated at one time, but the flapping and buffeting of the sails had worked through the rudder of the wheel and had dragged him to and fro, so that the cords with which he was tied had cut the flesh to the bone.

Accurate note was made of the state of things, and a doctor—Surgeon J. M. Caffyn, of 33, East Elliot Place—who came immediately after me, declared, after making examination, that the man must have been dead for quite two days.

In his pocket was a bottle, carefully corked, empty save for a little roll of paper, which proved to be the addendum to the log.

The coastguard said the man must have tied up his own hands, fastening the knots with his teeth. The fact that a coastguard was the first on board may save some complications, later on, in the Admiralty Court; for coastguards cannot claim the salvage which is the right of the first civilian entering on a derelict. Already, however, the legal tongues are wagging, and one young law student is loudly asserting that the rights of the owner are already completely sacrificed, his property being held in contravention of the statues of mortmain, since the tiller, as emblemship, if not proof, of delegated possession, is held in a *dead hand*.

It is needless to say that the dead steersman has been reverently removed from the place where he held his honourable watch and ward till death—a steadfastness as noble as that of the young Casabianca—and placed in the mortuary to await inquest.

Already the sudden storm is passing, and its fierceness is abating; the crowds are scattering homeward, and the sky is beginning to redden over the Yorkshire wolds.

I shall send, in time for your next issue, further details of the derelict ship which found her way so miraculously into harbour in the storm.

WHITBY.

9 August.—The sequel to the strange arrival of the derelict in the storm last night is almost more startling than the thing itself. It turns out that the schooner is Russian from Varna, and is called the *Demeter*. She is almost entirely in ballast of silver sand, with only a small amount of cargo, a number of great wooden boxes filled with mould.

This cargo was consigned to a Whitby solicitor, Mr. S. F. Billington, of 7, The Crescent, who this morning went aboard and took formal possession of the goods consigned to him.

The Russian consul, too, acting for the charter-party, took formal possession of the ship, and paid all harbour dues, etc.

Nothing is talked about here to-day except the strange coincidence; the officials of the Board of Trade have been most exacting in seeing that every compliance has been made with existing regulations. As the matter is to be a "nine days' wonder," they are evidently determined that there shall be no cause of other complaint.

A good deal of interest was abroad concerning the dog which landed when the ship struck, and more than a few of the members of the S.P.C.A., which is very strong in Whitby, have tried to befriend the animal. To the general disappointment, however, it was not to be found; it seems to have disappeared entirely from the town. It may be that it was frightened and made its way on to the moors, where it is still hiding in terror.

There are some who look with dread on such a possibility, lest later on it should in itself become a danger, for it is evidently a fierce brute. Early this morning a large dog, a half-bred mastiff belonging to a coal merchant close to Tate Hill Pier, was found dead in the roadway opposite its master's yard. It had been fighting, and manifestly had had a savage opponent, for its throat was torn away, and its belly was slit open as if with a savage claw.

Later.—By the kindness of the Board of Trade inspector, I have been permitted to look over the log-book of the *Demeter*, which was in order up to within three days, but contained nothing of special interest except as to facts of missing men. The greatest interest, however, is with regard to the paper found in the bottle, which was to-day produced at the inquest; and a more strange narrative than the two between them unfold it has not been my lot to come across.

As there is no motive for concealment, I am permitted to use them, and accordingly send you a rescript, simply omitting technical details of seamanship and supercargo. It almost seems as though the captain had been seized with some kind of mania before he had got well into blue water, and that this had developed persistently throughout the voyage. Of course my statement must be taken *cum grano*, since I am writing from the dictation of a clerk of the Russian consul, who kindly translated for me, time being short.

LOG OF THE DEMETER
Varna to Whitby.

Written 18 July, things so strange happening, that I shall keep accurate note henceforth till we land.

On *6 July* we finished taking in cargo, silver sand and boxes of earth. At noon set sail. East wind, fresh. Crew, five hands…two mates, cook, and myself, (captain).

On *11 July* at dawn entered Bosphorus. Boarded by Turkish Customs officers. Backsheesh. All correct. Under way at 4 P.M.

On *12 July* through Dardanelles. More Customs officers and flagboat of guarding squadron. Backsheesh again. Work of officers thorough, but quick. Want us off soon. At dark passed into Archipelago.

On *13 July* passed Cape Matapan. Crew dissatisfied about something. Seemed scared, but would not speak out.

On *14 July* was somewhat anxious about crew. Men all steady fellows, who sailed with me before. Mate could not make out what was wrong. They only told him there was *something*, and crossed themselves. Mate lost temper with one of them that day and struck him. Expected fierce quarrel, but all was quiet.

On *16 July* mate reported in the morning that one of the crew, Petrofsky, was missing. Could not account for it. Took larboard watch eight bells last night; was relieved by Abramoff, but did not go to bunk. Men more downcast than ever. All said they expected something of the kind, but would not say more than there was *something* aboard. Mate getting very impatient with them. Feared some trouble ahead.

On *17 July*, yesterday, one of the men, Olgaren, came to my cabin, and in an awestruck way confided to me that he thought there was a strange man aboard the ship. He said that in his watch he had been sheltering behind the deckhouse, as there was a rain-storm, when he saw a tall, thin man, who was not like any of the crew, come up the companionway, and go along the deck forward, and disappear. He followed cautiously, but when he got to bows found no one, and the hatchways were all closed. He was in a panic of superstitious fear, and I am afraid the panic may spread. To allay it, I shall today search the entire ship carefully from stem to stern.

Later in the day I got together the whole crew, and told them, as they evidently thought there was some one in the ship, we would search from stem to stern. First mate angry, said it was folly, and to yield to such foolish ideas would demoralise the men; said he would engage to keep them out of trouble with the handspike. I let him take the helm, while the rest began a thorough search, all keeping abreast, with lanterns. We left no corner unsearched. As there were only the big wooden boxes, there were no odd corners where a man could hide. Men much relieved when search over, and went back to work cheerfully. First mate scowled, but said nothing.

22 July.—Rough weather last three days—and all hands busy with sails—no time to be frightened. Men seem to have forgotten their dread. Mate cheerful again, and all on good terms. Praised men for work in bad weather. Passed Gibraltar and out through Straits. All well.

24 July.—There seems some doom over this ship. Already a hand short, and entering the Bay of Biscay with wild weather ahead, and yet last night another man lost—disappeared. Like the first, he came off his watch and was not seen again. Men all in a panic of fear, sent a round robin, asking to have double watch, as they fear to be alone. Mate angry. Fear there will be some trouble, as either he or the men will do some violence.

28 July.—Four days in hell, knocking about in a sort of malestrom, and the wind a tempest. No sleep for any one. Men all worn out. Hardly know how to set a watch, since no one fit to go on. Second mate volunteered to steer and watch, and let men snatch a few hours sleep. Wind abating; seas still terrific, but feel them less, as ship is steadier.

29 July.—Another tragedy. Had single watch to-night, as crew too tired to double. When morning watch came on deck could find no one except steersman. Raised outcry, and all came on deck. Thorough search, but no one found. Are now without second mate, and crew in a panic. Mate and I agreed to go armed henceforth and wait for any sign of cause.

30 July.—Last night. Rejoiced we are nearing England. Weather fine, all sails set. Retired worn out; slept soundly; awakened by mate telling me that both man of watch and steersman missing. Only self and mate and two hands left to work ship.

1 August.—Two days of fog, and not a sail sighted. Had hoped when in the English Channel to be able to signal for help or get in somewhere. Not having power to work sails, have to run before wind. Dare not lower, as could not raise them again. We seem to be drifting to some terrible doom. Mate now more demoralised than either of men. His stronger nature seems to have worked inwardly against himself. Men are beyond fear, working stolidly and patiently, with minds made up to worst. They are Russian, he Roumanian.

2 August, midnight.—Woke up from few minutes' sleep by hearing a cry, seemingly outside my port. Could see nothing in fog. Rushed on deck, and ran against mate. Tells me he heard cry and ran, but no sign of man on watch. One more gone. Lord, help us! Mate says we must be past Straits of Dover, as in a moment of fog lifting he saw North Foreland, just as he heard the man cry out. If so we are now off in the North Sea, and only God can guide us in the fog, which seems to move with us, and God seems to have deserted us.

3 August.—At midnight I went to relieve the man at the wheel and when I got to it found no one there. The wind was steady, and as we ran before it there was no yawing. I dared not leave it, so shouted for the mate. After a few seconds, he rushed up on deck in his flannels. He looked wild-eyed and haggard, and I greatly fear his reason has given way. He came close to me and whispered hoarsely, with his mouth to my ear, as though fearing the very air might hear. "It is here; I know it now. On the watch last night I saw It, like a man, tall and thin, and ghastly pale. It was in the bows, and looking out. I crept behind It, and gave it my knife, but the knife went through It, empty as the air." And as he spoke he took the knife and drove it savagely into space. Then he went on: "But *It* is here, and I'll find It. It is in the hold, perhaps in one of those boxes. I'll unscrew them one by one and see. You work the helm." And with a warning look and his finger on his lip, he went below. There was springing up a choppy wind, and I could not leave the helm. I saw him come out on deck again with a tool-chest and lantern, and go down the forward hatchway. He is mad, stark, raving mad, and it's no use my trying to stop him. He can't hurt those big boxes, they are invoiced as "clay," and to pull them about is as harmless a thing as he can do. So here I stay, and mind the helm, and write these notes. I can only trust in God and wait till the fog clears. Then, if I can't steer to any harbour with the wind that is, I shall cut down sails, and lie by, and signal for help....

It is nearly all over now. Just as I was beginning to hope that the mate would come out calmer—for I heard him knocking away at something in the hold, and work is good for him—there came up the hatchway a sudden, startled scream, which made my blood run cold, and up on the deck he came as if shot from a gun—a raging madman, with his eyes rolling and his face convulsed with fear. "Save me! save me!" he cried, and then looked round on the blanket of fog. His horror turned to despair, and in a steady voice he said: "You had better come too, captain, before it is too late. *He* is there! I know the secret now. The sea will save me from Him, and it is all that is left!" Before I could say a word, or move forward to seize him, he sprang on the bulwark and deliberately threw himself into the sea. I suppose I know the secret too, now. It was this madman who had got rid of the men one by one, and now he has followed them himself. God help me! How am I to account for all these horrors when I get to port? *When* I get to port! Will that ever be?

4 August.—Still fog, which the sunrise cannot pierce, I know there is sunrise because I am a sailor, why else I know not. I dared not go below, I dared not leave the helm; so here all night I stayed, and in the dimness of the night I saw It—Him! God, forgive me, but the mate was right to jump overboard. It was better to die like a man; to die like a sailor in blue water, no man can object. But I am captain, and I must not leave my ship. But I shall baffle this fiend or monster, for I shall tie my hands to the wheel when my strength begins to fail, and along with them I shall tie that which He—It!—dare not touch; and then, come good wind or foul, I shall save my soul, and my honour as a captain. I am growing weaker, and the night is coming on. If He can look me in the face again, I may not have time to act.... If we are wrecked, mayhap this bottle may be found, and those who find it may under- stand; if not,...well, then all men shall know that I have been true to my trust. God and the Blessed Virgin and the saints help a poor ignorant soul trying to do his duty...."

Of course the verdict was an open one. There is no evidence to adduce, and whether or not the man himself committed the murders there is now none to say. The folk here hold almost universally that the captain is simply a hero, and he is to be given a public funeral. Already it is arranged that his body is to be taken with a train of boats up the Esk for a piece and then brought back to Tate Hill Pier and up the Abbey steps; for he is to be buried in the churchyard on the cliff. The owners of more than a hundred boats have already given in their names as wishing to follow him to the grave.

No trace has ever been found of the great dog; at which there is much mourning, for, with public opinion in its present state, he would, I believe, be adopted by the town. Tomorrow will see the funeral, and so will end this one more "mystery of the sea."

THE PHANTOM SHIP

BY WILLIAM BUTLER YEATS

Flames the shuttle of the lightning across the driving
    sleet,
Ay, and shakes in sea-green waverings along the fishers'
    street;
Gone the stars and gone the white moon, gone and
    puffed away and dead.
Never storm arose so swiftly; scarce the children were
    in bed,
Scarce the old and wizen houses had their doors and
    windows shut.
Ah! it dwelt within the twilight as the worm within
    the nut.
"Waken, waken, sleepy fishers; no hour is this for sleep,"
Cries a voice at roaring midnight beside the moonless
    deep.
Half dizzy with the lightning there runs a gathering
    band—
"Watcher, wherefore have ye called us?" Eyes go after
    his lean hand,

And the fisher men and women from the dripping
    harbour wall
See the darkness slow disgorging a vessel blind with
    squall.
"Bring the ropes now! Stand ye by now! See, she rounds
    the harbour clear.
God! they're mad to fly such canvas!" Ah! what bell-notes
    do they hear?
Say what ringer rings at midnight; for, in the belfry high,
Slow the chapel bell is tolling as though the dead
    passed by.
Round she comes in stays before them; cease the winds,
    and on their poles
Cease the sails their flapping uproar, and the hull no
    longer rolls.
Now a scream from all those fishers, for there on deck
    there be
All the drowned that ever were drowned from that
    village by the sea;
And the ghastly ghost-flames glimmer all along the
    taffrail rails
On the drowned men's hands and faces, on the spars
    and on the sails.
Hush'd the fishers, till a mother calls by name her
    drowned son;
Then each wife and maid and mother calls by name
    some drowned one.
Stands each grey and silent phantom on the same
    regardless spot—
Joys and fears in their grey faces that the live earth
    knoweth not;
Down the vapours fall and hide them from the children
    of a day,

And the winds come down and blow them with the
vapours far away.
Hang the mist-threads for a little while like cobwebs
in the air;
Then the stars grow out of heaven with their
countenances fair.

"Pray for the souls in purgatory," the pale priest
trembling cries.

* * *

Prayed those forgotten fishers, till in the eastern skies
Came olive fires of morning and on the darkness fed,
By the slow heaving ocean—mumbling mother of
the dead.

Man Overboard

by Winston Churchill

It was a little after half-past nine when the man fell overboard. The mail steamer was hurrying through the Red Sea in the hope of making up the time which the currents of the Indian Ocean had stolen.

The night was clear, though the moon was hidden behind clouds. The warm air was laden with moisture. The still surface of the waters was only broken by the movement of the great ship, from whose quarter the long, slanting undulations struck out like the feathers from an arrow shaft, and in whose wake the froth and air bubbles churned up by the propeller trailed in a narrowing line to the darkness of the horizon.

There was a concert on board. All the passengers were glad to break the monotony of the voyage and gathered around the piano in the companion-house. The decks were deserted. The man had been listening to the music and joining in the songs, but the room was hot and he came out to smoke a cigarette and enjoy a breath of the wind which the speedy passage of the liner created. It was the only wind in the Red Sea that night.

The accommodation-ladder had not been unshipped since leaving Aden and the man walked out on to the platform, as on to a balcony. He leaned his back against the rail and blew a puff of smoke into the air reflectively. The piano struck

141

up a lively tune and a voice began to sing the first verse of "The Rowdy Dowdy Boys". The measured pulsations of the screw were a subdued but additional accompaniment. The man knew the song, it had been the rage at all the music halls when he had started for India seven years before. It reminded him of the brilliant and busy streets he had not seen for so long, but was soon to see again. He was just going to join in the chorus when the railing, which had been insecurely fastened, gave way suddenly with a snap and he fell backwards into the warm water of the sea amid a great splash.

For a moment he was physically too much astonished to think. Then he realised he must shout. He began to do this even before he rose to the surface. He achieved a hoarse, inarticulate, half-choked scream. A startled brain suggested the word, "Help!" and he bawled this out lustily and with frantic effort six or seven times without stopping. Then he listened.

> "Hi! hi! clear the way
> For the Rowdy Dowdy Boys."

The chorus floated back to him across the smooth water for the ship had already completely passed by. And as he heard the music a long stab of terror drove through his heart. The possibility that he would not be picked up dawned for the first time on his consciousness. The chorus started again:

> "Then—I—say—boys,
> Who's for a jolly spree?
> Rum—tum—tiddley—um,
> Who'll have a drink with me?"

"Help! Help! Help!" shrieked the man, now in desperate fear.

> "Fond of a glass now and then,
> Fond of a row or noise;
> Hi! hi! clear the way
> For the Rowdy Dowdy Boys!"

The last words drawled out fainter and fainter. The vessel was steaming fast. The beginning of the second verse was confused and broken by the ever-growing distance. The dark outline of the great hull was getting blurred. The stern light dwindled.

Then he set out to swim after it with furious energy, pausing every dozen strokes to shout long wild shouts. The disturbed waters of the sea began to settle again to their rest and widening undulations became ripples. The aerated confusion of the screw fizzed itself upwards and out. The noise of motion and the sounds of life and music died away.

The liner was but a single fading light on the blackness of the waters and a dark shadow against the paler sky.

At length full realisation came to the man and he stopped swimming. He was alone—abandoned. With the understanding the brain reeled. He began again to swim, only now instead of shouting he prayed—mad, incoherent prayers, the words stumbling into one another.

Suddenly a distant light seemed to flicker and brighten.

A surge of joy and hope rushed through his mind. They were going to stop—to turn the ship and come back. And with the hope came gratitude. His prayer was answered. Broken words of thanksgiving rose to his lips. He stopped and stared after the light—his soul in his eyes. As he watched it, it grew gradually but steadily smaller. Then the man knew that his fate was certain. Despair succeeded hope; gratitude gave place to curses. Beating the water with his arms, he raved impotently. Foul oaths burst from him, as broken as his prayers—and as unheeded.

The fit of passion passed, hurried by increasing fatigue. He became silent—silent as was the sea, for even the ripples were subsiding into the glassy smoothness of the surface. He swam on mechanically along the track of the ship, sobbing quietly to himself in the misery of fear. And the stern light became a tiny speck, yellower but scarcely bigger than some of the stars, which here and there shone between the clouds.

Nearly twenty minutes passed and the man's fatigue began to change to exhaustion. The overpowering sense of the inevitable pressed upon him. With the weariness came a strange comfort—he need not swim all the long way to Suez. There was another course. He would die. He would resign his existence since he was thus abandoned. He threw up his hands impulsively and sank.

Down, down he went through the warm water. The physical death took hold of him and he began to drown. The pain of that savage grip recalled his anger. He fought with it furiously. Striking out with arms and legs he sought to get back to the air. It was a hard struggle, but he escaped victorious and gasping to the surface. Despair awaited him. Feebly splashing with his hands, he moaned in bitter misery:

"I can't—I must. O God! let me die."

The moon, then in her third quarter, pushed out from behind the concealing clouds and shed a pale, soft glitter upon the sea. Upright in the water, fifty yards away, was a black triangular object. It was a fin. It approached him slowly.

His last appeal had been heard.

Hell Gate

by Washington Irving

About six miles from the renowned city of the Manhattoes, and in that Sound, or arm of the sea, which passes between the main land and Nassau or Long Island, there is a narrow strait, where the current is violently compressed between shouldering promontories, and horribly irritated and perplexed by rocks and shoals. Being at the best of times a very violent, hasty, current, its takes these impediments in mighty dudgeon; boiling in whirlpools; brawling and fretting in ripples and breakers; and, in short, indulging in all kinds of wrong headed paroxysms. At such times, woe to any unlucky vessel that ventures within its clutches.

This termagant humor is said to prevail only at half tides. At low water it is as pacific as any other stream. As the tide rises, it begins to fret; at half tide it rages and roars as if bellowing for more water; but when the tide is full it relapses again into quiet, and for a time seems almost to sleep as soundly as an alderman after dinner. It may be compared to an inveterate hard drinker, who is a peaceable fellow enough when he has no liquor at all, or when he has a full, but when half seas over plays the very devil.

This mighty, blustering, bullying little strait was a place of great difficulty arid danger to the Dutch navigators of ancient days; hectoring their tub built barks in a most unruly style; whirling them about, in a manner to make any but a Dutchman giddy, and not unfrequently stranding them upon and reefs.

Whereupon out of sheer spleen they denominated it Hellegat (literally Hell Gut) and solemnly gave it over to the devil. This appellation has since been aptly rendered into English by the name of Hell Gate; and into nonsense by the name of Hurl Gate, according to certain foreign intruders who neither understood Dutch nor English.—May St. Nicholas confound them!

From this strait to the city of the Manhattoes the borders of the Sound are greatly diversified; in one part, on the eastern shore of the island of Manhata and opposite Blackwell's Island; being very much broken and indented by rocky nooks, over hung with trees which give them a wild and romantic look.

The flux and reflux of the tide through this part of the Sound is extremely rapid, and the navigation troublesome, by reason of the whirling eddies and counter currents. I speak this from experience, having been much of a navigator of these small seas in my boyhood, and having more than once run the risk of shipwreck and drowning in the course of divers holiday voyages, to which in common with the Dutch urchins I was rather prone.

In the midst of this perilous strait, and hard by a group of rocks called "the Hen and Chickens," there lay in my boyish days the wreck of a vessel which had been entangled in the whirlpools and stranded during a storm. There was some wild story about this being the wreck of a pirate, and of bloody murder, connected with it, which I cannot now recollect. Indeed, the desolate look of this forlorn hulk, and the fearful place where it lay rotting, were sufficient to awaken strange notions concerning it. A row of timber heads, blackened by time, peered above the surface at high water; but low tide a considerable part of the hull was bare, and its ribs or timbers, partly stripped of their planks, looked like the skeleton of some sea monster. There was also the stump of a mast, with a few ropes and blocks swinging about and whistling in the wind, while the sea gull wheeled and screamed around this melancholy carcass.

The Phantom Light of the Baie des Chaleurs

by Arthur Wentworth Hamilton Eaton

'Tis the laughter of pines that swing and sway
Where the breeze from the land meets the breeze from the bay,
'Tis the silvery foam of the silver tide
In ripples that reach to the forest side;
'Tis the fisherman's boat, in the track of sheen,
Plying through tangled seaweed green,
    O'er the Baie des Chaleurs.

Who has not heard of the phantom light
That over the moaning waves at night
Dances and drifts in endless play,
Close to the shore, then far away,
Fierce as the flame in sunset skies,
Cold as the winter light that lies
    On the Baie des Chaleurs.

They tell us that many a year ago,
From lands where the palm and olive grow,
Where vines with their purple clusters creep
Over the hillsides gray and steep,
A knight in his doublet, slashed with gold,
Famed in that chivalrous time of old,
For valorous deeds and courage rare,
Sailed with a princess wondrous fair
    To the Baie des Chaleurs.

That a pirate crew from some isle of the sea,
A murderous band as e'er could be,
With a shadowy sail, and a flag of night,
That flaunted and flew in heaven's sight,
Swept in the wake of the lovers there,
And sank the ship and its freight so fair
    In the Baie des Chaleurs.

Strange is the tale that the fishermen tell,—
They say that a ball of fire fell
Straight from the sky, with crash and roar,
Lighting the bay from shore to shore;
That the ship with a shudder and a groan,
Sank through the waves to the caverns lone
    Of the Baie des Chaleurs.

That was the last of the pirate crew,
But many a night a black flag flew
From the mast of a spectre vessel, sailed
By a spectre band that wept and wailed,
For the wreck they had wrought on the sea and the land,
For the innocent blood they had spilt on the sand,
    Of the Baie des Chaleurs.

This is the tale of the phantom light,

That fills the mariner's heart at night,

With dread as it gleams o'er his path on the bay,

Now by the shore, then far away,

Fierce as the flame in sunset skies,

Cold as the winter moon that lies

    On the Baie des Chaleurs.

The Story of the Haunted Ship

by Wilhelm Hauff

My father kept a small shop at Balsora. He was neither poor nor rich, and one of those people who are afraid of venturing anything lest they should lose the little they possess. He brought me up plainly and virtuously, and soon I was enabled to assist him in his trade. Scarcely had I reached my eighteenth year, and hardly had he made his first large speculation, when he died, probably from grief at having confided a thousand pieces of gold to the sea.

I could not help thinking him lucky afterwards on account of his death, for a few weeks later the news arrived that the ship to which my father had entrusted his goods had sunk. This mishap, however, did not curb my youthful courage. I converted everything that my father had left into money, and set forth to try my fortune abroad, accompanied only by my father's old servant, who from long attachment would not separate himself from me and my fate.

We took ship at Balsora and left the haven with a favourable wind. The ship in which we embarked was bound for India. When we had sailed some fifteen days over the ordinary track, the Captain predicted a storm. He looked very serious, for it appeared that he was not sufficiently acquainted with the course in these parts to await a storm with composure. He had all sail furled, and we drifted along quite gently. The night had fallen. It was cold and clear, and the Captain began to think he had been deceived by false indications of the storm. All at once a ship which we had not observed before drove past at a little distance from our own. Wild shouts and cheers resounded from her deck; at which, in such an anxious hour before a tempest, I wondered not a little. The Captain, who stood by my side, turned as pale as death. "My ship is doomed!" he cried; "yonder sails death." Before I could question him as to the meaning of this strange exclamation, the sailors came running towards us, howling and crying. "Have you seen it?" they cried. "It is all over with us."

But the Captain caused some consolatory verses to be read out the Koran, and placed himself at the helm. All in vain! Visibly the storm increased in fury, and before an hour had passed the ship crashed and stuck fast. The boats were lowered, and scarcely had the last sailors saved themselves, when the ship sank before our eyes, and I was launched on the sea, a beggar. Further miseries awaited us. The storm raged more furiously, our boat became unmanageable. I had clasped my old servant tightly, and we vowed never to part from one another. At length day broke. But at the first dawn of morning a squall caught the boat in which we were seated and capsized it. I never saw my shipmates again. I was stunned by the shock; and when I awoke, I found myself in the arms of my old and faithful servant, who had saved himself on the overturned boat and dragged me after him. The tempest had subsided. Nothing more was seen of our ship. We discovered, however, not far from us another ship, towards which the waves were drifting us. As we drew near I recognized it as the same ship that had dashed past us on the preceding night, and which had terrified our Captain so much. I was inspired with a singular horror at the sight of this vessel. The expression of the Captain which had been so terribly fulfilled, the desolate aspect of the ship, on which, near as we were and loudly as we shouted, no one appeared, frightened me. However, this was our only means of safety, therefore we praised the Prophet who had so wonderfully preserved us.

Over the ship's bow hung a long cable. We paddled with hands and feet towards it in order to grasp it. At length we succeeded. Loudly I raised my voice, but all was silent on board. We then climbed up by the rope, I as the youngest going first. Oh, horror! What a spectacle met my gaze as I stepped upon the deck! The planks were reddened with blood; twenty or thirty corpses in Turkish dresses lay on the deck. Close to the mainmast stood a man, richly attired, a sabre in his hand, but with features pale and distorted; a great nail driven through his forehead pinning him to the mainmast. He also was dead.

Terror shackled my steps. I scarcely ventured to breathe. At last my companion had also come up. He too was struck at the sight of the deck, on which nothing living was to be seen, only so many frightful corpses. After a time we ventured, after having invoked the aid of the Prophet in anguish of heart, to go forward. At each step we glanced around expecting to discover something new and yet more terrible. But all was the same. Far and wide nothing was living but ourselves and the ocean. We dared not even speak aloud, lest the dead Captain spitted to the mast should turn his ghastly eyes upon us, or one of the corpses move its head. At last we reached a hatchway which led to the ship's hold. There we both stopped, involuntarily, and looked at each other, for neither dared to speak his thoughts.

"O Master," said my faithful servant, "something awful has happened here! Yet, though the hold below be full of murderers, I would rather give myself up to their mercy than remain here any longer among these corpses." I thought the same. We grew bold and, full of expectation, descended. But here likewise all was still as death, and only our steps sounded on the ladder. We stood at the door of the cabin. I placed my ear against it and listened. Nothing could be heard. I opened it, and the cabin presented a disorderly appearance. Dresses, weapons, and other things lay in confusion. Everything was out of its place. The crew, or at least the Captain, must have been carousing not long since, for all was still lying about.

We went from place to place and from cabin to cabin, and everywhere found splendid stores of silk, pearls, sugar, and the like. I was beside myself with joy at this sight, for since no one was on board, I thought I had a right to appropriate all to myself; but Ibrahim reminded me that we were doubtless far from land, which we could never reach without the help of man.

We refreshed ourselves with the meats and drinks, of which we found an ample supply, and finally ascended again to the deck. But here we shuddered at the sight of the ghastly corpses. We resolved upon freeing ourselves from them by throwing them overboard. But how awful was the dread which we felt when we found that not one could be moved from his position! So firmly fixed were they to the flooring, that we should have had to take up the planks of the deck in order to remove them, and for this purpose we had no tools. Neither could we loose the Captain from the mainmast, nor wrest his sabre from his rigid grasp.

We passed the day in sad contemplation of our position, and when night began to fall I allowed old Ibrahim to lie down to sleep, while I kept watch on deck spying for some means of deliverance.

But when the moon had come out, and I reckoned by the stars that it was about eleven o'clock, such an irresistible sleep took possession of me that I involuntarily fell behind a cask that stood on the deck. However, this was more stupefaction than sleep, for I distinctly heard the sea beating against the side of the ship, and the sails creaking and whistling in the wind. All of a sudden I thought I heard voices and men's footsteps on the deck. I endeavoured to get up to see what it was, but an invisible power held my limbs fettered; I could not even open my eyes. The voices, however, grew more distinct, and it appeared to me as if a merry crew was rushing about on the deck. Now and then I thought I heard the sonorous voice of a commander, and also distinctly the hoisting and lowering of cordage and sails. But by degrees my senses left me, I sank into a deeper sleep, in which I only thought I could hear a clatter of arms, and only awoke when the sun was far above the horizon and scorching my face.

I stared about in astonishment. Storm, ship, the dead, and what I had heard during the night, appeared to me like a dream, but when I glance around I found everything as on the previous day. Immovable lay the dead, immovable stood the Captain spitted to the mast. I laughed over my dream, and rose up to seek the old man. He was seated, absorbed in reflection in the cabin. "Oh, Master," he exclaimed, as I entered, "I would rather lie at the bottom of the sea than pass another night in this bewitched ship." I inquired the cause of his trouble, and he thus answered me: "After I had slept some hours, I awoke and heard people running about above my head. I thought at first it was you, but there were at least twenty, rushing to and fro, aloft, and I also heard calling and shouting. At last heavy steps came down the cabin. Upon this I became insensible, and only now and then my consciousness returned for a few moments, and then I saw the same man who is nailed to the mast overhead, sitting there at that table, singing and drinking, while the man in the scarlet dress, who is close to him on the floor, sat beside him and drank with him." Such was my old servant's narrative.

Believe me, my friends, I did not feel at all at ease, for it was no illusion. I had also heard the dead men quite plainly. To sail in such company was gruesome to me. My Ibrahim, however, relapsed into profound meditation. "I have just hit it!" he exclaimed at last. He recalled a little formula, which his grandfather, a man of experience and a great traveller, had taught him, which was a charm against ghosts and sorcery. He likewise affirmed that we might ward off the unnatural sleep during the coming night, by diligently saying verses from the Koran.

The proposal of the old man pleased me. In anxious expectation we saw the night approach.

Adjoining the cabin was a narrow berth, into which we resolved to retire. We bored several holes through the door, large enough to overlook the whole cabin; we then locked the door as well as we could inside, and Ibrahim wrote the name of the Prophet in all four corners. Thus we awaited the terrors of the night. It might be about eleven o'clock when I began to feel very drowsy. My companion therefore advised me to say some verses from the Koran, which indeed helped me. All at once everything grew animated above, the cordage creaked, feet paced the deck, and several voices became clearly heard. We had thus sat for some time in intense expectation, when we heard something descending the steps of the cabin stairs. The old man on hearing this commenced to recite the formula which his grandfather had taught him against ghosts and sorcery:—

> *"If you are spirits from the air,*
> *Or come from depths of sea,*
> *Have in dark sepulchres your lair,*
> *Or if from fire you be.*
> *Allah is your God and Lord,*
> *All spirits must obey His word."*

I must confess I did not quite believe in this charm, and my hair stood on end as the door opened. In stepped that tall majestic man whom I had seen nailed to the mainmast. The nail still passed through his skull, but his sword was sheathed. Behind him followed another person less richly dressed; him also I had seen stretched on deck. The Captain, for there was no doubt it was he, had a pale face, a large black beard and fiery eyes, with which he looked around the whole cabin. I could see him quite distinctly as he passed our door; but he did not seem to notice the door at all, which hid us. Both seated themselves at the table which stood in the middle of the cabin, speaking loudly and almost shouting to one another in an unknown tongue. They grew more and more hot and excited, until at last the Captain brought his fist down upon the table, so that the cabin shook. The other jumped up with a wild laugh and beckoned the Captain to follow him. The latter rose, tore his sabre out of its sheath, and both left the cabin.

After they had gone we breathed more freely, but our alarm was not to terminate yet. Louder and louder grew the noise on deck. We heard rushing backwards and forwards, shouting, laughing and howling. At last a most fiendish noise was heard, so we thought the deck together with all its sails was coming down on us, clashing of arms and shrieks—and suddenly a dead silence followed. When, after many hours, we ventured to ascend, we found everything as before; not one had shifted his place; all lay as stiff as wood.

Thus we passed many days on board this ship, and constantly steered on an eastern course, where according to my calculation land should be found; but although we seemed to cover many miles by day, yet at night it seemed to go back, for we were always in the same place at the rising of the sun. We could not understand this, except that the dead crew each night navigated the ship in a directly opposite course with full sails. In order to prevent this, we furled all the sails before night fell, and employed the same means as we had used on the cabin door. We wrote the name of the prophet, and the formula prescribed by Ibrahim's grandfather, upon a scroll of parchment, and wound it round the furled sails. Anxiously we awaited the result in our berths. The noise now seemed to increase more violently than ever; but behold, on the following morning, the sails were still furled, as we had left them. By day we only hoisted as many sails as were needed to carry the ship gently along, and thus in five days we covered a considerable tract.

At last on the sixth morning we discovered land at a short distance, and thanked Allah and his Prophet for our miraculous deliverance. This day and on the following night we sailed along a coast, and on the seventh morning we thought at a short distance we saw a town. With much difficulty we dropped our anchor, which at once struck ground, lowered a little boat, which was on deck, and rowed with all our strength towards the town. After the lapse of half-an-hour we entered a river which ran into the sea, and landed. On entering the gate of the town we asked the name of it, and learnt that it was an Indian town, not far from where I had intended to land at first. We went towards a caravanserai and refreshed ourselves after our adventurous journey. I also inquired there after some wise and intelligent man, intimating to the landlord that I wished to consult one on matters relating to sorcery. He led me to some remote street to a mean-looking house and knocked. I was allowed to enter, and simply told to ask for Muley.

In the house I met a little old man, with a grey beard and a long nose, who asked me what I wanted. I told him I desired to see the wise Muley, and he answered me that he was Muley. I now asked his advice what I should do with the corpses, and how I was to set about to remove them from the ship. He answered me that very likely the ship's crew were spell-bound on the ocean on account of some crime; and he believed the charm might be broken by bringing them on land, which, however, could only be done by taking up the planks on which they lay. The ship, together with all its goods, by divine and human law belonged to me, because I had as it were found it. I was, however, to keep all very secret, and make him a little present of my abundance, in return for which he and his slaves would assist me in removing the dead. I promised to reward him richly, and we set forth followed by five slaves provided with saws and hatchets. On the road the magician Muley could not sufficiently laud the happy thought of tacking the Koran verses upon the sails. He said that this had been the only means of our deliverance.

It was yet early morning when we reached the vessel. We all set to work immediately, and in an hour four lay already in the boat. Some of the slaves had to row them to land to bury them there. They related on their return that the corpses had saved them the trouble of burial, for hardly had they been put on the ground when they crumbled into dust. We continued sawing off the corpses, and before evening all had been removed to land except one, namely he who was nailed to the mast. In vain we endeavoured to draw the nail out of the wood. Every effort could not displace it a hair's-breadth. I did not know what to do, for it was impossible to cut down the mast to bring him to land. Muley, however, devised an expedient. He ordered a slave quickly to row to land, in order to bring him a pot filled with earth. When it was brought, the magician pronounced some mystic words over it, and emptied the earth upon the head of the corpse. Immediately he opened his eyes, heaved a deep sigh, and the wound of the nail in his forehead began to bleed. We now extracted the nail easily, and the wounded man fell into the arms of one of the slaves.

"Who has brought me hither?" he said, after having slightly recovered. Muley pointed to me, and I approached him. "Thanks be to thee, unknown stranger, for thou hast rescued me from a long martyrdom. For fifty years has my corpse been floating upon these waves, and my spirit was condemned to reanimate it each night; but now earth having touched my head, I can return to my fathers reconciled." I begged him to tell us how he had fallen into this awful condition, and he answered: "Fifty years ago I was a man of power and rank, and lived in Algiers. The longing after gain induced me to fit out a vessel in order to engage in piracy. I had already carried on this business for some time, when one day I took on board at Zante a Dervish, who asked for a free passage. My companions and myself were wild fellows, and paid no respect to the sanctity of the man, but rather mocked him. But one day, when he had reproached me in his holy zeal with my sinful mode of living, I became furious at night, after having drunk a great deal with my steersman in my cabin. Enraged at what a Dervish had told me, and what I would not even allow a Sultan to tell me, I rushed upon deck, and plunged my dagger in his breast. As he died, he cursed me and my crew, that we might neither live nor die till our heads should touch the earth. The Dervish died, and we threw him into the sea, laughing at his menaces; but in the very same night his words were fulfilled.

"Some of my crew mutinied against me. We fought with insane fury until my adherents were defeated, and I was nailed to the mainmast. But the mutineers also expired of their wounds, and my ship soon became but an immense tomb. My eyes also grew dim, my breathing ceased, I thought I was dying. But it was only a kind of numbness that seized me. The very next night, and at the precise hour that we had thrown the Dervish into the sea, I and all my companions awoke, we were alive, but we could only do and say what we had said and done on that night. Thus we have been sailing these fifty years unable to live or die: for how could we reach land? It was with a savage joy that we sailed many times with full sail in the storm, hoping that at length we might strike some rock, and rest our wearied heads at the bottom of the sea. We did not succeed. But now I shall die. Thanks once more, my unknown deliverer, and if treasures can reward thee, accept my ship as a mark of my gratitude."

After having said this, the Captain's head fell upon his breast, and he expired. Immediately his body also, like the crew's, crumbled to dust. We collected it in a little urn and buried him on shore. I engaged, however, workmen from the town, who repaired my ship thoroughly. After having bartered the goods which I had on board for others at a great profit, I collected a crew, rewarded my friend Muley handsomely, and set sail towards my native place. I made, however, a detour, and landed on many islands and countries where I sold my goods. The Prophet blessed my enterprise. After a lapse of nine months, twice as wealthy as the dying Captain had made me, I reached Balsora. My fellow-citizens were astonished at my riches and my fortune, and did not believe anything else but that I must have found the diamond valley of the celebrated traveller Sinbad. I left their belief undisturbed, but henceforth the young people of Balsora, when they were scarcely eighteen years old, were obliged to go out into the word in order like myself to seek their fortune. But I lived quietly and peacefully, and every five years undertook a journey to Mecca, in order to thank the Lord for His blessing at this sacred shrine, and pray for the Captain and his crew that He might receive them into His Paradise.

THE PALATINE

BY JOHN GREENLEAF WHITTIER

*Block Island in Long Island Sound, called by the Indians Manisees,
the isle of the little god, was the scene of a tragic incident a hundred
years or more ago, when* The Palatine, *an emigrant ship bound for
Philadelphia, driven off its course, came upon the coast at this point.
A mutiny on board, followed by an inhuman desertion on the part of
the crew, had brought the unhappy passengers to the verge of starvation
and madness. Tradition says that wreckers on shore, after rescuing all
but one of the survivors, set fire to the vessel, which was driven out to
sea before a gale which had sprung up. Every twelvemonth, according
to the same tradition, the spectacle of a ship on fire is visible to the
inhabitants of the island.*

—AUTHOR

Leagues north, as fly the gull and auk,
Point Judith watches with eye of hawk;
Leagues south, thy beacon flames, Montauk!

Lonely and wind-shorn, wood-forsaken,
With never a tree for Spring to waken,
For tryst of lovers or farewells taken,

Circled by waters that never freeze,
Beaten by billow and swept by breeze,
Lieth the island of Manisees,

Set at the mouth of the Sound to hold
The coast lights up on its turret old,
Yellow with moss and sea-fog mould.

Dreary the land when gust and sleet
At its doors and windows howl and beat,
And Winter laughs at its fires of peat!

But in summer time, when pool and pond,
Held in the laps of valleys fond,
Are blue as the glimpses of sea beyond;

When the hills are sweet with the brier-rose,
And, hid in the warm, soft dells, unclose
Flowers the mainland rarely knows;

When boats to their morning fishing go,
And, held to the wind and slanting low,
Whitening and darkening the small sails show,—

Then is that lonely island fair;
And the pale health-seeker findeth there
The wine of life in its pleasant air.

No greener valleys the sun invite,
On smoother beaches no sea-birds light,
No blue waves shatter to foam more white!

There, circling ever their narrow range,
Quaint tradition and legend strange
Live on unchallenged, and know no change.

Old wives spinning their webs of tow,
Or rocking weirdly to and fro
In and out of the peat's dull glow,

And old men mending their nets of twine,
Talk together of dream and sign,
Talk of the lost ship *Palatine,*—

The ship that, a hundred years before,
Freighted deep with its goodly store,
In the gales of the equinox went ashore.

The eager islanders one by one
Counted the shots of her signal gun,
And heard the crash when she drove right on!

Into the teeth of death she sped
(May God forgive the hands that fed
The false lights over the rocky Head!)

O men and brothers! what sights were there!
White upturned faces, hands stretched in prayer!
Where waves had pity, could ye not spare?

Down swooped the wreckers, like birds of prey
Tearing the heart of the ship away,
And the dead had never a word to say.

And then, with ghastly shimmer and shine
Over the rocks and the seething brine,
They burned the wreck of the *Palatine*.

In their cruel hearts, as they homeward sped,
"The sea and the rocks are dumb," they said
"There 'll be no reckoning with the dead."

But the year went round, and when once more
Along their foam-white curves of shore
They heard the line-storm rave and roar,

Behold! again, with shimmer and shine,
Over the rocks and the seething brine,
The flaming wreck of the *Palatine*!

So, haply in fitter words than these,
Mending their nets on their patient knees
They tell the legend of Manisees.

Nor looks nor tones a doubt betray;
"It is known to us all," they quietly say;
"We too have seen it in our day."

Is there, then, no death for a word once spoken?
Was never a deed but left its token
Written on tables never broken?

Do the elements subtle reflections give?
Do pictures of all the ages live
On Nature's infinite negative,

Which, half in sport, in malice half,
She shows at times, with shudder or laugh,
Phantom and shadow in photograph?

For still, on many a moonless night,
From Kingston Head and from Montauk light
The spectre kindles and burns in sight.

Now low and dim, now clear and higher,
Leaps up the terrible Ghost of Fire,
Then, slowly sinking, the flames expire.

And the wise Sound skippers, though skies be fine,
Reef their sails when they see the sign
Of the blazing wreck of the *Palatine*!

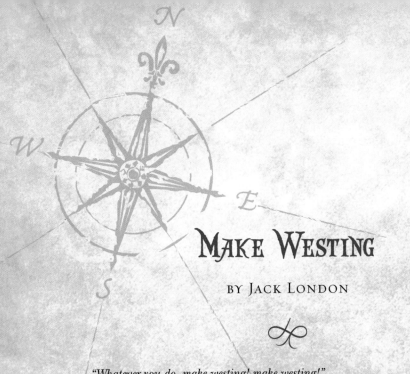

Make Westing

by Jack London

"Whatever you do, make westing! make westing!"
—Sailing directions for Cape Horn

For seven weeks the *Mary Rogers* had been 50° south in the Atlantic and 50° south in the Pacific, which meant that for seven weeks she had been struggling to round Cape Horn. For seven weeks she had been either in dirt, or close to dirt, save once, and then, following upon six days of excessive dirt, which she had ridden out under the shelter of the redoubtable Terra del Fuego coast, she had almost gone ashore during a heavy swell in the dead calm that had suddenly fallen. For seven weeks she had wrestled with the Cape Horn greybeards, and in return had been buffeted and smashed by them. She was a wooden ship, and her ceaseless straining had opened her seams, so that twice a day the watch took its turn at the pumps.

The *Mary Rogers* was strained, the crew was strained, and big Dan Cullen, master, was likewise strained. Perhaps he was strained most of all, for upon him rested the responsibility of that titanic struggle. He slept most of the time in his clothes, though he rarely slept. He haunted the deck at night, a great, burly, robust ghost, black with the sunburn of thirty years of sea and hairy as an orang-outang. He, in turn, was haunted by one thought of action, a sailing direction for the

165

Horn: *Whatever you do, make westing! make westing!* It was an obsession. He thought of nothing else, except, at times, to blaspheme God for sending such bitter weather.

Make Westing! He hugged the Horn, and a dozen times lay hove to with the iron Cape bearing east-by-north, or north-north-east, a score of miles away. And each time the eternal west wind smote him back and he made easting. He fought gale after gale, south to 64°, inside the antarctic drift-ice, and pledged his immortal soul to the Powers of darkness, for a bit of westing, for a slant to take him around. And he made easting. In despair, he had tried to make the passage through the Straits of Le Mazre. Halfway through, the wind hauled to the north'ard of north-west, the glass dropped to 28·88, and he turned and ran before a gale of cyclonic fury, missing, by a hair's breadth, piling up the *Mary Rogers* on the black-toothed rocks. Twice he had made west to the Diego Ramirez Rocks, one of the times saved between two snow-squalls by sighting the gravestones of ships a quarter of a mile dead ahead.

Blow! Captain Dan Cullen instanced all his thirty years at sea to prove that never had it blown so before. The *Mary Rogers* was hove to at the time he gave the evidence, and, to clinch it, inside half an hour the *Mary Rogers* was hove down to the hatches. Her new maintopsail and brand new spencer were blown away like tissue paper; and five sails, furled and fast under double gaskets, were blown loose and stripped from the yards. And before morning the *Mary Rogers* was hove down twice again, and holes were knocked in her bulwarks to ease her decks from the weight of ocean that pressed her down.

On an average of once a week Captain Dan Cullen caught glimpses of the sun. Once, for ten minutes, the sun shone at midday, and ten minutes afterwards a new gale was piping up, both watches were shortening sail, and all was buried in the obscurity of a driving snow-squall. For a fortnight, once, Captain Dan Cullen was without a meridian or a chronometer sight. Rarely did he know his position within half of a degree, except when in sight of land; for sun and stars remained hidden behind the sky, and it was so gloomy that even at the best the horizons were poor for accurate observations. A grey gloom shrouded the world. The clouds were grey; the great driving seas were leaden grey; the smoking crests were a grey churning; even the occasional albatrosses were grey, while the snow-flurries were not white, but grey, under the sombre pail of the heavens.

Life on board the *Mary Rogers* was grey—grey and gloomy. The faces of the sailors were blue grey; they were afflicted with sea-cuts and sea-boils, and suffered exquisitely. They were shadows of men. For seven weeks, in the forecastle or on deck, they had not known what it was to be dry. They had forgotten what it was to sleep out a watch, and all watches it was, "All hands on deck!" They caught the snatches of agonized sleep, and they slept in their oil-skins ready for the everlasting call. So weak and worn were they that it took both watches to do the work of one. That was why both watches were on deck so much of the time. And no shadow of a man could shirk duty. Nothing less than a broken leg could enable a man to knock off work; and there were two such, who had been mauled and pulped by the seas that broke overboard.

One other man who was the shadow of a man was George Dorety. He was the only passenger on board, a friend of the firm, and he had elected to make the voyage for his health. But seven weeks off Cape Horn had not bettered his health. He gasped and panted in his bunk through the long, heaving nights; and when on deck he was so bundled up for warmth that he resembled a peripatetic old-clothes shop. At midday, eating at the cabin table in a gloom so deep that the swinging sea-lamps burned always, he looked as blue-grey as the sickest, saddest man for'ard. Nor did gazing across the table at Captain Dan Cullen have any cheering effect upon him. Captain Cullen chewed and scowled and kept silent. The scowls were for God, and with every chew he reiterated the sole thought of his existence, which was *make westing*. He was a big, hairy brute, and the sight of him was not stimulating to the other's appetite. He looked upon George Dorety as a Jonah, and told him so once each meal savagely transferring the scowl from God to the passenger and back again.

Nor did the mate prove a first aid to a languid appetite. Joshua Higgins by name, a seamen by profession and pull, but a pot-walloper by capacity, he was a loose-jointed, sniffling creature, heartless and selfish and cowardly, without a soul, in fear of his life of Dan Cullen, and a bully over the sailors, who knew that behind the mate was Captain Cullen, the law-giver and compeller, the driver and the destroyer, the incarnation of a dozen bucko mates. In that wild weather at the southern end of the earth, Joshua Higgins ceased washing. His grimy face usually robbed George Dorety of what little appetite he managed to accumulate. Ordinarily this lavatorial dereliction would have caught Captain Cullen's eye and vocabulary, but in the present his mind was filled with making westing, to the exclusion of all other things not contributory thereto. Whether the mate's face was clean or dirty had no bearing upon westing. Later on, when 50° south in the Pacific had been reached, Joshua Higgins would wash his face very abruptly. In the meantime, at the cabin table, where grey twilight alternated with lamplight while the lamps were being filled, George Dorety sat between the two men, one a tiger and the other a hyena, and wondered why God had made them. The second mate, Matthew Turner, was a true sailor and a man, but George Dorety did not have the solace of his company, for he ate by himself, solitary, when they had finished.

On Saturday morning, July 24, George Dorety awoke to a feeling of life and headlong movement. On deck he found the *Mary Rogers* running off before a howling south-easter. Nothing was set but the lower topsails and the foresail. It was all she could stand, yet she was making fourteen knots, as Mr. Turner shouted in Dorety's ear when he came on deck. And it was all westing. She was going round the Horn at last…if the wind held. Mr. Turner looked happy. he end of the struggle was in sight. But Captain Cullen did not look happy. He scowled at Dorety in passing. Captain Cullen did not want God to know that he was pleased with that wind. He had a conception of a malicious God, and believed in his secret soul that if God knew it was a desirable wind, God would promptly efface it and send a snorter from the west. So he walked softly before God, smothering his joy down under scowls and muttered curses, and, so, fooling God, for God was the only thing in the universe of which Dan Cullen was afraid.

All Saturday and Saturday night the *Mary Rogers* raced her westing. Persistently she logged her fourteen knots, so that by Sunday morning she had covered three hundred and fifty miles. If the wind held, she would make around. If it failed, and the snorter came from anywhere between southwest and north, back the *Mary Rogers* would be hurled and be no better off than she had been seven weeks before. And on Sunday morning the wind was failing. The big sea was going down and running smoother. Both watches were on deck setting sail after sail as fast as the ship could stand it. And now Captain Cullen went around brazenly before God, smoking a big cigar, smiling jubilantly, as if the failing wind delighted him, while down underneath he was raging against God for

taking the life out of the blessed wind. *Make westing!* So he would, if God would only leave him alone. Secretly, he pledged himself to the Powers of Darkness, if they would let him make westing. He pledged himself so easily because he did not believe in the Powers of Darkness. He really believed only in God, though he did not know it. And in his inverted theology God was really the Prince of Darkness. Captain Cullen was a devil-worshipper, but he called the devil by another name, that was all.

At midday, after calling eight bells, Captain Cullen ordered the royals on. The men went aloft faster than they had gone in weeks. Not alone were they nimble because of the westing, but a benignant sun was shining down and limbering their stiff bodies. George Dorety stood aft, near Captain Cullen, less bundled in clothes than usual, soaking in the grateful warmth as he watched the scene. Swiftly and abruptly the incident occurred. There was a cry from the foreroyal-yard of "Man overboard!" Somebody threw a life-buoy over the side, and at the same instant the second mate's voice came aft, ringing and peremptory:—

"Hard down your helm!"

The man at the wheel never moved a spoke. He knew better, for Captain Dan Cullen was standing alongside of him. He wanted to move a spoke, to move all the spokes, to grind the wheel down, hard down, for his comrade drowning in the sea. He glanced at Captain Dan Cullen, and Captain Dan Cullen gave no sign.

"Down! Hard down!" the second mate roared, as he sprang aft.

But he ceased springing and commanding, and stood still, when he saw Dan Cullen by the wheel. And big Dan Cullen puffed at his cigar and said nothing. Astern, and going astern fast, could be seen the sailor. He had caught the life-buoy and was clinging to it. Nobody spoke. Nobody moved. The men aloft clung to the royal yards and watched with terror-stricken faces. And the *Mary Rogers* raced on, making her westing. A long, silent minute passed.

"Who was it?" Captain Cullen demanded.

"Mops, sir," eagerly answered the sailor at the wheel.

Mops topped a wave astern and disappeared temporarily in the trough. It was a large wave, but it was no greybeard. A small boat could live easily in such a sea, and in such a sea the *Mary Rogers* could easily come to. But she could not come to and make westing at the same time.

For the first time in all his years, George Dorety was seeing a real drama of life and death—a sordid little drama in which the scales balanced an unknown sailor named Mops against a few miles of longitude. At first he had watched the man astern, but now he watched big Dan Cullen, hairy and black, vested with power of life and death, smoking a cigar.

Captain Dan Cullen smoked another long, silent minute. Then he removed the cigar from his mouth. He glanced aloft at the spars of the *Mary Rogers*, and overside at the sea.

"Sheet home the royals!" he cried.

Fifteen minutes later they sat at table, in the cabin, with food served before them. On one side of George Dorety sat Dan Cullen, the tiger, on the other side, Joshua Higgins, the hyena. Nobody spoke. On deck the men were sheeting home the skysails. George Dorety could hear their cries, while a persistent vision haunted him of a man called Mops, alive and well, clinging to a lifebuoy miles astern in that lonely ocean. He glanced at Captain Cullen, and experienced a feeling of nausea, for the man was eating his food with relish, almost bolting it.

"Captain Cullen," Dorety said, "you are in command of this ship, and it is not proper for me to comment now upon what you do. But I wish to say one thing. There is a hereafter, and yours will be a hot one."

Captain Cullen did not even scowl. In his voice was regret as he said:—

"It was blowing a living gale. It was impossible to save the man."

"He fell from the royal-yard," Dorety cried hotly. "You were setting the royals at the time. Fifteen minutes afterwards you were setting the skysails."

"It was a living gale, wasn't it, Mr. Higgins?" Captain Cullen said, turning to the mate.

"If you'd brought her to, it'd have taken the sticks out of her" was the mate's answer. "You did the proper thing, Captain Cullen. The man hadn't a ghost of a show."

George Dorety made no answer, and to the meal's end no one spoke. After that, Dorety had his meals served in his state-room. Captain Cullen scowled at him no longer, though no speech was exchanged between them, while the *Mary Rogers* sped north toward warmer latitudes. At the end of the week, Dan Cullen cornered Dorety on deck.

"What are you going to do when we get to 'Frisco?" he demanded bluntly.

"I am going to swear out a warrant for your arrest," Dorety answered quietly. "I am going to charge you with murder, and I am going to see you hanged for it."

"You're almighty sure of yourself," Captain Cullen sneered, turning on his heel.

A second week passed, and one morning found George Dorety standing in the coach-house companionway at the for'ard end of the long poop, taking his first gaze around the deck. The *Mary Rogers* was reaching full-and-by, in a stiff breeze. Every sail was set and drawing, including the staysails. Captain Cullen strolled for'ard along the poop. He strolled carelessly, glancing at the passenger out of the corner of his eye. Dorety was looking the other way, standing with head and shoulders outside the companionway, and only the back of his head was to be seen. Captain Cullen, with swift eye, embraced the mainstaysail-block and the head and estimated the distance. He glanced about him. Nobody was looking. Aft, Joshua Higgins, pacing up and down, had just turned his back and was going the other way. Captain Cullen bent over suddenly and cast the staysail-sheet off from its pin. The heavy block hurtled through the air, smashing Dorety's head like an egg-shell and hurtling on and back and forth as the staysail whipped and slatted in the wind. Joshua Higgins turned around to see what had carried away, and met the full blast of the vilest portion of Captain Cullen's profanity.

"I made the sheet fast myself," whimpered the mate in the first lull, "with an extra turn to make sure. I remember it distinctly."

"Made fast?" the Captain snarled back, for the benefit of the watch as it struggled to capture the flying sail before it tore to ribbons. "You couldn't make your grandmother fast, you useless hell's scullion. If you made that sheet fast with an extra turn, why in hell didn't it stay fast? That's what I want to know. Why in hell didn't it stay fast?"

The mate whined inarticulately.

"Oh, shut up!" was the final word of Captain Cullen.

Half an hour later he was as surprised as any when the body of George Dorety was found inside the companionway on the floor. In the afternoon, alone in his room, he doctored up the log.

"*Ordinary seaman, Karl Brun,*" he wrote, "*lost overboard from foreroyal-yard in a gale of wind. Was running at the time, and for the safety of the ship did not dare to come up the wind. Nor could a boat have lived in the sea that was running.*"

On another page he wrote:

"Had often warned Mr. Dorety about the danger he ran because of his carelessness on deck. I told him, once, that some day he would get his head knocked off by a block. A carelessly fastened mainstaysail sheet was the cause of the accident, which was deeply to be regretted because Mr. Dorety was a favourite with all of us."

Captain Dan Cullen read over his literary effort with admiration, blotted the page, and closed the log. He lighted a cigar and stared before him. He felt the *Mary Rogers* lift, and heel, and surge along, and knew that she was making nine knots. A smile of satisfaction slowly dawned on his black and hairy face. Well, anyway, he had made his westing and fooled God.

The Flying Dutchman

by Charles Godfrey Leland

We met the *Flying Dutchman*,
　　By midnight he came,
His hull was all of hell fire,
　　His sails were all aflame;
Fire on the main-top,
　　Fire on the bow,
Fire on the gun-deck,
　　Fire down below.

Four-and-twenty dead men,
　　Those were the crew,
The devil on the bowsprit,
　　Fiddled as she flew,
We gave her the broadside,
　　Right in the dip,
Just like a candle,
　　Went out the ship.

THE STRIPED CHEST

BY SIR ARTHUR CONAN DOYLE

"What do you make of her, Allardyce?" I asked.

My second mate was standing beside me upon the poop, with his short, thick legs astretch, for the gale had left a considerable swell behind it, and our two quarter-boats nearly touched the water with every roll. He steadied his glass against the mizzen-shrouds, and he looked long and hard at this disconsolate stranger every time she came reeling up on to the crest of a roller and hung balanced for a few seconds before swooping down upon the other side. She lay so low in the water that I could only catch an occasional glimpse of a pea-green line of bulwark.

She was a brig, but her mainmast had been snapped short off some ten feet above the deck, and no effort seemed to have been made to cut away the wreckage, which floated, sails and yards, like the broken wing of a wounded gull upon the water beside her. The foremast was still standing, but the foretopsail was flying loose, and the headsails were streaming out in long, white pennons in front of her. Never have I seen a vessel which appeared to have gone through rougher handling.

But we could not be surprised at that, for there had been times during the last three days when it was a question whether our own barque would ever see land again. For thirty-six hours we had kept her nose to it, and if the *Mary Sinclair* had not been as good a seaboat as ever left the Clyde, we could not have gone through. And yet here we were at the end of it with the loss only of our gig and of part of the starboard bulwark. It did not astonish us, however, when the smother had cleared away, to find that others had been less lucky, and that this mutilated brig staggering about upon a blue sea and under a cloudless sky, had been left, like a blinded man after a lightning flash, to tell of the terror which is past.

Allardyce, who was a slow and methodical Scotchman, stared long and hard at the little craft, while our seamen lined the bulwark or clustered upon the fore shrouds to have a view of the stranger. In latitude 20° and longitude 10°, which were about our bearings, one becomes a little curious as to whom one meets, for one has left the main lines of Atlantic commerce to the north. For ten days we had been sailing over a solitary sea.

"She's derelict, I'm thinking," said the second mate.

I had come to the same conclusion, for I could see no signs of life upon her deck, and there was no answer to the friendly wavings from our seamen. The crew had probably deserted her under the impression that she was about to founder.

"She can't last long," continued Allardyce, in his measured way. "She may put her nose down and her tail up any minute. The water's lipping up to the edge of her rail."

"What's her flag?" I asked.

"I'm trying to make out. It's got all twisted and tangled with the halyards. Yes, I've got it now, clear enough. It's the Brazilian flag, but it's wrong side up."

She had hoisted a signal of distress, then, before her people had abandoned her. Perhaps they had only just gone. I took the mate's glass and looked round over the tumultuous face of the deep blue Atlantic, still veined and starred with white lines and spoutings of foam. But nowhere could I see anything human beyond ourselves.

"There may be living men aboard," said I.

"There may be salvage," muttered the second mate.

"Then we will run down upon her lee side, and lie to."

We were not more than a hundred yards from her when we swung our fore-yard aback, and there we were, the barque and the brig, ducking and bowing like two clowns in a dance.

"Drop one of the quarter-boats," said I. "Take four men, Mr. Allardyce, and see what you can learn of her."

But just at that moment my first officer, Mr. Armstrong, came on deck, for seven bells had struck, and it was but a few minutes off his watch. It would interest me to go myself to this abandoned vessel and to see what there might be aboard of her. So, with a word to Armstrong, I swung myself over the side, slipped down the falls, and took my place in the sheets of the boat.

It was but a little distance, but it took some time to traverse, and so heavy was the roll that often when we were in the trough of the sea, we could not see either the barque which we had left or the brig which we were approaching. The sinking sun did not penetrate down there, and it was cold and dark in the hollows of the waves, but each passing billow heaved us up into the warmth and the sunshine once more. At each of these moments, as we hung upon a white-capped ridge between the two dark valleys, I caught a glimpse of the long, pea-green line, and the nodding foremast of the brig, and I steered so as to come round by her stern, so that we might determine which was the best way of boarding her. As we passed her we saw the name *Nossa Sehnora da Vittoria* painted across her dripping counter.

"The weather side, sir," said the second mate. "Stand by with the boathook, carpenter!" An instant later we had jumped over the bulwarks, which were hardly higher than our boat, and found ourselves upon the deck of the abandoned vessel. Our first thought was to provide for our own safety in case—as seemed very probable—the vessel should settle down beneath our feet. With this object two of our men held on to the painter of the boat, and fended her off from the vessel's side, so that she might be ready in case we had to make a hurried retreat. The carpenter was sent to find out how much water there was, and whether it was still gaming, while the other seaman, Allardyce and myself, made a rapid inspection of the vessel and her cargo.

The deck was littered with wreckage and with hen-coops, in which the dead birds were washing about. The boats were gone, with the exception of one, the bottom of which had been stove, and it was certain that the crew had abandoned the vessel. The cabin was in a deck-house, one side of which had been beaten in by a heavy sea. Allardyce and I entered it, and found the captain's table as he had left it, his books and papers—all Spanish or Portuguese—scattered over it, with piles of cigarette ash everywhere. I looked about for the log, but could not find it.

"As likely as not he never kept one," said Allardyce. "Things are pretty slack aboard a South American trader, and they don't do more than they can help. If there was one it must have been taken away with him in the boat."

"I should like to take all these books and papers," said I. "Ask the carpenter how much time we have."

His report was reassuring. The vessel was full of water, but some of the cargo was buoyant, and there was no immediate danger of her sinking. Probably she would never sink, but would drift about as one of those terrible unmarked reefs which have sent so many stout vessels to the bottom.

"In that case there is no danger in your going below, Mr. Allardyce," said I. "See what you can make of her and find out how much of her cargo may be saved. I'll look through these papers while you are gone."

The bills of lading, and some notes and letters which lay upon the desk, sufficed to inform me that the Brazilian brig *Nossa Sehnora da Vittoria* had cleared from Bahia a month before. The name of the captain was Texeira, but there was no record as to the number of the crew. She was bound for London, and a glance at the bills of lading was sufficient to show me that we were not likely to profit much in the way of salvage. Her cargo consisted of nuts, ginger, and wood, the latter in the shape of great logs of valuable tropical growths. It was these, no doubt, which had prevented the ill-fated vessel from going to the bottom, but they were of such a size as to make it impossible for us to extract them. Besides these, there were a few fancy goods, such as a number of ornamental birds for millinery purposes, and a hundred cases of preserved fruits. And then, as I turned over the papers, I came upon a short note in English, which arrested my attention.

"It is requested," said the note, "that the various old Spanish and Indian curiosities, which came out of the Santarem collection, and which are consigned to Prontfoot & Neuman of Oxford Street, London, should be put in some place where there may be no danger of these very valuable and unique articles being injured or tampered with. This applies most particularly to the treasure-chest of Don Ramirez di Leyra, which must on no account be placed where anyone can get at it."

The treasure-chest of Don Ramirez! Unique and valuable articles! Here was a chance of salvage after all! I had risen to my feet with the paper in my hand when my Scotch mate appeared in the doorway.

"I'm thinking all isn't quite as it should be aboard of this ship, sir," said he. He was a hard-faced man, and yet I could see that he had been startled.

"What's the matter?"

"Murder's the matter, sir. There's a man here with his brains beaten out."

"Killed in the storm?" said I.

"May be so, sir, but I'll be surprised if you think so after you have seen him."

"Where is he, then?"

"This way, sir; here in the main-deck house."

There appeared to have been no accommodation below in the brig, for there was the afterhouse for the captain, another by the main hatchway, with the cook's galley attached to it, and a third in the forecastle for the men. It was to this middle one that the mate led me. As you entered, the galley, with its litter of tumbled pots and dishes, was upon the right, and upon the left was a small room with two bunks for the officers. Then beyond there was a place about twelve foot square, which was littered with flags and spare canvas. All round the walls were a number of packets done up in coarse cloth and carefully lashed to the woodwork. At the other end was a great box, striped red and white, though the red was so faded and the white so dirty that it was only where the light fell directly upon it that one could see the colouring. The box was, by subsequent measurement, four feet three inches in length, three feet two inches in height, and three feet across—considerably larger than a seaman's chest.

But it was not to the box that my eyes or my thoughts were turned as I entered the store-room. On the floor, lying across the litter of bunting, there was stretched a small, dark man with a short, curling beard. He lay as far as it was possible from the box, with his feet towards it and his head away. A crimson patch was printed upon the white canvas on which his head was resting, and little red ribbons wreathed themselves round his swarthy neck and trailed away on to the floor, but there was no sign of a wound that I could see, and his face was as placid as that of a sleeping child.

It was only when I stooped that I could perceive his injury, and then I turned away with an exclamation of horror. He had been pole-axed; apparently by some person standing behind him. A frightful blow had smashed in the top of his head and penetrated deeply into his brains. His face might well be placid, for death must have been absolutely instantaneous, and the position of the wound showed that he could never have seen the person who had inflicted it.

"Is that foul play or accident, Captain Barclay?" asked my second mate, demurely.

"You are quite right, Mr. Allardyce. The man has been murdered—struck down from above by a sharp and heavy weapon. But who was he, and why did they murder him?"

"He was a common seaman, sir," said the mate. "You can see that if you look at his fingers." He turned out his pockets as he spoke and brought to light a pack of cards, some tarred string, and a bundle of Brazilian tobacco.

"Hello, look at this!" said he.

It was a large, open knife with a stiff spring blade which he had picked up from the floor. The steel was shining and bright, so that we could not associate it with the crime, and yet the dead man had apparently held it in his hand when he was struck down, for it still lay within his grasp.

"It looks to me, sir, as if he knew he was in danger and kept his knife handy," said the mate. "However, we can't help the poor beggar now. I can't make out these things that are lashed to the wall. They seem to be idols and weapons and curios of all sorts done up in old sacking."

"That's right," said I. "They are the only things of value that we are likely to get from the cargo. Hail the barque and tell them to send the other quarter-boat to help us to get the stuff aboard."

While he was away I examined this curious plunder which had come into our possession. The curiosities were so wrapped up that I could only form a general idea as to their nature, but the striped box stood in a good light where I could thoroughly examine it. On the lid, which was clamped and cornered with metal-work, there was engraved a complex coat of arms, and beneath it was a line of Spanish which I was able to decipher as meaning, "The treasure-chest of Don Ramirez di Leyra, Knight of the Order of Saint James, Governor and Captain-General of Terra Firma and of the Province of Veraquas." In one corner was the date, 1606, and on the other a large white label, upon which was written in English, "You are earnestly requested, upon no account, to open this box." The same warning was repeated underneath in Spanish. As to the lock, it was a very complex and heavy one of engraved steel, with a Latin motto, which was above a seaman's comprehension.

By the time I had finished this examination of the peculiar box, the other quarter-boat with Mr. Armstrong, the first officer, had come alongside, and we began to carry out and place in her the various curiosities which appeared to be the only objects worth moving from the derelict ship. When she was full I sent her back to the barque, and then Allardyce and I, with the carpenter and one seaman, shifted the striped box, which was the only thing left, to our boat, and lowered it over, balancing it upon the two middle thwarts, for it was so heavy that it would have given the boat a dangerous tilt had we placed it at either end. As to the dead man, we left him where we had found him.

The mate had a theory that, at the moment of the desertion of the ship, this fellow had started plundering, and that the captain, in an attempt to preserve discipline, had struck him down with a hatchet or some other heavy weapon. It seemed more probable than any other explanation, and yet it did not entirely satisfy me either. But the ocean is full of mysteries, and we were content to leave the fate of the dead seaman of the Brazilian brig to be added to that long list which every sailor can recall.

The heavy box was slung up by ropes on to the deck of the Mary Sinclair, and was carried by four seamen into the cabin, where, between the table and the after-lockers, there was just space for it to stand. There it remained during supper, and after that meal the mates remained with me, and discussed over a glass of grog the event of the day. Mr. Armstrong was a long, thin, vulture-like man, an excellent seaman, but famous for his nearness and cupidity. Our treasure-trove had excited him greatly, and already he had begun with glistening eyes to reckon up how much it might be worth to each of us when the shares of the salvage came to be divided.

"If the paper said that they were unique, Mr. Barclay, then they may be worth anything that you like to name. You wouldn't believe the sums that the rich collectors give. A thousand pounds is nothing to them. We'll have something to show for our voyage, or I am mistaken."

"I don't think that," said I. "As far as I can see, they are not very different from any other South American curios."

"Well, sir, I've traded there for fourteen voyages, and I have never seen anything like that chest before. That's worth a pile of money, just as it stands. But it's so heavy that surely there must be something valuable inside it. Don't you think that we ought to open it and see?"

"If you break it open you will spoil it, as likely as not," said the second mate.

Armstrong squatted down in front of it, with his head on one side, and his long, thin nose within a few inches of the lock.

"The wood is oak," said he, "and it has shrunk a little with age. If I had a chisel or a strong-bladed knife I could force the lock back without doing any damage at all."

The mention of a strong-bladed knife made me think of the dead seaman upon the brig.

"I wonder if he could have been on the job when someone came to interfere with him," said I.

"I don't know about that, sir, but I am perfectly certain that I could open the box. There's a screwdriver here in the locker. Just hold the lamp, Allardyce, and I'll have it done in a brace of shakes."

"Wait a bit," said I, for already, with eyes which gleamed with curiosity and with avarice, he was stooping over the lid. "I don't see that there is any hurry over this matter. You've read that card which warns us not to open it. It may mean anything or it may mean nothing, but somehow I feel inclined to obey it. After all, whatever is in it will keep, and if it is valuable it will be worth as much if it is opened in the owner's offices as in the cabin of the *Mary Sinclair*."

The first officer seemed bitterly disappointed at my decision.

"Surely, sir, you are not superstitious about it," said he, with a slight sneer upon his thin lips. "If it gets out of our own hands, and we don't see for ourselves what is inside it, we may be done out of our rights; besides—"

"That's enough, Mr. Armstrong," said I, abruptly. "You may have every confidence that you will get your rights, but I will not have that box opened tonight."

"Why, the label itself shows that the box has been examined by Europeans," Allardyce added. "Because a box is a treasure-box is no reason that it has treasures inside it now. A good many folk have had a peep into it since the days of the old Governor of Terra Firma."

Armstrong threw the screwdriver down upon the table and shrugged his shoulders.

"Just as you like," said he; but for the rest of the evening, although we spoke upon many subjects, I noticed that his eyes were continually coming round, with the same expression of curiosity and greed, to the old striped box.

And now I come to that portion of my story which fills me even now with a shuddering horror when I think of it. The main cabin had the rooms of the officers round it, but mine was the farthest away from it at the end of the little passage which led to the companion. No regular watch was kept by me, except in cases of emergency, and the three mates divided the watches among them. Armstrong had the middle watch, which ends at four in the morning, and he was relieved by Allardyce. For my part I have always been one of the soundest of sleepers, and it is rare for anything less than a hand upon my shoulder to arouse me.

And yet I was aroused that night, or rather in the early grey of the morning. It was just half-past four by my chronometer when something caused me to sit up in my berth wide awake and with every nerve tingling. It was a sound of some sort, a crash with a human cry at the end of it, which still jarred on my ears. I sat listening, but all was now silent. And yet it could not have been imagination, that hideous cry, for the echo of it still rang in my head, and it seemed to have come from some place quite close to me. I sprang from my bunk, and, pulling on some clothes, I made my way into the cabin.

At first I saw nothing unusual there. In the cold, grey light I made out the red-clothed table, the six rotating chairs, the walnut lockers, the swinging barometer, and there, at the end, the big striped chest. I was turning away, with the intention of going upon deck and asking the second mate if he had heard anything, when my eyes fell suddenly upon something which projected from under the table. It was the leg of a man—a leg with a long sea-boot upon it. I stooped, and there was a figure sprawling upon his face, his arms thrown forward and his body twisted. One glance told me that it was Armstrong, the first officer, and a second that he was a dead man. For a few moments I stood gasping. Then I rushed on to the deck, called Allardyce to my assistance, and came back with him into the cabin.

Together we pulled the unfortunate fellow from under the table, and as we looked at his dripping head we exchanged glances, and I do not know which was the paler of the two.

"The same as the Spanish sailor," said I.

"The very same. God preserve us! It's that infernal chest! Look at Armstrong's hand!"

He held up the mate's right hand, and there was the screwdriver which he had wished to use the night before.

"He's been at the chest, sir. He knew that I was on deck and you were asleep. He knelt down in front of it, and he pushed the lock back with that tool. Then something happened to him, and he cried out so that you heard him."

"Allardyce," I whispered, "what *could* have happened to him?"

The second mate put his hand upon my sleeve and drew me into his cabin.

"We can talk here, sir, and we don't know who may be listening to us in there. What do you suppose is in that box, Captain Barclay?"

"I give you my word, Allardyce, that I have no idea."

"Well, I can only find one theory which will fit all the facts. Look at the size of the box. Look at all the carving and metal-work which may conceal any number of holes. Look at the weight of it; it took four men to carry it. On top of that, remember that two men have tried to open it, and both have come to their end through it. Now, sir, what can it mean except one thing?"

"You mean there is a man in it?"

"Of course there is a man in it. You know how it is in these South American States, sir. A man may be president one week and hunted like a dog the next— they are for ever flying for their lives. My idea is that there is some fellow in hiding there, who is armed and desperate, and who will fight to the death before he is taken."

"But his food and drink?"

"It's a roomy chest, sir, and he may have some provisions stowed away. As to his drink, he had a friend among the crew upon the brig who saw that he had what he needed."

"You think, then, that the label asking people not to open the box was simply written in his interest?"

"Yes, sir, that is my idea. Have you any other way of explaining the facts?"

I had to confess that I had not.

"The question is what we are to do?" I asked.

"The man's a dangerous ruffian, who sticks at nothing. I'm thinking it wouldn't be a bad thing to put a rope round the chest and tow it alongside for half an hour; then we could open it at our ease. Or if we just tied the box up and kept him from getting any water maybe that would do as well. Or the carpenter could put a coat of varnish over it and stop all the blowholes."

"Come, Allardyce," said I, angrily. "You don't seriously mean to say that a whole ship's company are going to be terrorized by a single man in a box. If he's there, I'll engage to fetch him out!" I went to my room and came back with my revolver in my hand. "Now, Allardyce," said I, "do you open the lock, and I'll stand on guard."

"For God's sake, think what you are doing, sir!" cried the mate. "Two men have lost their lives over it, and the blood of one not yet dry upon the carpet."

"The more reason why we should revenge him."

"Well, sir, at least let me call the carpenter. Three are better than two, and he is a good stout man."

He went off in search of him, and I was left alone with the striped chest in the cabin. I don't think that I'm a nervous man, but I kept the table between me and this solid old relic of the Spanish Main. In the growing light of morning the red and white striping was beginning to appear, and the curious scrolls and wreaths of metal and carving which showed the loving pains which cunning craftsmen had expended upon it. Presently the carpenter and the mate came back together, the former with a hammer in his hand.

"It's a bad business, this, sir," said he, shaking his head, as he looked at the body of the mate. "And you think there's someone hiding in the box?"

"There's no doubt about it," said Allardyce, picking up the screwdriver and setting his jaw like a man who needs to brace his courage. "I'll drive the lock back if you will both stand by. If he rises let him have it on the head with your hammer, carpenter! Shoot at once, sir, if he raises his hand. Now!"

He had knelt down in front of the striped chest, and passed the blade of the tool under the lid. With a sharp snick the lock flew back. "Stand by!" yelled the mate, and with a heave he threw open the massive top of the box. As it swung up we all three sprang back, I with my pistol levelled, and the carpenter with the hammer above his head. Then, as nothing happened, we each took a step forward and peeped in. The box was empty.

Not quite empty either, for in one corner was lying an old yellow candle-stick, elaborately engraved, which appeared to be as old as the box itself. Its rich yellow tone and artistic shape suggested that it was an object of value. For the rest there was nothing more weighty or valuable than dust in the old striped treasure-chest.

"Well, I'm blessed!" cried Allardyce, staring blankly into it. "Where does the weight come in, then?"

"Look at the thickness of the sides, and look at the lid. Why, it's five inches through. And see that great metal spring across it."

"That's for holding the lid up," said the mate. "You see, it won't lean back. What's that German printing on the inside?"

"It means that it was made by Johann Rothstein of Augsburg, in 1606."

"And a solid bit of work, too. But it doesn't throw much light on what has passed, does it, Captain Barclay? That candlestick looks like gold. We shall have something for our trouble after all."

He leant forward to grasp it, and from that moment I have never doubted as to the reality of inspiration, for on the instant I caught him by the collar and pulled him straight again. It may have been some story of the Middle Ages which had come back to my mind, or it may have been that my eye had caught some red which was not that of rust upon the upper part of the lock, but to him and to me it will always seem an inspiration, so prompt and sudden was my action.

"There's devilry here," said I. "Give me the crooked stick from the corner."

It was an ordinary walking-cane with a hooked top. I passed it over the candlestick and gave it a pull. With a flash a row of polished steel fangs shot out from below the upper lip, and the great striped chest snapped at us like a wild animal. Clang came the huge lid into its place, and the glasses on the swinging rack sang and tinkled with the shock. The mate sat down on the edge of the table and shivered like a frightened horse.

"You've saved my life, Captain Barclay!" said he.

So this was the secret of the striped treasure-chest of old Don Ramirez di Leyra, and this was how he preserved his ill-gotten gains from the Terra Firma and the

Province of Veraquas. Be the thief ever so cunning he could not tell that golden candlestick from the other articles of value, and the instant that he laid hand upon it the terrible spring was unloosed and the murderous steel pikes were driven into his brain, while the shock of the blow sent the victim backward and enabled the chest to automatically close itself. How many, I wondered, had fallen victims to the ingenuity of the mechanic of Ausgburg? And as I thought of the possible history of that grim striped chest my resolution was very quickly taken.

"Carpenter, bring three men, and carry this on deck."

"Going to throw it overboard, sir?"

"Yes, Mr. Allardyce. I'm not superstitious as a rule, but there are some things which are more than a sailor can be called upon to stand."

"No wonder that brig made heavy weather, Captain Barclay, with such a thing on board. The glass is dropping fast, sir, and we are only just in time."

So we did not even wait for the three sailors, but we carried it out, the mate, the carpenter, and I, and we pushed it with our own hands over the bulwarks. There was a white spout of water, and it was gone. There it lies, the striped chest, a thousand fathoms deep, and if, as they say, the sea will some day be dry land, I grieve for the man who finds that old box and tries to penetrate into its secret.

An Encounter with a Ghost

by W. Clark Russell

I t is a great many years now since the Phantom Ship was last sighted; so long indeed that one might fairly suppose Vanderdecken had got to windward at last, doubled the Cape, and settled down somewhere in his native land to enjoy a well-earned repose after his centuries of conflict with the Pacific gales. It turns out, however, that the poor old skipper is still afloat. His vessel has not only been sighted, but boarded—a quite unprecedented incident in the history of this marine apparition. The countenance of Vanderdecken has been surveyed by human eyes, and, what is of some importance, the vexed question of the rig of his craft has been set at rest once and for good. She is not a ship, it seems, but a brig with stump topgallantmasts and single topsail yards. The yarn of one of the crew of the barque who sighted the *Flying Dutchman* and boarded her is curious, rather graphic, and full of singular particulars. Perhaps were an engraving of the mariner who related the story to accompany this account the interest would be heightened—for so queer a looking sailor I never before set eyes on. He is what the young ladies of Limehouse and Poplar would call a 'shell-back,' his shoulders being as round as the shell of a turtle; his hair hangs over his forehead and down the back of his neck in masses of minute ringlets; he broke the bridge of his nose

189

when a youth by falling down the main hold of a ship, and that feature submits but little more to the eye than a pair of nostrils; his small eyes are lodged very deep, and twinkle in their caverns like glowworms, and under his chin stands a lump of coarse black hair. He masticated a large junk of tobacco as he gave me his story, which may have added a deeper note to his hoarse and wheezing voice. He began thus:

"The *Sally G.*'s an American barque; Captain Prodgers was the master, Mr. Anderson chief mate, and there were sixteen hands. We was bound from Palermo to New London with a cargo of fruit, and on the 11th of April last we reckoned ourselves to be somewhere near about 1,500 miles to the east'ards of Montauk Point. We was rather a mixed company. I'm an Englishman myself, and there was Tom, a Gravesend man. Us two made all the Englishmen aboard. But there was three Scotchmen and six Irishmen; so Britannia mustered middling strong. There was likewise a Swede, and chaps we call Mediterranean scowbanks, who'll pass for Portuguese, or Spaniards, or Hi-talians, just as they're wanted.

"The 11th of April was a werry fine morning: a light breeze from the south'ard and east'ard, sea calm, and sky blue. I was in the port watch, and came on deck at eight o'clock. The barque was under all plain sail; and soon after we had turned out, Mr. Anderson, the chief mate, sings out to some of us to jump aloft and get the stun'sail booms rigged out. I lay aloft, and got on to the foretopsail yard; but, as I was stepping from the rigging on to foot-ropes, I caught sight of a bit of white shining upon the horizon about two points on the starboard bow. I turned my head and bawled down 'Sail ho!' and pointed, and the mate crossed the deck to look; but he had to wait a bit to see her; for it required half-an-hour more of sailing to heave the stranger up wisible from the deck. You may reckon no one took much notice of the wessel ahead while she remained small. Having set the stun'sails, we went on quietly with our different jobs, and the mate walked up and down the weather side o' the deck, sometimes squinting aloft, sometimes taking a look at the compass, and now and again casting his eyes upon the stranger. But the *Sally G.*'s a quick boat in smooth water; the stun'sails were helping her along, and we came up with the old sawed-off square wagon ahead as though she had been a lighthouse. I thought she'd h'ist her ensign as we came along, but she never showed no colours.

"When we was close enough to see her plain we all stood lookin' and wonderin'. I don't know as ever I saw a queerer-looking wessel. Her stern was up and down in the water; she'd a great sheer aft that made her look sagged: her sides were as rusty as an old kettle; her rigging was grey; she had short topgallant masts, and a man named Maloney told me the canvas was so thin that he could see the sky looking blue through it. This might ha'been, but I took no notice o' that myself, I saw the mate working away at the brig's stern with a spyglass, and then he turns to the captain, who had come on deck, and says, 'Captain,' says he, 'I can't see no name.' 'Here, give me hold,' says the captain, and he took the glass and looked himself, and then says, 'No; there's no name. But I'll tell 'ee what, Mr. Anderson, there's bin a name there, but the water's washed the letterin' away.' 'Well,' says the mate, 'I reckon she must be a diving job. They've fished her up out o' deep water, and ye may take her to be a showman's speculation, sir.' The cook was standing near the pumps looking at her, and he says to me who was anigh him, 'Bill,' he says, 'd'ye notice her deck-house is green?' 'Yes,' says I, 'I see that, cook,' I says. 'That means, Bill,' says he in a slow way, and looking strange, 'that she's a Dutchman.' 'She ought to be,' says I. 'I don't know that we ought to be glad that we met her, Bill,' says the cook. 'I'd as lief be shipmates with a Fin as keep that wessel company.' 'Why, what ails ye, cook?' says I. 'What's the matter with the brig?' 'Look at her,' says he, shaking his head and speaking hollow like. I thought he wasn't worth while paying attention to. The cook, sir, was a man as believed in ghosts, and was a werry ignorant person. He couldn't read nor write, but he was extraordinary positive. He'd quote things wrong, and 'ud refuse to be corrected, saying he knew better, and that books was full o' lies. Yet he was a good cook, and there was more conscience in the duff he biled for the men than I can recollect meeting with in any sea-mess. Well, I let him shake his head, and stood watchin' the brig.

"As we came up with her she backed her main yards and lowered a boat. This was a pretty strong hint to us to stop; so we boom-ended our stun'sails, brought the barque to the wind, and hove her to. Two men got into the boat, and a man squatted hisself in the stern sheets, and the boat headed for us. It were difficult to guess what they could want, for the vessel looked right enough aloft, nothin' wanting up there, and if they was in distress it was queer they didn't signalize us in the morning, when we hove in sight.

"All hands knocked off work to see the Dutchman, as the cook called him, come aboard. The boat hooked on, and the man in charge of her climbed over the side. He was a shortish man with a werry Dutch face on him, and there was no getting at his age by staring. His skin had the greyish, washed-out look o' the brig's rigging. He'd got on a bell-shaped fur cap with a peak to it, that lay flat on his forehead, sea-boots, a round jacket, big breeches which he filled out handsomely, and the stem of a long Dutch pipe sticking out of his coat pocket werry strangely ornamented. I noticed a sort o' eagerness in the way some of our men—'specially the Swede and two o' the Scotchmen—stared at him as if he wan't a wholesome sight. The cook never took his eyes off him for an instant.

"Arter gazing slowly round at us, he singled out the captain with ne're a man to tell him who was skipper, and going up to Captain Prodgers, he makes a long speech. While he talked, the captain and Mr. Anderson twisted their heads about like hens trying to look aloft, first bringing one ear to bear and then another, but they couldn't understand him no more than if he had spoke Chinaman's lingo. He spoke to 'em for ten minutes, never stoppin', goin' along slow and regular, without e'er a movement in his face, and his arms hanging up and down alongside of him without a stir. I see him now, and I likewise see the skipper and Mr. Anderson a listenin' and lookin' just as they'd appear if they was trying to see into the bottom of a well. At last he stopped, and then nobody spoke, and all hands looked at each other, savin' the cook, who wouldn't take his eyes away from the Dutchman. Suddenly the skipper sings out, 'Call the watch below on deck.' I ran forward and bawled down the scuttle for the men to rouse up smartly, and presently all the crew were on deck looking at the Dutchman.

'Look ye, men,' says Captain Prodgers, 'among you all there's enough of you, to make out seven languages; Irish, Scotch, English, Swedish Portugee, Spanish, and Hi-talian. Let all hands turn to and listen their hardest whilst I make this man say his speech over again. Now, then, fix your hattentions, bullies.' And with that he signs to the Dutchman to begin again. He didn't seem to know what was wanted at first, but after the skipper and Mr. Anderson had motioned and flourished to him like a pair of windmills for about five minutes, he gravely nods his head and goes through his speech, all hands listening hard, bobbing their noses together as they leans forward, and all o' them werry anxious to make out the man's meaning.

In ten minutes he made an end; and then Captain Prodgers, looking at us, says, 'Well?' Nobody answered. 'Is it Irish?' says he. 'No, it isn't Irish, sor,' says Micky O'Connor. 'Is it English or Scotch?' says he. 'No, sir,' says I. 'Is it, Swedish?' says Captain Prodgers. The Swede says, 'Not it,' and the scowbanks said it wasn't Portuguese, nor Hi-talian, nor any lingo that's spoke down in their part o' Europe. 'Then, what the deuce can it be?' says Captain Prodgers. 'A languidge,' answers the cook, in a faint voice, 'as is buried and forgot.'

'Well, sir, this being the sitiwation, what was to be done? Some skippers, I daresay, would ha' waved the Dutchman into his boat, filled the main topsail, and stood on. But Captain Prodgers is a humane man. 'Look here, Mr. Anderson,' says he, 'it's pretty clear that whatever may be the matter with that there brig, this Dutch sailor man, if so be he is a Dutchman, can't tell us what's wrong. So,' says he, 'get that starboard quarter boat manned and go aboard the brig yourself, and see if you can make out what's amiss.'

'No sooner said than done. The boat was lowered, and me and two o' the scowbanks and one o' the Scotchmen, makin' four men, tumbled into her, and we rowed Mr. Anderson on board the brig. I took notice of Mr. Anderson looking and looking werry hard at the wessel as we went along, as a man might who didn't much fancy the job he was put upon. We had our backs to the brig, but when we threw in our oars and got alongside, I'm blessed if the sight o' that old hull and the queer appearance o' the rigging didn't give me a kind o' crawling sensation. It might ha' been what the cook had said, or it might ha' been the faded paint and the brig's sides, that looked like a man's face arter he's cured o' the smallpox, or like a bit of French cheese I once saw, that might ha' passed for a muffin. But whatever it was, I didn't like the feeling, and rather wished I had let Sammy Saunders shove in front of me and get my place when we all run to man the boat. However, there I was, and bein' there I thought I might as well see all that was going to happen, so I followed the mate aboard, he taking no notice. Indeed, I reckon he wished me to come, not liking to be the only one o' us 'twixt the rails of that strange old brig.

"I took a look forward and saw four men standing together, and leaning against the side o' the galley, where the sun shone. I didn't like their appearance at all. They hung there like coves fairly wore out. They all seemed middlin' old, but for that matter their faces was just as puzzling as the Dutchman's who had boarded us; ye might ha' called them old or young as you please, and both 'ud ha' been right. They all stared at us as we got over the side, but barring this twisting of their eyes round they was quite lifeless, and a melancholy row of men they seemed. There was a dim and grey-lookin' old man at the tiller, and him that was the skipper stood at the gangway to meet Mr. Anderson. Did ye ever see a dried apple—a werry old 'un, sir? Well, that skipper's face were like that. It was all brownness and wrinkles, with a bit of a withered nose amidships, and under it a slit that stood for a mouth, and a pair of eyes that I calculate 'ud shine red in the dark. He'd a fur cap on, and an old coat that came down to the calves of his legs, and I never see skinnier fingers nor legs with such a sheer at the joints as though his body stood on a hoop. His boots was like a pair of shovels. He bobbed to the mate and smiled away like clockwork and then droppin' his arms down as t'other Dutchman had done, he up and spoke a speech that must ha' lasted eight minutes by any man's watch.

"When he began to talk the mate looked round and was glad enough to see me standing close astern of him, I believe; he fell back a step to draw nearer to me, and listened with his head dropped. But the strange bosh, sir, were harder to follow than 'ead t'other man's had been; this old man's pipes were cracked, and he made a noise like a saw. The men forrards never moved; there they stood sunning themselves, and the dim old cove as steered looked at nothin' but the leech o' the topgallant sail, and though the wessel was hove-to, mind.

"As soon as the skipper had done, Mr. Anderson he says in a loud strong voice, 'Mister,' says he, 'all that you've bin saying is no doubt past contradicting of, but I'm bound to tell 'ee I don't understand your lingo. Yonder barque's the *Sally G.*, Captain Prodgers, and I'm her mate. If ye'll tell me what you want, we'll try to do it for you;' and here he stopped and looked at the little man, who made no answer, but kept on smilin' away as if somebody was tickling of him. 'What's the name o' this wessel?' says Mr. Anderson in a werry powerful woice. The skipper only smiled. The mate looked forrards at the men, and sings out sternly, 'Anybody understand me there?' Says he, 'I say, what's the name o' this wessel, and what d'ye want?' Ne'er a one took notice, and the skipper he kept on smiling. 'Come you along with me,' says Mr. Anderson, after takin' a long look round, and speaking to me. 'We'll overhaul his old sugar-box for ourselves, and see what's wrong.'

"So away we went to the harness-cask, the old skipper arter us, smiling all the time, and we looks into it, and sees it full o' pieces of meat. The mate he smelt of these wittles, and says, 'They're sweet enough. Nothin' wrong in here.' Then we goes over to the scuttle-butts and drops the dipper in, and finds 'em full o' fresh water. 'Well, they can't be in want o' water,' says the mate. Then, stopping a minute, he pulls out a piece o' chalk and stoops down and writes down the latitood and longitood in big letters, and then gets up and points to the marks, looking at the skipper. But this wasn't it either, for the skipper, always smiling, shakes his head so quickly that I thought it would ha' dropped off. Then we sounded the well, but that was right enough; no water there to take notice of. 'Come along with me,' says the mate, and down we bundles into the cabin, the skipper behind us. A strange old place it was, with a smell of snuff about. It looked to me to be wisibly decayin'. It made me feel as a diver does when he finds hisself in the cabin of a wessel that's been under water for years and years. I wondered to see no barnacles. We opens a door or two until we comes to the pantry, looks in, and sees plenty o' grub knocking about the shelves. 'Well, they ain't starvin',' says the mate. 'An' there's no water comin' in,' says I. 'And they don't want our reckonin',' says the mate. 'Perhaps they've got the cholera aboard,' says I. 'Let's go forrard and see,' says the mate.

"We went up the companion steps, the skipper followin' of us like a shadder, and walks to the fore hatch, and drops into the forecastle. A rummier place even than the cabin: full of ancient bunks covered with a wild flourish o' carving, and scores o' cockroaches blackening the timbers, with three or four sea-chests and an odd boot or two, and the likes o' that. 'If the cholera's aboard,' says the mate, 'it ain't in this fo'cs'le, for there's nobody here.' With that we scrambles on deck again. The skipper lay in wait for us at the fore scuttle, and when he sees us he falls a-smiling. 'Capt'en,' says Mr. Anderson, 'we've overhauled your wessel fore and aft, and can't find anything wrong. There's plenty o' meat and water aboard, the wessel's tight, ye don't want our reckonings, and there ain't no disease perceptible. That bein' so, I don't see what good we can do by stopping.'

"The skipper looked at him narrowly and smilingly as he said this, and when he were done, he began another speech; but this Mr. Anderson cut short by saying that there was nothing to thank him for, and that what we had done wasn't worth mentioning, and then calling to me, we drops into our boat and returns to the *Sally G.* None of us spoke as we rowed back, no man feelin' comfortable. On reaching the barque, I went forrard, followed by all hands, who wanted to know what we had seen; but their questions was stopped by the order being given to swing the main yards and get the stunsails on her agin.

"No sooner was this done than the cook tailed on to me and wouldn't let me go. 'What did ye see?' says he. 'A brig,' says I. 'And what else,' says he. 'Four strange men standing in the sun,' says I, 'and a dim old man at the tiller, and a skipper like a marmozeet,' says I. 'And what was his langwidge,' says the cook. 'Unbeknown,' says I. 'Bill,' says he, in a low woice, which made the others, who stood listening, lean forrards to hear, 'Bill,' says he, 'I'm sorry for you,' says he, 'I don't want to alarm you, Bill, but you've been aboard the *Flying Dutchman*,' says he, 'and take notice of what I'm going to say,' says the cook; 'and if I'm wrong I'll give any man leave to bile me in my own coppers. There'll be a gale o' wind,' he says, 'within the next twenty-four hours.'

"D'ye see this hand, sir,' said the mariner who favoured me with this narrative, laying his large paw upon his knee, with the tar-stained palm uppermost. 'Well, as true as that there hand of mine is a-lying on my leg at this minute, did a wiolent gale o' wind bust down upon us heighteen hours arter we parted company with that Dutch brig. It blew from the west'ards, and drove us one hundred mile out o' our course. So there ye have it, sir. That's the naked truth. I don't ask you to mind what the cook said. You may forget him. Here's a fact to speak for itself. Heighteen hours arter we left that brig, a hurricane bust down upon us. If that ain't conclusive there's nothin' more to say."

Written on Passing Deadman's Island,

In the Gulf of St. Lawrence, Late in the Evening, September, 1804.

BY SIR THOMAS MOORE

This is one of the Magdalen Islands, and, singularly enough, is the property of Sir Isaac Coffin. The above lines were suggested by a superstition very common among sailors, who called this ghost-ship, I think, "The Flying Dutchman."

—AUTHOR

See you, beneath yon cloud so dark,
Fast gliding along a gloomy bark?
Her sails are full,—though the wind is still,
And there blows not a breath her sails to fill!

Say, what doth that vessel of darkness bear?
The silent calm of the grave is there,
Save now and again a death-knell rung,
And the flap of the sails with night-fog hung.

There lieth a wreck on the dismal shore
Of cold and pitiless Labrador;
Where, under the moon, upon mounts of frost,
Full many a mariner's bones are tost.

Yon shadowy bark hath been to that wreck,
And the dim blue fire, that lights her deck,
Doth play on as pale and livid a crew,
As ever yet drank the churchyard dew.

To Deadman's Isle, in the eye of the blast,
To Deadman's Isle, she speeds her fast;
By skeleton shapes her sails are furled,
And the hand that steers is not of this world!

Oh! hurry thee on—oh! hurry thee on,
Thou terrible bark, ere the night be gone,
Nor let morning look on so foul a sight
As would blanch for ever her rosy light!

THE DERELICT NEPTUNE

BY MORGAN ROBERTSON

A cross the Atlantic Ocean from the Gulf of Guinea to Cape St. Rogue moves a great body of water—the Main Equatorial Current—which can be considered a motive power, or mainspring, of the whole Atlantic current system, as it obtains its motion directly from the ever-acting push of the tradewinds. At Cape St. Rogue this broad current splits into two parts, one turning north, the other south. The northern part contracts, increases its speed, and, passing up the northern coast of South America as the Guiana Current, enters through the Caribbean Sea into the Gulf of Mexico, where it circles around to the northward; then, colored a deep blue from the fine river silt of the Mississippi, and heated from its long surface exposure under a tropical sun to an average temperature of eighty degrees, it emerges into the Florida Channel as the Gulf Stream.

From here it travels northeast, following the trend of the coast line, until, off Cape Hatteras, it splits into three divisions, one of which, the westernmost, keeps on to lose its warmth and life in Baffin's Bay. Another impinges on the Hebrides, and is no more recognizable as a current; and the third, the eastern and largest part of the divided stream, makes a wide sweep to the east and south, enclosing the Azores and the dead water called the Sargasso Sea, then, as the African Current, runs down the coast until, just below the Canary Isles, it merges into the Lesser Equatorial Current, which, parallel to the parent stream, and separated from it by a narrow band of backwater, travels west and filters through the West Indies, making puzzling combinations with the tides, and finally bearing so heavily on the young Gulf Stream as to give to it the sharp turn to the northward through the Florida Channel.

In the South Atlantic, the portion of the Main Equatorial Current split off by Cape St. Rogue and directed south leaves the coast at Cape Frio, and at the latitude of the River Plate assumes a due easterly direction, crossing the ocean as the Southern Connecting Current. At the Cape of Good Hope it meets the cold, northeasterly Cape Horn Current, and with it passes up the coast of Africa to loin the Equatorial Current at the starting point in the Gulf of Guinea, the whole constituting a circulatory system of ocean rivers, of speed value varying from eighteen to ninety miles a day.

On a bright morning in November, 1894, a curious looking craft floated into the branch current which, skirting Cuba, flows westward through the Bahama Channel. A man standing on the highest of two points enclosing a small bay near Cape Maisi, after a critical examination through a telescope, disappeared from the rocks, and in a few moments a light boat, of the model used by whalers, emerged from the mouth of the bay, containing this man and another. In the boat also was a coil of rope.

The one who had inspected the craft from the rocks was a tall young fellow, dressed in flannel shirt and trousers, the latter held in place by a cartridge belt, such as is used by the American cowboy. To this was hung a heavy revolver. On his head was a broad-brimmed cork helmet, much soiled, and resembling in shape the Mexican sombrero. Beneath this headgear was a mass of brown hair, which showed a non acquaintance with barbers for, perhaps, months, and under this hair a sun tanned face, lighted by serious gray eyes. The most noticeable feature of this face was the extreme arching of the eyebrows—a never-failing index of the highest form of courage. It was a face that would please. The face of the other was equally pleasing in its way. It was red, round, and jolly, with twinkling eyes, the whole borrowing a certain dignity from closely cut white hair and mustaches. The man was about fifty, dressed and armed like the other.

"What do you want of pistols, Boston?" he said to the younger man. "One might think this an old-fashioned, piratical cutting out."

"Oh, I don't know, Doc. It's best to have them. That hulk may be full of Spaniards, and the whole thing nothing but a trick to draw us out. But she looks like a derelict. I don't see how she got into this channel, unless she drifted up past Cape Maisi from the southward, having come in with the Guiana Current. It's all rocks and shoals to the eastward."

The boat, under the impulse of their oars, soon passed the fringing reef and came in sight of the strange craft, which lay about a mile east and half a mile off shore. "You see," resumed the younger man, called Boston, "there's a back-water inside Point Mulas, and if she gets into it she may come ashore right here."

"Where we can loot her. Nice business for a respectable practitioner like me to be engaged in! Doctor Bryce, of Havana, consorting with Fenians from Canada, exiled German socialists, Cuban horse-thieves who would be hung in a week if they went to Texas, and a long-legged sailor man who calls himself a retired naval officer, but who looks like a pirate; and all shouting for *Cuba Libre! Cuba Libre!* It's plunder you want."

"But none of us ever manufactured dynamite," answered Boston, with a grin. "How long did they have you in Moro Castle, Doc?"

"Eight months," snapped the doctor, his face clouding. "Eight months in that rathole, with the loss of my property and practice—all for devotion to science. I was on the brink of the most important and beneficent discovery in explosives the world ever dreamed of. Yes, sir, 'twould have made me famous and stopped all warfare."

"The captain told me this morning that he'd heard from Marti," said Boston, after an interval. "Good news, he said, but that's all I learned. Maybe it's from Gomez. If he'll only take hold again we can chase the Spanish off the island now. Then we'll put some of your stuff under Moro and lift it off the earth."

In a short time, details of the craft ahead, hitherto hidden by distance, began to show. There was no sign of life aboard; her spars were gone, with the exception of the foremast, broken at the hounds, and she seemed to be of about a thousand tons burden, colored a mixed brown and dingy gray, which, as they drew near, was shown as the action of iron rust on black and lead colored paint. Here and there were outlines of painted ports. Under the stump of a shattered bowsprit projected from between bluff bows a weather-worn figurehead, representing the god of the sea. Above on the bows were wooden-stocked anchors stowed inboard, and aft on the quarters were iron davits with blocks intact—but no falls. In a few of the dead-eyes in the channels could be seen frayed rope-yarns, rotten with age, and, with the stump of the foremast, the wooden stocks of the anchors, and the teak wood rail, of a bleached gray color. On the round stern, as they pulled under it, they spelled, in raised letters, flecked, here and there with discolored gilt, the name "Neptune, of London." Unkempt and forsaken, she had come in from the mysterious sea to tell her story.

They climbed the channels, fastened the painter, and peered over the rail. There was no one in sight, and they sprang down, finding themselves on a deck that was soft and spongy with time and weather.

"She's an old tub," said Boston, scanning the gray fabric fore and aft; "one of the first iron ships built, I should think. They housed the crew under the t'gallant forecastle. See the doors forward, there? And she has a full decked cabin—that's old style. Hatches are all battened down, but I doubt if this tarpaulin holds water." He stepped on the main hatch, brought his weight on the ball of one foot, and turned around. The canvas crumbled to threads, showing the wood beneath. "Let's go below. If there were any Spaniards here they'd have shown themselves before this."

The cabin doors were latched but not locked, and they opened them.

"Hold on," said the doctor, "this cabin may have been closed for years, and generated poisonous gases. Open, that upper door, Boston."

Boston ran up the shaky poop ladder and opened the companion-way above, which let a stream of the fresh morning air and sunshine into the cabin, then, after a moment or two, descended and joined the other, who had entered from the main-deck. They were in an ordinary ship's cabin, surrounded by staterooms, and with the usual swinging lamp and tray; but the table, chairs, and floor were covered with fine dust.

"Where the deuce do you get so much dust at sea?" coughed the doctor.

"Nobody knows, Doc. Let's hunt for the manifest and the articles. This must have been the skipper's room." They entered the largest stateroom, and Boston opened an old fashioned desk. Among the discolored documents it contained; he found one and handed it to the doctor. "Articles," he said; "look at it." Soon he took out another. "I've got it. Now we'll find what she has in her hold, and if it's worth bothering about."

"Great Scott!" exclaimed the doctor; "this paper is dated 1844, fifty years ago." Boston looked over his shoulder.

"That's so; she signed her crew at Boston, too. Where has she been all this time? Let's see this one."

The manifest was short, and stated that her cargo was 3,000 barrels of lime, 8,000 kids of tallow, and 2,500 carboys of acid, 1,700 of which were sulphuric, the rest of nitric acid. "That cargo won't be much good to us, Doc. I'd hoped to find something we could use. Let's find the log book, and see what happened to her." Boston rummaged what seemed to be the firstmate's room. "Plenty of duds here," he said; "but they're ready to fall to pieces. Here's the log."

He returned with the book, and, seated at the dusty table, they turned the yellow leaves. "First departure, Highland Light, March 10, 1844," read Boston. "We'll look in the remarks column."

Nothing but the ordinary incidents of a voyage were found until they reached the date June 1st, where entry was made of the ship being "caught aback" and dismasted off the Cape of Good Hope in a sudden gale. Then followed daily "remarks" of the southeasterly drift of the ship, the extreme cold (which, with the continuance of the bad weather, prevented saving the wreck for jury masts), and the fact that no sails were sighted.

June 6th told of her being locked in soft, slushy ice, and still being pressed southward by the never ending gale; June 10th said that the ice was hard, and at June 15th was the terrible entry: "Fire in the hold!"

On June 16th was entered this: "Kept hatches battened down and stopped all air holes, but the deck is too hot to stand on, and getting hotter. Crew insist on lowering the boats and pulling them northward over the ice to open water in hopes of being picked up. Good bye." In the position columns of this date the latitude was given as 62° 44´ S. and the longitude as 30° 50´ E. There were no more entries.

"What tragedy does this tell of?" said the doctor. "They left this ship in the ice fifty years ago. Who can tell if they were saved?"

"Who indeed?" said Boston. "The mate hadn't much hope. He said 'Good bye.' But one thing is certain; we are the first to board her since. I take it she stayed down there in the ice until she drifted around the Pole, and thawed out where she could catch the Cape Horn Current, which took her up to the Hope. Then she came up with the South African Current till she got into the Equatorial drift, then west, and up with the Guiana Current into the Caribbean Sea to the southward of us, and this morning the flood tide brought her through. It isn't a question of winds; they're too variable. It's currents, though it may have taken her years to get here. But the surprising part of it is that she hasn't been boarded. Let's look in the hold and see what the fire has done."

When they boarded the hulk, the sky, with the exception of a filmy haze overhanging the eastern end of the island, was clear. Now, as they emerged from the cabin, this haze had solidified and was coming—one of the black and vicious squalls of the West India seas.

"No man can tell what wind there is in them," remarked Boston, as he viewed it. "But it's pretty close to the water, and dropping rain. Hold on, there, Doc. Stay aboard. We couldn't pull ashore in the teeth of it." The doctor had made a spasmodic leap to the rail. "If the chains were shackled on, we might drop one of the hooks and hold her; but it's two hours' work for a full crew."

"But we're likely to be blown away, aren't we?" asked the doctor.

"Not far. I don't think it'll last long. We'll make the boat fast astern and get out of the wet." They did so, and entered the cabin. Soon the squall, coming with a shock like that of a solid blow, struck the hulk broadside to and careened her. From the cabin door they watched the nearly horizontal rain as it swished across the deck, and listened to the screaming of the wind, which prevented all conversation. Silently they waited—one hour—two hours—then Boston said: "This is getting serious. It's no squall. If it wasn't so late in the season I'd call it a hurricane. I'm going on deck."

He climbed the companionway stairs to the poop, and shut the scuttle behind him—for the rain was flooding the cabin—then looked around. The shore and horizon were hidden by a dense wall of gray, which seemed not a hundred feet distant. From to windward this wall was detaching great waves or sheets of almost solid water, which bombarded the ship in successive blows, to be then lost in the gray whirl to leeward. Overhead was the same dismal hue, marked by hurrying masses of darker cloud, and below was a sea of froth, white and flat; for no waves could raise their heads in that wind. Drenched to the skin, he tried the wheel and found it free in its movements. In front of it was a substantial binnacle, and within a compass, which, though sluggish, as from a well worn pivot, was practically in good condition. "Blowing us about nor'west by west," he muttered, as he looked at it—"straight up the coast. It's better than the beach in this weather, but may land us in Havana." He examined the boat. It was full of water, and tailing to windward, held by its painter. Making sure that this was fast, he went down.

"Doc," he said, as he squeezed the water from his limp cork helmet and flattened it on the table, "have you any objections to being rescued by some craft going into Havana?"

"I have—decided objections."

"So have I; but this wind is blowing us there sideways. Now, such a blow as this, at this time of year, will last three days at least, and I've an idea that it'll haul gradually to the south, and west towards the end of it. Where'll we be then? Either piled up on one of the Bahama keys or interviewed by the Spaniards. Now I've been thinking of a scheme on deck. We can't get back to camp for a while— that's settled. This iron hull is worth something, and if we can take it into an American port we can claim salvage. Key West is the nearest, but Fernandina is the surest. We've got a stump of a foremast and a rudder and a compass. If we can get some kind of sail up forward and bring her 'fore the wind, we can steer any course within thirty degrees of the wind line."

"But I can't steer. And how long will this voyage take? What will we eat?"

"Yes, you can steer—good enough. And, of course, it depends on food, and water, too. We'd better catch some of this that's going to waste."

In what had been the steward's storeroom they found a harness-cask with bones and dry rust in the bottom. "It's salt meat, I suppose," said the doctor, "reduced to its elements." With the handles of their pistols they carefully hammered down the rusty hoops over the shrunken staves, which were well preserved by the brine they had once held, and taking the cask on deck, cleaned it thoroughly under the scuppers—or drain holes—of the poop, and let it stand under the stream of water to swell and sweeten itself.

"If we find more casks we'll catch some more," said Boston; "but that will last us two weeks. Now we'll hunt for her stores. I've eaten salt-horse twenty years old,

but I can't vouch for what we may find here." They examined all the rooms adjacent to the cabin, but found nothing.

"Where's the lazarette in this kind of a ship?" asked Boston. "The cabin runs right aft to the stern. It must be below us." He found that the carpet was not tacked to the floor, and, raising the after end, discovered a hatch, or trap door, which he lifted. Below, when their eyes were accustomed to the darkness, they saw boxes and barrels—all covered with the same fine dust which filled the cabin.

"Don't go down there, yet, Boston," said the doctor. "It may be full of carbonic acid gas. She's been afire, you know. Wait." He tore a strip from some bedding in one of the rooms, and, lighting one end by means of a flint and steel which he carried, lowered the smouldering rag until it rested on the pile below. It did not go out.

"Safe enough, Boston," he remarked. "But you go down; you're younger."

Boston smiled and sprang down on the pile, from which he passed up a box. "Looks like tinned stuff, Doc. Open, it, and I'll look over here."

The doctor smashed the box with his foot, and found, as the other had thought, that it contained cylindrical cans; but the labels were faded with age. Opening one with his jack-knife, he tasted the contents. It was a mixture of meat and a fluid, called by sailors "soup-and-bully," and as fresh and sweet as though canned the day before.

"We're all right, Boston," he called down the hatch. "Here's as good a dish as I've tasted for months. Ready cooked, too."

Boston soon appeared. "There are some beef or pork barrels over in the wing," he said, "and plenty of this canned stuff. I don't know what good the salt meat is. The barrels seem tight, but we won't need to broach one for a while. There's a bag of coffee—gone to dust, and some hard bread that isn't fit to eat; but this'll do." He picked up the open can.

"Boston," said the doctor, "if those barrels contain meat, we'll find it cooked—boiled in its own brine, like this."

"Isn't it strange," said Boston, as he tasted the contents of the can, "that this stuff should keep so long?"

"Not at all. It was cooked thoroughly by the heat, and then frozen. If your barrels haven't burst from the expansion of the brine under the heat or cold, you'll find the meat just as good."

"But rather salty, if I'm a judge of salt-horse. Now, where's the sail-locker? We want a sail on that fore mast. It must be forward."

In the forecastle they found sailor's chests and clothing in all stages of ruin, but none of the spare sails that ships carry. In the boatswain's locker, in one corner of the forecastle, however, they found some iron strapped blocks in fairly good condition, which Boston noted. Then they opened the main-hatch, and discovered a mixed pile of boxes, some showing protruding necks of large bottles, or carboys, others nothing but the circular opening. Here and there in the tangled heap were sections of canvas sails—rolled and unrolled, but all yellow and worthless. They closed the hatch and returned to the cabin, where they could converse.

"They stowed their spare canvas in the 'tween-deck on top of the cargo," said Boston; "and the carboys—"

"And the carboys burst from the heat and ruined the sails," broke in the doctor. "But another question is, what became of that acid?"

"If it's not in the 'tween-deck yet, it must be in the hold—leaked through the hatches."

"I hope it hasn't reached the iron in the hull, Boston, my boy. It takes a long time for cold acids to act on iron after the first oxidation, but in fifty years mixed nitric and sulphuric will do lots of work."

"No fear, Doc; it had done its work when you were in your cradle. What'll we do for canvas? We must get this craft before the wind. How'll the carpet do?" Boston lifted the edge, and tried the fabric in his fingers. "It'll go," he said; "we'll double it. I'll hunt for a palm-and-needle and some twine." These articles he found in the mate's room. "The twine's no better than yarn," said he, "but we'll use four parts."

Together they doubled the carpet diagonally, and with long stitches joined the edges. Then Boston sewed into each corner a thimble—an iron ring—and they had a triangular sail of about twelve feet hoist. "It hasn't been exposed to the action of the air like the ropes in the locker forward," said Boston, as he arose and took off the palm; "and perhaps it'll last till she pays off. Then we can steer. You get the big pulley-blocks from the locker, Doc, and I'll get the rope from the boat. It's lucky I thought to bring it; I expected to lift things out of the hold with it."

At the risk of his life Boston obtained the coil from the boat, while the doctor brought the blocks. Then, together, they rove off a tackle. With the handles of their pistols they knocked bunk-boards to pieces and saved the nails; then Boston climbed the foremast, as a painter climbs a steeple—by nailing successive billets of wood above his head for steps. Next he hauled up and secured the tackle to the forward side of the mast, with which they pulled up the upper corner of their sail, after lashing the lower corners to the windlass and fife rail.

It stood the pressure, and the hulk paid slowly off and gathered headway. Boston took the wheel and steadied her at northwest by west—dead before the wind— while the doctor, at his request, brought the open can of soup and lubricated the wheel-screw with the only substitute for oil at their command; for the screw worked hard with the rust of fifty years.

Their improvised sail, pressed steadily on but one side, had held together, but now, with the first flap as the gale caught it from another direction, appeared a rent; with the next flap the rag went to pieces.

"Let her go!" sang out Boston gleefully; "we can steer now. Come here, Doc, and learn to steer."

The doctor came; and when he left that wheel, three days later, he had learned. For the wind had blown a continuous gale the whole of this time, which, with the ugly sea raised as the ship left the lee of the land, necessitated the presence of both men at the helm. Only occasionally was there a lull during which one of them could rush below and return with a can of soup. During one of these lulls Boston had examined the boat, towing half out of water; and concluded that a short painter was best with a water logged boat, had reinforced it with a few turns of his rope from forward. In the three days they had sighted no craft except such as their own—helpless—hove-to or scudding.

Boston had judged rightly in regard to the wind. It had hauled slowly to the southward, allowing him to make the course he wished—through the Bahama and up the Florida Channel with the wind over the stern. During the day he could guide himself by landmarks, but at night, with a darkened binnacle, he could only steer blindly on with the wind at his back. The storm centre, at first to the south of Cuba, had made a wide circle, concentric with the curving course of the ship, and when the latter had reached the upper end of the Florida Channel, had spurted ahead and whirled out to sea across her bows. It was then that the undiminished gale, blowing nearly west, had caused Boston, in despair, to throw the wheel down and bring the ship into the trough of the sea—to drift. Then the two wet, exhausted, hollow-eyed men slept the sleep that none but sailors and soldiers know; and when they awakened, twelve hours later, stiff and sore, it was to look out on a calm, starlit evening, with an eastern moon silvering the surface of the long, northbound rollers, and showing in sharp relief a dark horizon, on which there was no sign of land or sail.

They satisfied their hunger; then Boston, with a rusty iron pot from the galley, to which he fastened the end of his rope, dipped up some of the water from over the side. It was warm to the touch, and, aware that they were in the Gulf Stream, they crawled under the musty bedding in the cabin berths and slept through the night. In the morning there was no promise of the easterly wind that Boston hoped would come to blow them to port, and they secured their boat—reeving off davit tackles, and with the plug out, pulling it up, one end at a time while the water drained out through the hole in the bottom.

"Now, Boston," said the doctor, "here we are, as you say, on the outer edge of the Gulf Stream, drifting out into the broad Atlantic at the rate of four miles an hour. We've got to make the best of it until something comes along; so you hunt through that store-room and see what else there is to eat, and I'll examine the cargo. I want to know where that acid went."

They opened all the hatches, and while Boston descended to the lazarette, the doctor, with his trousers rolled up, climbed down the notched steps in a stanchion. In a short time he came up with a yellow substance in his hand, which he washed thoroughly with fresh water in Boston's improvised draw bucket, and placed in the sun to dry. Then he returned to the 'tweendeck. After a while, Boston, rummaging the lazarette, heard him calling through the bulkhead, and joined him.

"Look here, Boston," said the doctor; "I've cleared away the muck over this hatch. It's 'corked,' as you sailormen call it. Help me get it up."

They dug the compacted oakum from the seams with their knives, and by iron rings in each corner, now eaten with rust to almost the thinness of wire, they lifted the hatch. Below was a filthy-looking layer of whitish substance, protruding from which were charred, half burned staves. First they repeated the experiment with the smouldering rag, and finding that it burned, as before, they descended. The whitish substance was hard enough to bear their weight, and they looked around. Overhead, hung to the under side of the deck and extending the length of the hold, were wooden tanks, charred, and in some places burned through.

"She must have been built for a passenger or troop ship," said Boston. "Those tanks would water a regiment."

"Boston," answered the doctor, irrelevantly, "will you climb up and bring down an oar from the boat? Carry it down—don't throw it, my boy." Boston obliged him, and the doctor, picking his way forward, then aft, struck each tank with the oar. "Empty—all of them," he said.

He dug out with his knife a piece of the whitish substance under foot, and examined it closely in the light from the hatch.

"Boston," he said, impressively, "this ship was loaded with lime, tallow, and acids—acids above, lime and tallow down here. This stuff is neither; it is lime-soap. And, moreover, it has not been touched by acids." The doctor's ruddy face was ashen.

"Well?" asked Boston.

"Lime soap is formed by the cauticizing action of lime on tallow in the presence of water and heat. It is easy to understand this fire. One of those tanks leaked and dribbled down on the cargo, attacking the lime—which was stowed underneath, as all these staves we see on top are from tallow-kids. The heat generated by the slaking lime set fire to the barrels in contact, which in turn set fire to others, and they burned until the air was exhausted, and then went out. See, they are but partly consumed. There was intense heat in this hold, and expansion of the water in all the tanks. Are tanks at sea filled to the top?"

"Chock full, and a cap screwed down on the upper end of the pipes."

"As I thought. The expanding water burst every tank in the hold, and the cargo was deluged with water, which attacked every lime barrel in the bottom layer, at least. Result—the bursting of those barrels from the ebullition of slaking lime, the melting of the tallow—which could not burn long in the closed up space—and the mixing of it in the interstices of the lime barrels with water and lime—a boiling hot mess. What happens under such conditions?"

"Give it up," said Boston, laconically.

"Lime soap is formed, which rises, and the water beneath is in time all taken up by the lime."

"But what of it?" interrupted the other.

"Wait. I see that this hold and the 'tween deck are lined with wood. Is that customary in iron ships?"

"Not now. It used to be a notion that an iron skin damaged the cargo; so the first iron ships were ceiled with wood."

"Are there any drains in the 'tween-deck to let water out, in case it gets into that deck from above—a sea, for instance?"

"Yes, always; three or four scupper-holes each side amidships. They lead the water into the bilges, where the pumps can reach it."

"I found up there," continued the doctor, "a large piece of wood, badly charred by acid for half its length, charred to a lesser degree for the rest. It was oval in cross section, and the larger end was charred most."

"Scupper plug. I suppose they plugged the 'tween deck scuppers to keep any water they might ship out of the bilges and away from the lime."

"Yes, and those plugs remained in place for days, if not weeks or months, after the carboys burst, as indicated by the greater charring of the larger end of the plug. I burrowed under the debris, and found the hole which that plug fitted. It was worked loose, or knocked out of the hole by some internal movement of the broken carboys, perhaps. At any rate, it came out, after remaining in place long enough for the acids to become thoroughly mixed and for the hull to cool down. She was in the ice, remember. Boston, the mixed acid went down that hole, or others like it. Where is it now?"

"I suppose," said Boston, thoughtfully, "that it soaked up into the hold, through the skin."

"Exactly. The skin is calked with oakum, is it not?" Boston nodded.

"That oakum would contract with the charring action, as did the oakum in the hatch, and every drop of that acid—ten thousand gallons, as I have figured— has filtered up into the hold, with the exception of what remained between the frames under the skin. Have you ever studied organic chemistry?"

"Slightly."

"Then you can follow me. When tallow is saponified there is formed, from the palmitin, stearin, and olein contained, with the cauticizing agent—in this case, lime—a soap. But there are two ends to every equation, and at the bottom of this immense soap vat, held in solution by the water, which would afterwards be taken up by the surplus lime, was the other end of this equation; and as the yield from tallow of this other product is about thirty per cent., and as we start with eight thousand fifty-pound kids—four hundred thousand pounds—all of which has disappeared, we know that, sticking to the skin and sides of the barrels down here, is—or was once—one hundred and twenty thousand pounds, or sixty tons, of the other end of the equation—glycerine!"

"Do you mean, Doc," asked Boston, with a startled look, "that—"

"I mean," said the doctor, emphatically, "that the first thing the acids—mixed in the 'tween-deck to just about the right proportions, mind you—would attack, on oozing through the skin, would be this glycerine; and the certain product of this union under intense cold—this hull was frozen in the ice, remember—would be nitro glycerine; and, as the yield of the explosive is two hundred and twenty per cent. of the glycerine, we can be morally sure that in the bottom of this hold, each minute globule of it held firmly in a hard matrix of sulphate or nitrate of calcium— which would be formed next when the acids met the hydrates and carbonates of lime—is over one hundred and thirty tons of nitro glycerine, all the more explosive from not being washed of free acids. Come up on deck. I'll show you something else."

Limp and nerveless, Boston followed the doctor. This question was beyond his seamanship.

The doctor brought the yellow substance—now well dried. "I found plenty of this in the 'tween-deck," he said; "and I should judge they used it to pack between the carboy boxes. It was once cotton-batting. It is now, since I have washed it, a very good sample of gun cotton. Get me a hammer—crowbar—something hard."

Boston brought a marline spike from the locker, and the doctor, tearing off a small piece of the substance and placing it on the iron barrel of a gipsy winch, gave it a hard blow with the marline spike, which was nearly torn from his hand by the explosion that followed.

"We have in the 'tween-deck," said the doctor, as he turned, "about twice as many pounds of this stuff as they used to pack the carboys with; and, like the nitro-glycerine, is the more easily exploded from the impurities and free acids. I washed this for safe handling. Boston, we are adrift on a floating bomb that would pulverize the rock of Gibraltar!"

"But, doctor," asked Boston, as he leaned against the rail for support, "wouldn't there be evolution of heat from the action of the acids on the lime—enough to explode the nitro-glycerine just formed?"

"The best proof that it did not explode is the fact that this hull still floats. The action was too slow, and it was very cold down there. But I can't yet account for the acids left in the bilges. What have they been doing all these fifty years?"

Boston found a sounding-rod in the locker, which he scraped bright with his knife, then, unlaying a strand of the rope for a line, sounded the pump well. The rod came up dry, but with a slight discoloration on the lower end, which Boston showed to the doctor.

"The acids have expended themselves on the iron frames and plates. How thick are they?"

"Plates, about five-eighths of an inch; frames, like railroad iron."

"This hull is a shell! We won't get much salvage. Get up some kind of distress signal, Boston." Somehow the doctor was now the master-spirit.

A flag was nailed to the mast, union down, to be blown to pieces with the first breeze; then another, and another, until the flag locker was exhausted. Next they hung out, piece after piece, all they could spare of the rotten bedding, until that too was exhausted. Then they found, in a locker of their boat, a flag of Free Cuba, which they decided not to waste, but to hang out only when a sail appeared.

But no sail appeared, and the craft, buffeted by gales and seas, drifted eastward, while the days became weeks, and the weeks became months. Twice she entered the Sargasso Sea—the graveyard of derelicts—to be blown out by friendly gales and resume her travels. Occasional rains replenished the stock of fresh water, but the food they found at first, with the exception of some cans of fruit, was all that came to light; for the salt meat was leathery, and crumbled to a salty dust on exposure to the air. After a while their stomachs revolted at the diet of cold soup, and they ate only when hunger compelled them.

At first they had stood watch-and-watch, but the lonely horror of the long night vigils in the constant apprehension of instant death had affected them alike, and they gave it up, sleeping and watching together. They had taken care of their boat and provisioned it, ready to lower and pull into the track of any craft that might approach. But it was four months from the beginning of this strange voyage when the two men, gaunt and hungry—with ruined digestions and shattered nerves—saw, with joy which may be imagined, the first land and the first sail that gladdened their eyes after the storm in the Florida Channel.

A fierce gale from the southwest had been driving them, broadside on, in the trough of the sea, for the whole of the preceding day and night; and the land they now saw appeared to them a dark, ragged line of blue, early in the morning. Boston could only surmise that it was the coast of Portugal or Spain. The sail—which lay between them and the land, about three miles to leeward—proved to be the try-sail of a black craft, hove to, with bows nearly towards them.

Boston climbed the foremast with their only flag and secured it; then, from the high poop deck, they watched the other craft, plunging and wallowing in the immense Atlantic combers, often raising her forefoot into plain view, again descending with a dive that hid the whole forward half in a white cloud of spume.

"If she was a steamer I'd call her a cruiser," said Boston; "one of England's black ones, with a storm-sail on her military mainmast. She has a ram bow, and—yes, sponsons and guns. That's what she is, with her funnels and bridge carried away."

"Isn't she right in our track, Boston?" asked the doctor, excitedly. "Hadn't she better get out of our way?"

"She's got steam up—a full head; see the escape-jet? She isn't helpless. If she don't launch a boat, we'll take to ours and board her."

The distance lessened rapidly—the cruiser plunging up and down in the same spot, the derelict heaving to leeward in great, swinging leaps, as the successive seas caught her, each one leaving her half a length farther on. Soon they could make out the figures of men.

"Take us off," screamed the doctor, waving his arms; "and get out of our way!"

"We'll clear her," said Boston; "see, she's started her engine."

As they drifted down on the weather side of the cruiser they shouted repeatedly words of supplication and warning. They were answered by a solid shot from a secondary gun, which flew over their heads. At the same time, the ensign of Spain was run up on the flagstaff.

"They're Spanish, Boston. They're firing on us. Into that boat with you! If a shot hits our cargo, we won't know what struck us."

They sprang into the boat, which luckily hung on the lee side, and cleared the falls—fastened and coiled in the bow and stern. Often during their long voyage they had rehearsed the launching of the boat in a seaway—an operation requiring quick and concerted action.

"Ready, Doc?" sang out Boston. "One, two, three—let go!" The falls overhauled with a whir, and the falling boat, striking an uprising sea with a smack, sank with it. When it raised they unhooked the tackle blocks, and pushed off with the oars just as a second shot hummed over their heads.

"Pull, Boston; pull hard—straight to windward!" cried the doctor.

The tight whaleboat shipped no water, and though they were pulling in the teeth of a furious gale, the hulk was drifting away from them, so, in a short time, they were separated from their late home by a full quarter mile of angry sea. The cruiser had forged ahead in plain view, and, as they looked, took in the try-sail.

"She's going to wear," said Boston. "See, she's paying off."

"I don't know what 'wearing' means, Boston," panted the doctor, "but I know the Spanish nature. She's going to ram that hundred and thirty tons of nitro. Don't stop. Pull away. Hold on, there; hold on, you fools!" he shouted. "That's a torpedo; keep away from her!"

Forgetting his own injunction to "pull away," the doctor stood up, waving his oar frantically, and Boston assisted. But if their shouts and gestures were understood aboard the cruiser, they were ignored. She slowly turned in a wide curve and headed straight for the *Neptune* which had drifted to leeward of her.

What was in the minds of the officers on that cruiser's deck will never be known. Cruisers of all nations hold roving commissions in regard to derelicts, and it is fitting and proper for one of them to gently prod a "vagrant of the sea" with the steel prow and send her below to trouble no more. But it may be that the sight of the Cuban flag, floating defiantly in the gale, had something to do with the full speed at which the Spanish ship approached. When but half a length separated the two craft, a heavy sea lifted the bow of the cruiser high in air; then it sank, and the sharp steel ram came down like a butcher's cleaver on the side of the derelict.

A great semicircular wall of red shut out the gray of the sea and sky to leeward, and for an instant the horrified men in the boat saw—as people see by a lightning flash—dark lines radiating from the centre of this red wall, and near this centre poised on end in mid-air, with deck and sponsons still intact, a bowless, bottomless remnant of the cruiser. Then, and before the remnant sank into the vortex beneath, the spectacle went out in the darkness of unconsciousness; for a report, as of concentrated thunder, struck them down. A great wave had left the crater-like depression in the sea, which threw the boat on end, and with the inward rush of surrounding water rose a mighty gray cone, which then subsided to a hollow, while another wave followed the first. Again and again this gray pillar rose and fell, each subsidence marked by the sending forth of a wave. And long before these concentric waves had lost themselves in the battle with the storm-driven combers from the ocean, the half-filled boat, with her unconscious passengers, had drifted over the spot where lay the shattered remnant, which, with the splintered fragments of wood and iron strewn on the surface and bottom of the sea for a mile around, and the lessening cloud of dust in the air, was all that was left of the derelict *Neptune* and one of the finest cruisers in the Spanish navy.

A few days later, two exhausted, half-starved men pulled a whaleboat up to the steps of the wharf at Cadiz, where they told some lies and sold their boat. Six months after, these two men, sitting at a camp-fire of the Cuban army, read from a discolored newspaper, brought ashore with the last supplies, the following:

"By cable to the *Herald*.

"Cadiz, March 13, 1895.—Anxiety for the safety of the *Reina Regente* has grown rapidly to-day, and this evening it is feared, generally, that she went down with her four hundred and twenty souls in the storm which swept the southern coast on Sunday night and Monday morning. Despatches from Gibraltar say that pieces of a boat and several semaphore flags belonging to the cruiser came ashore at Ceuta and Tarifa this afternoon."

The Thing in the Weeds

by William Hope Hodgson

I

THIS IS AN EXTRAORDINARY TALE. WE HAD COME UP FROM THE CAPE, AND OWING to the Trades heading us more than usual, we had made some hundreds of miles more westing than I ever did before or since.

I remember the particular night of the happening perfectly. I suppose what occurred stamped it solid into my memory, with a thousand little details that, in the ordinary way, I should never have remembered an hour. And, of course, we talked it over so often among ourselves that this, no doubt, helped to fix it all past any forgetting.

I remember the mate and I had been pacing the weather side of the poop and discussing various old shellbacks' superstitions. I was third mate, and it was between four and five bells in the first watch, i.e. between ten and half-past. Suddenly he stopped in his walk and lifted his head and sniffed several times.

"My word, mister," he said, "there's a rum kind of stink somewhere about. Don't you smell it?"

I sniffed once or twice at the light airs that were coming in on the beam; then I walked to the rail and leaned over, smelling again at the slight breeze. And abruptly I got a whiff of it, faint and sickly, yet vaguely suggestive of something I had once smelt before.

"I can smell something, Mr. Lammart," I said. "I could almost give it name; and yet somehow I can't." I stared away into the dark to windward. "What do you seem to smell?" I asked him.

"I can't smell anything now," he replied, coming over and standing beside me. "It's gone again. No! By Jove! there it is again. My goodness! Phew!"

The smell was all about us now, filling the night air. It had still that indefinable familiarity about it, and yet it was curiously strange, and, more than anything else, it was certainly simply beastly.

The stench grew stronger, and presently the mate asked me to go for'ard and see whether the look-out man noticed anything. When I reached the break of the fo'c's'le head I called up to the man, to know whether he smelled anything.

"Smell anythin', sir?" he sang out. "Jumpin' larks! I sh'u'd think I do. I'm fair p'isoned with it."

I ran up the weather steps and stood beside him. The smell was certainly very plain up there, and after savouring it for a few moments I asked him whether he thought it might be a dead whale. But he was very emphatic that this could not be the case, for, as he said, he had been nearly fifteen years in whaling ships, and knew the smell of a dead whale, "like as you would the smell of bad whiskey, sir," as he put it. "'Tain't no whale yon, but the Lord He knows what 'tis. I'm thinking it's Davy Jones come up for a breather."

I stayed with him some minutes, staring out into the darkness, but could see nothing; for, even had there been something big close to us, I doubt whether I could have seen it, so black a night it was, without a visible star, and with a vague, dull haze breeding an indistinctness all about the ship.

I returned to the mate and reported that the look-out complained of the smell, but that neither he nor I had been able to see anything in the darkness to account for it.

By this time the queer, disgusting odour seemed to be in all the air about us, and the mate told me to go below and shut all the ports, so as to keep the beastly smell out of the cabins and the saloon.

When I returned he suggested that we should shut the companion doors, and after that we commenced to pace the poop again, discussing the extraordinary smell, and stopping from time to time to stare through our night-glasses out into the night about the ship.

"I'll tell you what it smells like, mister," the mate remarked once, "and that's like a mighty old derelict I once went aboard in the North Atlantic. She was a proper old-timer, an' she gave us all the creeps. There was just this funny, dank, rummy sort of century-old bilge-water and dead men an' seaweed. I can't stop thinkin' we're nigh some lonesome old packet out there; an' a good thing we've not much way on us!"

"Do you notice how almighty quiet everything's gone the last half-hour or so?" I said a little later. "It must be the mist thickening down."

"It is the mist," said the mate, going to the rail and staring out. "Good Lord, what's that?" he added.

Something had knocked his hat from his head, and it fell with a sharp rap at my feet. And suddenly, you know, I got a premonition of something horrid.

"Come away from the rail, sir!" I said sharply, and gave one jump and caught him by the shoulders and dragged him back. "Come away from the side!"

"What's up, mister?" he growled at me, and twisted his shoulders free. "What's wrong with you? Was it you knocked off my cap?" He stooped and felt around for it, and as he did so I *heard* something unmistakably fiddling away at the rail which the mate had just left.

"My God, sir!" I said "there's something there. Hark!"

The mate stiffened up, listening; then he heard it. It was for all the world as if something was feeling and rubbing the rail there in the darkness, not two fathoms away from us.

"Who's there?" said the mate quickly. Then, as there was no answer: "What the devil's this hanky-panky? Who's playing the goat there?" He made a swift step through the darkness towards he rail, but I caught him by the elbow.

"Don't go, mister!" I said, hardly above a whisper. "It's not one of the men. Let me get a light."

"Quick, then!" he said, and I turned and ran aft to the binnacle and snatched out the lighted lamp. As I did so I heard the mate shout something out of the darkness in a strange voice. There came a sharp, loud, rattling sound, and then a crash, and immediately the mate roaring to me to hasten with the light. His voice changed even whilst he shouted, and gave out something that was nearer a scream than anything else. There came two loud, dull blows and an extraordinary gasping sound; and then, as I raced along the poop, there was a tremendous smashing of glass and an immediate silence.

"Mr. Lammart!" I shouted. "Mr. Lammart!" And then I had reached the place where I had left the mate for forty seconds before; but he was not there.

"Mr. Lammart!" I shouted again, holding the light high over my head and turning quickly to look behind me. As I did so my foot glided on some slippery substance, and I went headlong to the deck with a tremendous thud, smashing the lamp and putting out the light.

I was on my feet again in an instant. I groped a moment for the lamp, and as I did so I heard the men singing out from the maindeck and the noise of their feet as they came running aft. I found the broken lamp and realised it was useless; then I jumped for the companion-way, and in half a minute I was back with the big saloon lamp glaring bright in my hands.

I ran for'ard again, shielding the upper edge of the glass chimney from the draught of my running, and the blaze of the big lamp seemed to make the weather side of the poop as bright as day, except for the mist, that gave something of a vagueness to things.

Where I had left the mate there was blood upon the deck, but nowhere any signs of the man himself. I ran to the weather rail and held the lamp to it. There was blood upon it, and the rail itself seemed to have been wrenched by some huge force. I put out my hand and found that I could shake it. Then I leaned out-board and held the lamp at arm's length, staring down over the ship's side.

"Mr. Lammart!" I shouted into the night and the thick mist. "Mr. Lammart! Mr. Lammart!" But my voice seemed to go, lost and muffled and infinitely small, away into the billowy darkness.

I heard the men snuffling and breathing, waiting to leeward of the poop. I whirled round to them, holding the lamp high,

"We heard somethin', sir," said Tarpley, the leading seaman in our watch. "Is anythin' wrong, sir?"

"The mate's gone," I said blankly. "We heard something, and I went for the binnacle lamp. Then he shouted, and I heard a sound of things smashing, and when I got back he'd gone clean." I turned and held the light out again over the unseen sea, and the men crowded round along the rail and stared, bewildered.

"Blood, sir," said Tarpley, pointing. "There's somethin' almighty queer out there." He waved a huge hand into the darkness. "That's what stinks—"

He never finished; for suddenly one of the men cried out something in a frightened voice: "Look out, sir! Look out, sir!"

I saw, in one brief flash of sight, something come in with an infernal flicker of movement; and then, before I could form any notion of what I had seen, the lamp was dashed to pieces across the poop deck. In that instant my perceptions cleared, and I saw the incredible folly of what we were doing; for there we were, standing up against the blank, unknowable night, and out there in the darkness there surely lurked some thing of monstrousness; and we were at its mercy. I seemed to feel it hovering—hovering over us, so that I felt the sickening creep of gooseflesh all over me.

"Stand back from the rail!" I shouted. "Stand back from the rail!" There was a rush of feet as the men obeyed, in sudden apprehension of their danger, and I gave back with them. Even as I did so I felt some invisible thing brush my shoulder, and an indescribable smell was in my nostrils from something that moved over me in the dark.

"Down into the saloon everyone!" I shouted. "Down with you all! Don't wait a moment!"

There was a rush along the dark weather deck, and then the men went helter-skelter down the companion steps into the saloon, falling and cursing over one another in the darkness. I sang out to the man at the wheel to join them, and then I followed.

I came upon the men huddled at the foot of the stairs and filling up the passage, all crowding each other in the darkness. The skipper's voice was filling the saloon, and he was demanding in violent adjectives the cause of so tremendous a noise. From the steward's berth there came also a voice and the splutter of a match, and then the glow of a lamp in the saloon itself.

I pushed my way through the men and found the captain in the saloon in his sleeping gear, looking both drowsy and angry, though perhaps bewilderment topped every other feeling. He held his cabin lamp in his hand, and shone the light over the huddle of men.

I hurried to explain, and told him of the incredible disappearance of the mate, and of my conviction that some extraordinary thing was lurking near the ship out in the mist and the darkness. I mentioned the curious smell, and told how the mate had suggested that we had drifted down near some old-time, sea-rotted derelict. And, you know, even as I put it into awkward words, my imagination began to awaken to horrible discomforts; a thousand dreadful impossibilities of the sea became suddenly possible.

The captain (Jeldy was his name) did not stop to dress, but ran back into his cabin, and came out in a few moments with a couple of revolvers and a handful of cartridges. The second mate had come running out of his cabin at the noise, and had listed intensely to what I had to say; and now he jumped back into his berth and brought out his own lamp and a large Smith and Wesson, which was evidently ready loaded.

Captain Jeldy pushed one of his revolvers into my hands, with some of the cartridges, and we began hastily to load the weapons. Then the captain caught up his lamp and made for the stairway, ordering the men into the saloon out of his way.

"Shall you want them, sir?" I asked.

"No," he said. "It's no use their running any unnecessary risks." He threw a word over his shoulder: "Stay quiet here, men; if I want you I'll give you a shout; then come spry!"

"Aye, aye, sir," said the watch in a chorus; and then I was following the captain up the stairs, with the second mate close behind.

We came up through the companion-way on to the silence of the deserted poop. The mist had thickened up, even during the brief time that I had been below, and there was not a breath of wind. The mist was so dense that it seemed to press in upon us, and the two lamps made a kind of luminous halo in the mist, which seemed to absorb their light in a most peculiar way.

"Where was he?" the captain asked me, almost in a whisper.

"On the port side, sir," I said, "a little foreside the charthouse and about a dozen feet in from the rail. I'll show you the exact place."

We went for'ard along what had been the weather side, going quietly and watchfully, though, indeed, it was little enough that we could see, because of the mist. Once, as I led the way, I thought I heard a vague sound somewhere in the mist, but was all unsure because of the slow creak, creak of the spars and gear as the vessel rolled slightly upon an odd, oily swell. Apart from this slight sound, and the far-up rustle of the canvas slatting gently against the masts, there was no sound of all throughout the ship. I assure you the silence seemed to me to be almost menacing, in the tense, nervous state in which I was.

"Hereabouts is where I left him," I whispered to the captain a few seconds later. "Hold your lamp low, sir. There's blood on the deck."

Captain Jeldy did so, and made a slight sound with his mouth at what he saw. Then, heedless of my hurried warning, he walked across to the rail, holding his lamp high up. I followed him, for I could not let him go alone; and the second mate came too, with his lamp. They leaned over the port rail and held their lamps out into the mist and the unknown darkness beyond the ship's side. I remember how the lamps made just two yellow glares in the mist, ineffectual, yet serving somehow to make extraordinarily plain the vastitude of the night and the *possibilities of the dark*. Perhaps that is a queer way to put it, but it gives you the effect of that moment upon my feelings. And all the time, you know, there was upon me the brutal, frightening expectancy of something reaching in at us from out of that everlasting darkness and mist that held all the sea and the night, so that we were just three mist-shrouded, hidden figures, peering nervously.

The mist was now so thick that we could not even see the surface of the water overside, and fore and aft of us the rail vanished away into the fog and the dark. And then, as we stood here staring, I heard something moving down on the maindeck. I caught Captain Jeldy by the elbow.

"Come away from the rail, sir," I said, hardly above a whisper; and he, with the swift premonition of danger, stepped back and allowed me to urge him well inboard. The second mate followed, and the three of us stood there in the mist, staring round about us and holding our revolvers handily, and the dull waves of the mist beating in slowly upon the lamps in vague wreathings and swirls of fog.

"What was it you heard, mister?" asked the captain after a few moments.

"Ssst!" I muttered. "There it is again. There's something moving down on the maindeck!"

Captain Jeldy heard it himself now, and the three of us stood listening intensely. Yet it was hard to know what to make of the sounds. And then suddenly there was the rattle of a deck ringbolt, and then again, as if something or someone were fumbling and playing with it.

"Down there on the maindeck!" shouted the captain abruptly, his voice seeming hoarse close to my ear, yet immediately smothered by the fog. "Down there on the maindeck! Who's there?"

But there came never an answering sound. And the three of us stood there, looking quickly this way and that, and listening. Abruptly the second mate muttered something:

"The look-out, sir! The look-out!"

Captain Jeldy took the hint on the instant.

"On the look-out there!" he shouted.

And then, far away and muffled-sounding, there came the answering cry of the look-out man from the fo'c'sle head:

"Sir-r-r?" A little voice, long drawn out through unknowable alleys of fog.

"Go below into the fo'c'sle and shut both doors, an' don't stir out till you're told!" sung out Captain Jeldy, his voice going lost into the mist. And then the man's answering "Aye, aye, sir!" coming to us faint and mournful. And directly afterwards the clang of a steel door, hollow-sounding and remote; and immediately the sound of another.

"That puts them safe for the present, anyway," said the second mate. And even as he spoke there came again that indefinite noise down upon the maindeck of something moving with an incredible and unnatural stealthiness.

"On the maindeck there!" shouted Captain Jeldy sternly. "If there is anyone there, answer, or I shall fire!"

The reply was both amazing and terrifying, for suddenly a tremendous blow was stricken upon the deck, and then there came the dull, rolling sound of some enormous weight going hollowly across the maindeck. And then an abominable silence.

"My God!" said Captain Jeldy in a low voice, "what was *that*?" And he raised his pistol, but I caught him by the wrist. "Don't shoot, sir!" I whispered. "It'll be no good. That—that—whatever it is I—mean it's something enormous, sir. I—I really wouldn't shoot." I found it impossible to put my vague idea into words; but I felt there was a force aboard, down on the maindeck, that it would be futile to attack with so ineffectual a thing as a puny revolver bullet.

And then, as I held Captain Jeldy's wrist, and he hesitated, irresolute, there came a sudden bleating of sheep and the sound of lashings being burst and the cracking of wood; and the next instant a huge crash, followed by crash after crash, and the anguished m-aa-a-a-ing of sheep.

"My God!" said the second mate, "the sheep-pen's being beaten to pieces against the deck. Good God! What sort of thing could do that?"

The tremendous beating ceased, and there was a splashing overside; and after that a silence so profound that it seemed as if the whole atmosphere of the night was full of an unbearable, tense quietness. And then the damp slatting of a sail, far up in the night, that made me start—a lonesome sound to break suddenly through that infernal silence upon my raw nerves.

"Get below, both of you. Smartly now!" muttered Captain Jeldy. "There's something run either aboard us or alongside; and we can't do anything till daylight."

We went below and shut the doors of the companion-way, and there we lay in the wide Atlantic, without wheel or look-out or officer in charge, and something incredible down on the dark maindeck.

II

FOR SOME HOURS WE SAT IN THE CAPTAIN'S CABIN TALKING THE MATTER OVER WHILST the watch slept, sprawled in a dozen attitudes on the floor of the saloon. Captain Jeldy and the second mate still wore their pyjamas, and our loaded revolvers lay handy on the cabin table. And so we watched anxiously through the hours for the dawn to come in.

As the light strengthened we endeavoured to get some view of the sea from the ports, but the mist was so thick about us that it was exactly like looking out into a grey nothingness, that became presently white as the day came.

"Now," said Captain Jeldy, "we're going to look into this."

He went out through the saloon to the companion stairs. At the top he opened the two doors, and the mist rolled in on us, white and impenetrable. For a little while we stood there, the three of us, absolutely silent and listening, with our revolvers handy; but never a sound came to us except the odd, vague slatting of a sail or the slight creaking of the gear as the ship lifted on some slow, invisible swell.

Presently the captain stepped cautiously out on to the deck; he was in his cabin slippers, and therefore made no sound. I was wearing gum-boots, and followed him silently, and the second mate after me in his bare feet. Captain Jeldy went a few paces along the deck, and the mist hid him utterly. "Phew!" I heard him mutter, "the stink's worse than ever!" His voice came odd and vague to me through the wreathing of the mist.

"The sun'll soon eat up all this fog," said the second mate at my elbow, in a voice little above a whisper.

We stepped after the captain, and found him a couple of fathoms away, standing shrouded in the mist in an attitude of tense listening.

"Can't hear a thing!" he whispered. "We'll go for'ard to the break, as quiet as you like. Don't make a sound."

We went forward, like three shadows, and suddenly Captain Jeldy kicked his shin against something and pitched headlong over it, making a tremendous noise. He got up quickly, swearing grimly, and the three of us stood there in silence, waiting lest any infernal thing should come upon us out of all that white invisibility. Once I felt sure I saw something coming towards me, and I raised my revolver, but saw in a moment that there was nothing. The tension of imminent, nervous expectancy eased from us, and Captain Jeldy stooped over the object on the deck.

"The port hencoop's been shifted out here!" he muttered. "It's all stove!"

"That must be what I heard last night when the mate went," I whispered. There was a loud crash just before he sang out to me to hurry with the lamp."

Captain Jeldy left the smashed hencoop, and the three of us tiptoed silently to the rail across the break of the poop. Here we leaned over and stared down into the blank whiteness of the mist that hid everything.

"Can't see a thing," whispered the second mate; yet as he spoke I could fancy that I heard a slight, indefinite, slurring noise somewhere below us; and I caught them each by an arm to draw them back.

"There's something down there," I muttered. "For goodness' sake come back from the rail."

We gave back a step or two, and then stopped to listen; and even as we did so there came a slight air playing through the mist.

"The breeze is coming," said the second mate. "Look, the mist is clearing already."

He was right. Already the look of white impenetrability had gone, and suddenly we could see the corner of the after-hatch coamings through the thinning fog. Within a minute we could see as far for'ard as the mainmast, and then the stuff blew away from us, clear of the vessel, like a great wall of whiteness, that dissipated as it went.

"*Look!*" we all exclaimed together. The whole of the vessel was now clear to our sight; but it was not at the ship herself that we looked, for, after one quick glance along the empty maindeck, we had seen something beyond the ship's side. All around the vessel there lay a submerged spread of weed, for, maybe, a good quarter of a mile upon every side.

"Weed!" sang out Captain Jeldy in a voice of comprehension. "Weed! Look! By Jove, I guess I know now what got the mate!"

He turned and ran to the port side and looked over. And suddenly he stiffened and beckoned silently over his shoulder to us to come and see. We had followed, and now we stood, one on each side of him, staring.

"Look!" whispered the captain, pointing. "See the great brute! Do you see it? There! Look!"

At first I could see nothing except the submerged spread of the weed, into which we had evidently run after dark. Then, as I stared intently, my gaze began to separate from the surrounding weed a leathery-looking something that was somewhat darker in hue than the weed itself.

"My God!" said Captain Jeldy. "What a monster! What a monster! Just look at the brute! Look at the thing's eyes! That's what got the mate. What a creature out of hell itself!"

I saw it plainly now; three of the massive feelers lay twined in and out among the clumpings of the weed; and then, abruptly, I realised that the two extraordinary round disks, motionless and inscrutable, were the creature's eyes, just below the surface of the water. It appeared to be staring, expressionless, up at the steel side of the vessel. I traced, vaguely, the shapeless monstrosity of what must be termed its head. "My God!" I muttered. "It's an enormous squid of some kind! What an awful brute! What—"

The sharp report of the captain's revolver came at that moment. He had fired at the thing, and instantly there was a most awful commotion alongside. The weed was hove upward, literally in tons. An enormous quantity was thrown aboard us by the thrashing of the monster's great feelers. The sea seemed almost to boil, in one great cauldron of weed and water, all about the brute, and the steel side of the ship resounded with the dull, tremendous blows that the creature gave in its struggle. And into all that whirling boil of tentacles, weed, and seawater the three of us emptied our revolvers as fast as we could fire and reload. I remember the feeling of fierce satisfaction I had in thus aiding to avenge the death of the mate.

Suddenly the captain roared out to us to jump back, and we obeyed on the instant. As we did so the weed rose up into a great mound over twenty feet in height, and more than a ton of it slopped aboard. The next instant three of the monstrous tentacles came in over the side, and the vessel gave a slow, sullen roll to port as the weight came upon her, for the monster had literally hove itself almost free of the sea against our port side, in one vast, leathery shape, all wreathed with weed-fronds, and seeming drenched with blood and curious black liquid.

The feelers that had come inboard thrashed round here and there, and suddenly one of them curled in the most hideous, snake-like fashion around the base of the mainmast. This seemed to attract it, for immediately it curled the two others about the mast, and forthwith wrenched upon it with such hideous violence that the whole towering length of spars, through all their height of a hundred and fifty feet, were shaken visibly, whilst the vessel herself vibrated with the stupendous efforts of the brute.

"It'll have the mast down, sir!" said the second mate, with a gasp. "My God! It'll strain her side open! My—"

"One of those blasting cartridges!" I said to Jeldy almost in a shout, as the inspiration took me. "Blow the brute to pieces!"

"Get one, quick!" said the captain, jerking his thumb towards the companion. "You know where they are."

In thirty seconds I was back with the cartridge. Captain Jeldy took out his knife and cut the fuse dead short; then, with a steady hand, he lit the fuse, and calmly held it, until I backed away, shouting to him to throw it, for I knew it must explode in another couple of seconds.

Captain Jeldy threw the thing like one throws a quoit, so that it fell into the sea just on the outward side of the vast bulk of the monster. So well had he timed it that it burst, with a stunning report, just as it struck the water. The effect upon the squid was amazing. It seemed literally to collapse. The enormous tentacles released themselves from the mast and curled across the deck helplessly, and were drawn inertly over the rail, as the enormous bulk sank away from the ship's side, out of sight, into the weed. The ship rolled slowly to starboard, and then steadied. "Thank God!" I muttered, and looked at the two others. They were pallid and sweating, and I must have been the same.

"Here's the breeze again," said the second mate, a minute later. "We're moving." He turned, without another word, and raced aft to the wheel, whilst the vessel slid over and through the weedfield.

"Look where that brute broke up the sheep-pen!" cried Jeldy, pointing. "And here's the skylight of the sail-locker smashed to bits!"

He walked across to it, and glanced down. And suddenly he let out a tremendous shout of astonishment:

"Here's the mate down here!" he shouted. "He's not overboard at all! He's *here!*"

He dropped himself down through the skylight on to the sails, and I after him; and, surely, there was the mate, lying all huddled and insensible on a hummock of spare sails. In his right hand he held a drawn sheath-knife, which he was in the habit of carrying A. B. fashion, whilst his left hand was all caked with dried blood, where he had been badly cut. Afterwards, we concluded he had cut himself in slashing at one of the tentacles of the squid, which had caught him round the left wrist, the tip of the tentacle being still curled tight about his arm, just as it had

been when he hacked it through. For the rest, he was not seriously damaged, the creature having obviously flung him violently away through the framework of the skylight, so that he had fallen in a studded condition on to the pile of sails.

We got him on deck, and down into his bunk, where we left the steward to attend to him. When we returned to the poop the vessel had drawn clear of the weed-field, and the captain and I stopped for a few moments to stare astern over the taffrail.

As we stood and looked something wavered up out of the heart of the weed— a long, tapering, sinuous thing, that curled and wavered against the dawn-light, and presently sank back again into the demure weed—a veritable spider of the deep, waiting in the great web that Dame Nature had spun for it in the eddy of her tides and currents.

And we sailed away northwards, with strengthening "trades," and left that patch of monstrousness to the loneliness of the sea.

A Greyport Legend

by Bret Harte

They ran through the streets of the seaport town,
They peered from the decks of the ships that lay;
The cold seafog that came whitening down
Was never as cold or white as they.
    "Ho, Starbuck and Pinckney and Tenterden!
     Run for your shallops, gather your men,
      Scatter your boats on the lower bay."

Good cause for fear! In the thick midday
The hulk that lay by the rotting pier,
Filled with the children in happy play,
Parted its moorings and drifted clear,
    Drifted clear beyond reach or call,—
    Thirteen children they were in all,—
     All adrift in the lower bay!

Said a hardfaced skipper, "God help us all!
She will not float till the turning tide!"
Said his wife, "My darling will hear my call,
Whether in sea or heaven she bide;"
 And she lifted a quavering voice and high,
 Wild and strange as a seabird's cry,
  Till they shuddered and wondered at her side.

The fog drove down on each laboring crew,
Veiled each from each and the sky and shore;
There was not a sound but the breath they drew,
And the lap of water and creak of oar;
 And they felt the breath of the downs, fresh blown
 O'er leagues of clover and cold gray stone,
  But not from the lips that had gone before.

They came no more. But they tell the tale
That, when fogs are thick on the harbor reef,
The mackerel fishers shorten sail
For the signal they know will bring relief;
 For the voices of children, still at play
 In a phantom hulk that drifts alway
  Through channels whose waters never fail.

It is but a foolish Shipman's tale,
A theme for a poet's idle page;
But still, when the mists of Doubt prevail,
And we lie becalmed by the shores of Age,
 We hear from the misty troubled shore
 The voice of the children gone before,
  Drawing the soul to its anchorage.

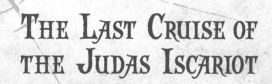

The Last Cruise of the Judas Iscariot

by Edward Page Mitchell

"**S**he formerly showed the name *Flying Sprite* on her starn moldin'," said Captain Trumbull Cram. "but I had thet gouged out and planed off, and *Judas Iscariot* in gilt sot thar instid."

"That was an extraordinary name," said I.

"'Strornary craft," replied the captain, as he absorbed another inch and a half of chewing tobacco. "I'm neither a profane man or an irreverend; but sink my jig if I don't believe the sperrit of Judas possessed thet schooner. Hey, Ammi?"

The young man addressed as Ammi was seated upon a mackerel barrel. He deliberately removed from his lips a black brierwood and shook his head with great gravity.

"The cap'n," said Ammi, "is neither a profane or an irreverend. What he says he mostly knows; but when he sinks his jig he's allers to be depended on."

Fortified with this neighborly estimate of character, Captain Cram proceeded. "You larf at the idea of a schooner's soul? Perhaps you hev sailed 'em forty-odd year up and down this here coast, an' 'quainted yourself with their dispositions an' habits of mind. Hey, Ammi?"

"The cap'n," explained the gentleman on the mackerel keg, "hez coasted an' hez fished for forty-six year. He's lumbered and he's iced. When the cap'n sees fit for to talk about schooners he understands the subjeck."

"My friend," said the captain, "a schooner has a soul like a human being, but considerably broader of beam, whether for good or for evil. I ain't a goin' to deny thet I prayed for the *Judas* in Tuesday 'n' Thursday evenin' meetin', week arter week an' month arter month. I ain't a goin' to deny thet I interested Deacon Plympton in the 'rastle for her redemption. It was no use, my friend; even the deacon's powerful p'titions were clear waste."

I ventured to inquire in what manner this vessel had manifested its depravity. The narrative which I heard was the story of a demon of treachery with three masts and a jib boom.

The *Flying Sprite* was the first three-master ever built at Newaggen, and the last. People shook their heads over the experiment. "No good can come of sech a critter," they said. "It's contrairy to natur. Two masts is masts enough." The *Flying Sprite* began its career of base improbity at the very moment of its birth. Instead of launching decently into the element for which it was designed, the three-masted schooner slumped through the ways into the mud and stuck there for three weeks, causing great expense to the owners, of whom Captain Trumbull Cram was one to the extent of an undivided third. The oracles of Newaggen were confirmed in their forebodings. "Two masts is masts enough to sail the sea," they said; "the third is the Devil's hitchin' post."

On the first voyage of the *Flying Sprite*, Captain Cram started her for Philadelphia, loaded with ice belonging to himself and Lawyer Swanton; cargo uninsured. Ice was worth six dollars a ton in Philadelphia; this particular ice had cost Captain Cram and Lawyer Swanton eighty-five cents a ton shipped, including sawdust. They were happy over the prospect. The *Flying Sprite* cleared the port in beautiful shape, and then suddenly and silently went to the bottom in Fiddler's Reach, in eleven feet of salt water. It required only six days to float her and pump her out, but owing to a certain incompatibility between ice and salt water, the salvage consisted exclusively of sawdust.

On her next trip the schooner carried a deckload of lumber from the St. Croix River. It was in some sense a consecrated cargo, for the lumber was intended for a new Baptist meeting-house in southern New Jersey. If the prayerful hopes of the navigators, combined with the prayerful expectations of the consignees had availed, this voyage, at least, would have been successfully made. But about sixty miles southeast of Nantucket the *Flying Sprite* encountered a mild September gale. She ought to have weathered it with perfect ease, but she behaved so abominably that the church timber was scattered over the surface of the Atlantic Ocean from about latitude 40° 15′ to about latitude 43° 50′. A month or two later she contrived to go on her beam ends under a gentle land breeze, dumping a lot of expensively carved granite from the Fox Island quarries into a deep hole in Long Island Sound. On the very next trip she turned deliberately out of her course in order to smash into the starboard bow of a Norwegian brig, and was consequently libeled for heavy damages.

It was after a few experiences of this sort that Captain Cram erased the old name from the schooner's stern and from her quarter, and substituted that of *Judas Iscariot*. He could discover no designation that expressed so well his contemptuous opinion of her moral qualities. She seemed animate with the spirit of purposeless malice, of malignant perfidy. She was a floating tub of cussedness.

A board of nautical experts sat upon the *Judas Iscariot*, but could find nothing the matter with her, physically. The lines of her hull were all right, she was properly planked and ceiled and calked, her spars were of good Oregon pine, she was rigged taut and trustworthy, and her canvas had been cut and stitched by a God-fearing sailmaker. According to all theory, she ought to have been perfectly responsible as to her keel. In practice, she was frightfully cranky. Sailing the *Judas Iscariot* was like driving a horse with more vices than hairs in his tail. She always did the unexpected thing, except when bad behavior was expected of her on general principles. If the idea was to luff, she would invariably fall off; if to jibe, she would come round dead in the wind and hang there like Mohammed's coffin. Sending a man to haul the jib sheet to windward was sending a man on a forlorn hope: the jib habitually picked up the venturesome navigator, and, after shaking him viciously in the air for a second or two, tossed him overboard. A boom never crossed the deck without breaking somebody's head. Start on whatever course she might, the schooner was certain to run before long into one of three things, namely, some other vessel, a fog bank, or the bottom. From the day on which she was launched her scent for a good, sticky mud bottom was unerring. In the clearest weather fog followed and enveloped her as misfortune follows wickedness. Her presence on the Banks was enough to drive every codfish to the coast of Ireland. The mackerel and porgies were always where the *Judas Iscariot* was not. It was impossible to circumvent the schooner's fixed purposes to ruin everybody who chartered her. If chartered to carry a deckload, she spilled it; if loaded between decks, she dived and spoiled the cargo. She was like one of the trick mules which, if they cannot otherwise dislodge the rider, get down and roll over and over. In short, the *Judas Iscariot* was known from Marblehead to the Bay of Chaleur as the consummate schooneration of malevolence, turpitude, and treachery.

After commanding the *Judas Iscariot* for five or six years, Captain Cram looked fully twenty years older. It was in vain that he had attempted to sell her at a sacrifice. No man on the coast of Maine, Massachusetts, or the British provinces would have taken the schooner as a gift. The belief in her demoniac obsession was as firm as it was universal.

Nearly at the end of a season, when the wretched craft had been even more unprofitable than usual a conference of the owners was held in the Congregational vestry one evening after the monthly missionary meeting. No outsider knows exactly what happened, but it is rumored that in the two hours during which these capital-ists were closeted certain arithmetical computations were effected which led to significant results and to a singular decision.

On the forenoon of the next Friday there was a general suspension of business at Newaggen. The *Judas Iscariot*, with her deck scoured and her spars scraped till they shone in the sun like yellow amber, lay at the wharf by Captain Cram's fish house. Since Monday the captain and his three boys and Andrew Jackson's son Tobias from Mackerel Cove had been busy loading the schooner deep. This time her cargo was an extraordinary one. It consisted of nearly a quarter of a mile of stone wall from the boundaries of the captain's shore pasture. "I calklet," remarked the commander of the *Judas Iscariot*, as he saw the last boulder disappearing down the main hatch, "thar's nigh two hundud'n fifty ton of stone fence aboard thet schoon'r."

Conjecture was wasted over this unnecessary amount of ballast. The owners of the *Judas Iscariot* stood up well under the consolidated wit of the village; they returned witticism for witticism, and kept their secret. "Ef you must know, I'll tell ye," said the captain. "I hear thar's a stone-wall famine over Machias way. I'm goin' to take mine over'n peddle it out by the yard." On this fine sunshiny Friday morning, while the luckless schooner lay on one side of the wharf, looking as bright and trim and prosperous as if she were the best-paying maritime investment in the world, the tug *Pug* of Portland lay under the other side, with steam up. She had come down the night before in response to a telegram from the owners of the *Judas Iscariot*. A good land breeze was blowing, with the promise of freshening as the day grew older.

At half past seven o'clock the schooner put off from the landing, carrying not only the captain's pasture wall, but also a large number of his neighbors and friends, including some of the solidest citizens of Newaggen. Curiosity was stronger than fear. "You know what the critter," the captain had said, in reply to numerous applications for passage. "Ef you're a mind to resk her antics, come along, an' welcome." Captain Cram put on a white shirt and a holiday suit for the occasion. As he stood at the wheel shouting directions to his boys and Andrew Jackson's son Tobias at the halyards, his guests gathered around him—a fair representation of the respectability, the business enterprise, and the piety of Newaggen Harbor. Never had the *Judas Iscariot* carried such a load. She seemed suddenly struck with a sense of decency and responsibility, for she came around into the wind without balking, dived her nose playfully into the brine, and skipped off on the short hitch to clear Tumbler Island, all in the properest fashion. The *Pug* steamed after her.

The crowd on the wharf and the boys in the small boats cheered this unexpectedly orthodox behavior, and they now saw for the first time that Captain Cram had painted on the side of the vessel in conspicuous white letters, each three or four feet long, the following legend:

THIS IS THE SCHOONER *JUDAS ISCARIOT* N.B.—GIVE HER A WIDE BERTH!!!

Hour after hour the schooner bounded along before the northwest wind, holding to her course as straight as an arrow. The weather continued fine. Every time the captain threw the log he looked more perplexed. Eight, nine, nine and a half knots! He shook his head as he whispered to Deacon Plympton: "She's meditatin' mischief o' some natur or other." But the *Judas* led the *Pug* a wonderful chase, and by half past two in the afternoon, before the demijohn which Andrew Jackson's son Tobias had smuggled on board was three quarters empty, and before Lawyer Swanton had more than three quarters finished his celebrated story about Governor Purington's cork leg, the schooner and the tug were between fifty and sixty miles from land.

Suddenly Captain Cram gave a grunt of intelligence. He pointed ahead, where a blue line just above the horizon marked a distant fog bank. "She smelt it an' she run for it," he remarked, sententiously. "Time for business."

Then ensued a singular ceremony. First Captain Cram brought the schooner to, and transferred all his passengers to the tug. The wind had shifted to the southeast, and the fog was rapidly approaching. The sails of the *Judas Iscariot* flapped as she lay head to the wind; her bows rose and fell gently under the influence of the long swell. The Pug bobbed up and down half a hawser's length away.

Having put his guests and crew aboard the tug, Captain Cram proceeded to make everything shipshape on the decks of the schooner. He neatly coiled a loose end of rope that had been left in a snarl. He even picked up and threw overboard the stopper of Andrew Jackson's son Tobias' demijohn. His face wore an expression of unusual solemnity. The people on the tug watched his movements eagerly, but silently. Next he tied one end of a short rope to the wheel and attached the other end loosely by means of a running bowline to a cleat upon the rail. Then he was seen to take up an ax, and to disappear down the companionway. Those on the tug distinctly heard several crashing blows. In a moment the captain reappeared on deck, walked deliberately to the wheel, brought the schooner around so that her sails filled, pulled the running bowline taut, and fastened the rope with several half hitches around the cleat, thus lashing the helm, jumped into a dory, and sculled over to the tug.

Left entirely to herself, the schooner rolled once or twice, tossed a few bucketfuls of water over her dancing bows, and started off toward the South Atlantic. But Captain Trumbull Cram, standing in the bow of the tugboat, raised his hand to command silence and pronounced the following farewell speech, being sentence, death warrant, and funeral oration, all in one:

"I ain't advancin' no theory to 'count for her cussedness. You all know the *Judas*. Mebbe thar was too much fore an' aff to her. Mebbe the inickerty of a vessel's in the fore an' aff, and the vartue in the squar' riggin'. Mebbe two masts *was* masts enough. Let that go; bygones is bygones. Yonder she goes, carryin' all sail on top, two hundred'n-odd ton o' stone fence in her bolt, an' a hole good two foot acrost stove in her belly. The way of the transgressor is hard. Don't you see her settlin'? It should be a lesson, my friends, for us to profit by; there's an end to the long-sufferin'est mercy, and unless—Oh, yer makin' straight for the fog, are ye? Well, it's your last fog bank. The bottom of the sea's the fust port you'll fetch, you critter, you! Git, and be damned to ye!"

This, the only occasion on which Captain Cram was ever known to say such a word, was afterward considered by a committee of discipline of the Congregational Church at Newaggen; and the committee, after pondering all the circumstances under which the word was uttered, voted unanimously to take no action.

Meanwhile, the fog had shut in around the tug, and the *Judas Iscariot* was lost to view. The tug was put about and headed for home. The damp wind chilled everybody through and through. Little was said. The contents of the demijohn had long been exhausted. From a distance to the south was heard at intervals the hoarse whistling of an ocean steamer.

"I hope that feller's well underwrit," said the captain grimly, "for the *Judas*'ll never go down afore she's sarched him out'n sunk him."

"And was the abandoned schooner ever heard of?" I asked, when my informant had reached this point in the narrative.

The captain took me by the arm and led me out of the grocery store down to the rocks. Across the mouth of the small cove back of his house, blocking the entrance to his wharf and fishhouse, was stretched a skeleton wreck.

"Thar she lays," he said, pointing to the blackened ribs. "That's the *Judas*. Did yer suppose she'd sink in deep water, where she could do no more damage? No, sir, not if all the rocks on the coast of Maine was piled onto her, and her hull bottom knocked clean out. She come home to roost. She come sixty mile in the teeth of the wind. When the tug got back next mornin' thar lay the *Judas Iscariot* acrost my cove, with her jib boom stuck though my kitchen winder. I say schooners has souls."

The Demon Frigate

An excerpt from Rokeby

by Sir Walter Scott

This is an allusion to a well-known nautical superstition concerning a fantastic vessel, called by sailors the Flying Dutchman, *and supposed to be seen about the latitude of the Cape of Good Hope. She is distinguished from earthly vessels by bearing a press of sail when all others are unable, from stress of weather, to show an inch of canvas. The cause of her wandering is not altogether certain; but the general account is, that she was originally a vessel loaded with great wealth, on board of which some horrid act of murder and piracy had been committed; that the plague broke out among the wicked crew who had perpetrated the crime, and that they sailed in vain from port to port; offering, as the price of shelter, the whole of their ill-gotten wealth; that they were excluded from every harbour, for fear of the contagion which was devouring them; and that, as a punishment of their crimes, the apparition of the ship still continues to haunt those seas in which the catastrophe took place, and is considered by the mariners as the worst of all possible omens.*

—Author

Bertram had listed many a tale
Of wonder in his native dale,
That in his secret soul retain'd
The credence they in childhood gain'd;
Nor less his wild adventurous youth
Believed in every legend's truth;
Learn'd when, beneath the tropic gale,
Full swell'd the vessel's steady sail,
And the broad Indian moon her light
Pour'd on the watch of middle night,
When seamen love to hear and tell
Of portent, prodigy, and spell;
What gales are sold on Lapland's shore,
How whistle rash bids tempests roar,
Of witch, of mermaid, and of sprite,
Of Erick's cap and Elmo s light;
Or of that Phantom Ship, whose form
Shoots like a meteor through the storm;
When the dark scud comes driving hard,
And lower'd is every topsail-yard,
And canvas, wove in earthly looms,
No more to brave the storm presumes!
Then, 'mid the war of sea and sky,
Top and top-gallant hoisted high,
Full spread and crowded every sail,
The Demon Frigate braves the gale;
And well the doom'd spectators know
The harbinger of wreck and woe.

Christmas Eve on a Haunted Hulk

by Frank Cowper

I shall never forget that night as long as I live.

It was during the Christmas vacation 187_. I was staying with an old college friend who had lately been appointed the curate of a country parish, and had asked me to come and cheer him up, since he could not get away at that time.

As we drove along the straight country lane from the little wayside station, it forcibly struck me that a life in such a place must be dreary indeed. I have always been much influenced by local colour; above all things, I am depressed by a dead level, and here was monotony with a vengeance. On each side of the low hedges, lichen-covered and wind-cropped, stretched bare fields, the absolute level of the horizon being only broken at intervals by some mournful tree that pointed like a decrepit finger-post towards the east, for all its western growth was nipped and blasted by the roaring south-west winds. An occasional black spot, dotted against the grey distance, marked a hay-rick or labourer's cottage, while some two miles ahead of us the stunted spire of my friend's church stood out against the wintry sky, amid the withered branches of a few ragged trees. On our right hand stretched dreary wastes of mud, interspersed here and there with firmer patches of land, but desolate and forlorn, cut off from all communication with the mainland by acres of mud and thin streaks of brown water.

A few sea-birds were piping over the waste, and this was the only sound, except the grit of our own wheels and the steady step of the horse, which broke the silence.

"Not lively is it?" said Jones; and I couldn't say it was. As we drove "up street," as the inhabitants fondly called the small array of low houses which bordered the highroad, I noticed the lack-lustre expression of the few children and untidy women who were loitering about the doors of their houses.

There was an old tumble-down inn, with a dilapidated sign-board, scarcely held up by its rickety ironwork. A daub of yellow and red paint, with a dingy streak of blue, was supposed to represent the Duke's head, although what exalted member of the aristocracy was thus distinguished it would be hard to say. Jones inclined to think it was the Duke of Wellington; but I upheld the theory that it was the Duke of Marlborough, chiefly basing my arguments on the fact that no artist who desired to convey a striking likeness would fail to show the Great Duke in profile, whereas this personage was evidently depicted full face, and wearing a three-cornered hat.

At the end of the village was the church, standing in an untidy churchyard, and opposite it was a neat little house, quite new, and of that utilitarian order of architecture which will stamp the Victorian age as one of the least imaginative of eras. Two windows flanked the front door, and three narrow windows looked out overhead from under a slate roof; variety and distinction being given to the facade by the brilliant blending of the yellow bricks with red, so bright as to suggest the idea of their having been painted. A scrupulously clean stone at the front door, together with the bright green of the little palings and woodwork, told me what sort of landlady to expect, and I was not disappointed. A kindly featured woman, thin, cheery, and active, received us, speaking in that encouraging tone of half-compassionate, half-proprietary patronage, which I have observed so many women adopt towards lone beings of the opposite sex.

"You will find it precious dull, old man," said Jones, as we were eating our frugal dinner. "There's nothing for you to do, unless you care to try a shot at the duck over the mud-flats. I shall be busy on and off nearly all to-morrow."

As we talked, I could not help admiring the cheerful pluck with which Jones endured the terrible monotony of his life in this dreary place. His rector was said to be delicate, and in order to prolong a life, which no doubt he considered valuable to the Church, he lived with his family either at Torquay or Cannes in elegant idleness, quite unable to do any duty, but fully equal to enjoying the pleasant society of those charming places, and quite satisfied that he had done his duty when he sacrificed a tenth of his income to provide for the spiritual needs of his parish. There was no squire in the place; no "gentlefolk," as the rustics called them, lived nearer than five miles; and there was not a single being of his own class with whom poor Jones could associate. And yet he made no complaint. The nearest approach to one being the remark that the worst of it was, it was so difficult, if not impossible, to be really understood. "The poor being so suspicious and ignorant, they look at everything from such a low standpoint, enthusiasm and freshness sink so easily into formalism and listlessness."

The next day, finding that I really could be of no use, and feeling awkward and bored, as a man always is when another is actively doing his duty, I went off to the marshes to see if I could get any sport.

I took some sandwiches and a flask with me, not intending to return until dinner. After wandering about for some time, crossing dyke after dyke by treacherous rails more or less rotten, I found myself on the edge of a wide mere. I could see some duck out in the middle, and standing far out in the shallow water was a heron. They were all out of shot, and I saw I should do no good without a duck-punt.

I sat down on an old pile left on the top of the sea-wall, which had been lately repaired. The duck looked very tempting; but I doubted if I should do much good in broad daylight, even if I had a duckpunt, without a duck-gun. After sitting disconsolately for some time, I got up and wandered on.

The dreariness of the scene was most depressing: everything was brown and grey. Nothing broke the monotony of the wide-stretching mere; the whole scene gave me the impression of a straight line of interminable length, with a speck in the centre of it. That speck was myself.

At last, as I turned an angle in the sea-wall, I saw something lying above high-water mark, which looked like a boat.

Rejoiced to see any signs of humanity, I quickened my pace. It was a boat, and, better still, a duckpunt. As I came nearer I could see that she was old and very likely leaky; but here was a prospect of adventure, and I was not going to be readily daunted. On examination, the old craft seemed more water-tight than I expected. At least she held water very well, and if she kept it in, she must equally well keep it out. I turned her over to run the water out, and then dragging the crazy old boat over the line of seaweed, launched her. But now a real difficulty met me. The paddles were nowhere to be seen. They had doubtless been taken away by the owner, and it would be little use searching for them. But a stout stick would do to punt her over the shallow water; and after some little search. I found an old stake which would answer well.

This was real luck. I had now some hope of bagging a few duck; at any rate, I was afloat, and could explore the little islets, which barely rose above the brown water. I might at least find some rabbits on them. I cautiously poled myself towards the black dots; but before I came within range, up rose first one, then another and another, like a string of beads, and the whole flight went, with outstretched necks and rapidly beating wings, away to my right, and seemed to pitch again beyond a low island some half-mile away. The heron had long ago taken himself off; so there was nothing to be done but pole across the mud in pursuit of the duck. I had not gone many yards when I found that I was going much faster than I expected, and soon saw the cause. The tide was falling, and I was being carried along with it. This would bring me nearer to my ducks, and I lazily guided the punt with the stake.

On rounding the island I found a new source of interest. The mere opened out to a much larger extent, and away towards my right I could see a break in the low land, as if a wide ditch had been cut through; while in this opening ever and anon dark objects rose up and disappeared again in a way I could not account for. The water seemed to be running off the mud-flats, and I saw that if I did not wish to be left high, but not dry, on the long slimy wastes, I must be careful to keep in the little channels or "lakes," which acted as natural drains to the acres of greasy mud.

A conspicuous object attracted my attention some mile or more towards the opening in the land. It was a vessel lying high up on the mud, and looking as if she was abandoned.

The ducks had pitched a hundred yards or so beyond the island, and I approached as cautiously as I could; but just as I was putting down the stake to take up my gun, there was a swift sound of beating wings and splashing water, and away my birds flew, low over the mud, towards the old hulk.

Here was a chance, I thought. If I could get on board and remain hidden, I might, by patiently waiting, get a shot. I looked at my watch; there was still plenty of daylight left, and the tide was only just beginning to leave the mud. I punted away, therefore, with renewed hope, and was not long in getting up to the old ship.

There was just sufficient water over the mud to allow me to approach within ten or twelve feet, but further I could not push the punt. This was disappointing; however, I noticed a deep lake ran round the other side, and determined to try my luck there. So with a slosh and a heave I got the flat afloat again, and made for the deeper water. It turned out quite successful, and I was enabled to get right under the square overhanging counter, while a little lane of water led alongside her starboard quarter. I pushed the nose of the punt into this, and was not long in clambering on board by the rusty irons of her fore-chains.

The old vessel lay nearly upright in the soft mud, and a glance soon told she would never be used again. Her gear and rigging were, all rotten, and everything valuable had been removed. She was a brig of some two hundred tons, and had been a fine vessel, no doubt. To me there is always a world of romance in a deserted ship. The places she has been to, the scenes she has witnessed, the possibilities of crime, of adventure—all these thoughts crowd upon me when I see an old hulk lying deserted and forgotten—left to rot upon the mud of some lonely creek.

In order to keep my punt afloat as long as possible, I towed her round and moored her under the stern, and then looked over the bulwarks for the duck. There they were, swimming not more than a hundred and fifty yards away, and they were coming towards me. I remained perfectly concealed under the high bulwark, and could see them paddling and feeding in the greasy weed. Their approach was slow, but I could afford to wait. Nearer and nearer they came; another minute, and they would be well within shot. I was already congratulating myself upon the success of my adventure, and thinking of the joy of Jones at this large accession to his larder, when suddenly there was a heavy splash, and with a wild spluttering rush the whole pack rose out of the water, and went skimming over the mud towards the distant sea. I let off both barrels after them, and tried to console myself by thinking that I saw the feathers fly from one; but not a bird dropped, and I was left alone in my chagrin.

What could have caused the splash, that luckless splash, I wondered. There was surely no one else on board the ship, and certainly no one could get out here without mud-pattens or a boat. I looked round. All was perfectly still Nothing broke the monotony of the grey scene—sodden and damp and lifeless. A chill breeze came up from the southwest, bringing with it a raw mist, which was blotting out the dark distance, and fast limiting my horizon. The day was drawing in, and I must be thinking of going home. As I turned round, my attention was arrested by seeing a duck-punt glide past me in the now rapidly falling water, which was swirling by the mud-bank on which the vessel lay. But there was no one in her. A dreadful thought struck me. It must be my boat, and how shall I get home? I ran to the stern and looked over. The duck-punt was gone.

The frayed and stranded end of the painter told me how it had happened. I had not allowed for the fall of the tide, and the strain of the punt, as the water fell away, had snapped the line, old and rotten as it was.

I hurried to the bows, and jumping on to the bitts, saw my punt peacefully drifting away, some quarter of a mile off. It was perfectly evident I could not hope to get her again.

It was beginning to rain steadily. I could see that I was in for dirty weather, and became a little anxious about how I was to get back, especially as it was now rapidly growing dark. So thick was it that I could not see the low land anywhere, and could only judge of its position by remembering that the stern of the vessel pointed that way.

The conviction grew upon me that I could not possibly get away from this doleful old hulk without assistance, and how to get it, I could not for the life of me see. I had not seen a sign of a human being the whole day. It was not likely any more would be about at night. However, I shouted as loud as I could, and then waited to hear if there were any response. There was not a sound, only the wind moaned slightly through the stumps of the masts, and something creaked in the cabin.

Well, I thought, at least it might be worse. I shall have shelter for the night; while had I been left on one of these islands, I should have had to spend the night exposed to the pelting rain. Happy thought! Go below before it gets too dark, and see what sort of a berth can be got, if the worst comes to the worst. So thinking, I went to the booby-hatch, and found as I expected that it was half broken open, and anyone could go below who liked.

As I stepped down the rotting companion, the air smelt foul and dank. I went below very cautiously, for I was not at all sure that the boards would bear me. It was fortunate I did so, for as I stepped off the lowest step the floor gave way under my foot, and had I not been holding on to the stair-rail, I should have fallen through. Before going any further, I took a look round.

The prospect was not inviting. The light was dim; I could scarcely make out objects near me, all else was obscurity. I could see that the whole of the inside of the vessel was completely gutted. What little light there was came through the stern ports. A small round speck of light looked at me out of the darkness ahead, and I could see that the flooring had either all given way or been taken out of her. At my feet a gleam of water showed me what to expect if I should slip through the floor-joists. Altogether, a more desolate, gloomy, ghostly place it would be difficult to find.

I could not see any bunk or locker where I could sit down, and everything movable had been taken out of the hulk. Groping my way with increasing caution, I stepped across the joists, and felt along the side of the cabin. I soon came to a bulkhead. Continuing to grope, I came to an opening. If the cabin was dim, here was blackness itself. I felt it would be useless to attempt to go further, especially as a very damp foul odour came up from the bilgewater in her hold. As I stood looking into the darkness, a creepy, chilly shudder passed over me, and with a shiver I turned round to look at the cabin. My eyes had now become used to the gloom. A deeper patch of darkness on my right suggested the possibility of a berth, and groping my way over to it, I found the lower bunk was still entire. Here at least I could rest, if I found it impossible to get to shore. Having some wax vestas in my pocket, I struck a light and examined the bunk. It was better than I expected. If I could only find something to burn, I should be comparatively cheerful.

Before reconciling myself to my uncomfortable position, I resolved to see whether I could not get to the shore, and went up the rickety stairs again. It was raining hard, and the wind had got up. Nothing could be more dismal. I looked over the side and lowered myself down from the main-chains, to see if it were possible to walk over the mud. I found I could not reach the mud at all; and fearful of being unable to climb back if I let go, I clambered up the side again and got on board.

It was quite clear I must pass the night here. Before going below I once more shouted at the top of my voice, more to keep up my own spirits than with any hope of being heard, and then paused to listen. Not a sound of any sort replied. I now prepared to make myself as comfortable as I could.

It was a dreary prospect. I would rather have spent the night on deck than down below in that foul cabin; but the drenching driving rain, as well as the cold, drove me to seek shelter below. It seemed so absurd to be in the position of a shipwrecked sailor, within two or three miles of a prosy country hamlet, and in a landlocked harbour while actually on land, if the slimy deep mud could be called land. I had not many matches left, but I had my gun and cartridges. The idea occurred to me to fire off minute-guns. "That's what I ought to do, of course. The red flash will be seen in this dark night," for it was dark now and no mistake. Getting up on to the highest part of the vessel, I blazed away. The noise sounded to me deafening; surely the whole countryside would be aroused. After firing off a dozen cartridges, I waited. But the silence only seemed the more oppressive, and the blackness all the darker. "It's no good; I'll turn in," I thought, dejectedly.

With great difficulty I groped my way to the top of the companion-ladder, and bumped dismally down the steps. If only I had a light I should be fairly comfortable, I thought. "Happy thought, make a 'spit-devil!' " as we used when boys to call a little cone of damp gunpowder.

I got out my last two cartridges, and emptying the powder carefully into my hand, I moistened it, and worked it up to a paste. I then placed it on the smooth end of the rail, and lighted it. This was brilliant: at least so it seemed by contrast with the absolute blackness around me. By its light I was able to find my way to the bunk, and it lasted just long enough for me to arrange myself fairly comfortably for the night. By contriving a succession of matches, I was enabled to have enough light to see to eat my frugal supper; for I had kept a little sherry and a few sandwiches to meet emergencies, and it was a fortunate thing I had. The light and the food made me feel more cheery, and by the time the last match had gone out, I felt worse might have happened to me by a long way.

As I lay still, waiting for sleep to come, the absurdity of the situation forced itself upon me. Here was I, to all intents and purposes as much cut off from all communication with the rest of the world as if I were cast away upon a desert island. The chances were that I should make some one see or hear me the next day. Jones would be certain to have the country searched, and at the longest I should only endure the discomfort of one night, and get well laughed at for my pains; but meanwhile I was absolutely severed from all human contact, and was as isolated as Robinson Crusoe, only "more so," for I had no other living thing whatever to share my solitude. The silence of the place was perfect; and if silence can woo sleep, sleep ought very soon to have come. But when one is hungry and wet, and in a strange uncanny kind of place, besides being in one's clothes, it is a very difficult thing to go to sleep. First, my head was too low; then, after resting it on my arms, I got cramp in them. My back seemed all over bumps; when I turned on my side, I appeared to have got a rather serious enlargement of the hipjoint; and I found my damp clothes smell very musty. After sighing and groaning for some time, I sat up for change of position, and nearly fractured my skull in so doing, against the remains of what had once been a berth above me. I didn't dare to move in the inky blackness, for I had seen sufficient to know that I might very easily break my leg or my neck in the floorless cabin.

There was nothing for it but to sit still, or lie down and wait for daylight. I had no means of telling the time. When I had last looked at my watch, before the last match had gone out, it was not more than six o'clock; it might be now about eight, or perhaps not so late. Fancy twelve long hours spent in that doleful black place, with nothing in the world to do to pass away the time! I *must* go to sleep; and so, full of this resolve, I lay down again.

I suppose I went to sleep. All I can recollect, after lying down, is keeping my mind resolutely turned inwards, as it were, and fixed upon the arduous business of counting an imaginary and interminable flock of sheep pass one by one through an ideal gate. This meritorious method of compelling sleep had, no doubt, been rewarded; but I have no means of knowing how long I slept, and I cannot tell at what hour of the night the following strange circumstances occurred—for occur they certainly did—and I am as perfectly convinced that I was the oral witness to some ghastly crime, as I am that I am writing these lines. I have little doubt I shall be laughed at, as Jones laughed at me—be told that I was dreaming, that I was overtired and nervous. In fact, so accustomed have I become to this sort of thing, that I now hardly ever tell my tale; or, if I do, I put it in the third person, and then I find people believe it, or at least take much more interest in it. I suppose the reason is, that people cannot bring themselves to think so strange a thing could have happened to such a prosy everyday sort of man as myself, and they cannot divest their minds of the idea that I am—well, to put it mildly—"drawing on my imagination for facts." Perhaps, if the tale appears in print, it will be believed, as a facetious friend of mine once said to a newly married couple, who had just seen the announcement of their marriage in the Times, "Ah, didn't know you were married till you saw it in print!"

Well, be the time what it may have been, all I know is that the next thing I can remember after getting my five-hundredth sheep through the gate is, that I heard two most horrible yells ring through the darkness. I sat bolt-upright; and as a proof that my senses were "all there," I did not bring my head this time against the berth overhead, remembering to bend it outwards so as to clear it.

There was not another sound. The silence was as absolute as the darkness. "I must have been dreaming," I thought; but the sounds were ringing in my ears, and my heart was beating with excitement. There must have been some reason for this. I never was "taken this way" before. I could not make it out, and felt very uncomfortable. I sat there listening for some time. No other sound breaking the deathly stillness, and becoming tired of sitting, I lay down again. Once more I set myself to get my interminable flocks through that gate, but I could not help myself listening.

There seemed to me a sound growing in the darkness, a something gathering in the particles of the air, as if molecules of the atmosphere were rustling together, and with stilly movement were whispering something. The wind had died down, and I would have gone on deck if I could move; but it was hazardous enough moving about in the light: it would have been madness to attempt to move in that blackness. And so I lay still and tried to sleep.

But now there was a sound, indistinct, but no mere fancy; a muffled sound, as of some movement in the forepart of the ship.

I listened intently and gazed into the darkness.

What was the sound? It did not seem like rats. It was a dull, shuffling kind of noise, very indistinct, and conveying no clue whatever as to its cause. It lasted only for a short time. But now the cold damp air seemed to have become more piercingly chilly. The raw iciness seemed to strike into the very marrow of my bones, and my teeth chattered. At the same time a new sense seemed to be assailed: the foul odour which I had noticed arising from the stagnant water in the bilge appeared to rise into more objectionable prominence, as if it had been stirred.

"I cannot stand this," I muttered, shivering in horrible aversion at the disgusting odour; "I will go on deck at all hazards."

Rising to put this resolve in execution, I was arrested by the noise beginning again. I listened. This time I distinctly distinguished two separate sounds: one, like a heavy soft weight being dragged along with difficulty; the other like the hard sound of boots on boards. Could there be others on board after all? If so, why had they made no sound when I clambered on deck, or afterwards, when I shouted and fired my gun?

Clearly, if there were people, they wished to remain concealed, and my presence was inconvenient to them. But how absolutely still and quiet they had kept! It appeared incredible that there should be anyone. I listened intently. The sound had ceased again, and once more the most absolute stillness reigned around. A gentle swishing, wobbling, lapping noise seemed to form itself in the darkness. It increased, until I recognised the chattering and bubbling of water. "It must be the tide which is rising," I thought; "it has reached the rudder, and is eddying round the stern-post." This also accounted, in my mind, for the other noises, because, as the tide surrounded the vessel, and she thus became water-borne, all kinds of sounds might be produced in the old hulk as she resumed her upright position.

However, I could not get rid of the chilly horrid feeling those two screams had produced, combined with the disgusting smell, which was getting more and more obtrusive. It was foul, horrible, revolting, like some carrion, putrid and noxious. I prepared to take my chances of damage, and rose up to grope my way to the companion-ladder.

It was a more difficult job than I had any idea of. I had my gun, it was true, and with it I could feel for the joists; but when once I let go of the edge of the bunk I had nothing to steady me, and nearly went headlong at the first step. Fortunately I reached back in time to prevent my fall; but this attempt convinced me that I had better endure the strange horrors of the unknown, than the certain miseries of a broken leg or neck.

I sat down, therefore, on the bunk.

Now that my own movements had ceased, I became aware that the shuffling noise was going on all the time. "Well," thought I, "they may shuffle. They won't hurt me, and I shall go to sleep again." So reflecting, I lay down, holding my gun, ready to use as a club if necessary.

Now it is all very well to laugh at superstitious terrors. Nothing is easier than to obtain a cheap reputation for brilliancy, independence of thought, and courage, by deriding the fear of the supernatural when comfortably seated in a drawing-room well lighted, and with company. But put those scoffers in a like situation with mine, and I don't believe they would have been any more free from a feeling the reverse of bold, mocking, and comfortable, than I was.

I had read that most powerful ghost-story, "The Haunted and the Haunters," by the late Lord Lytton, and the vividness of that weird tale had always impressed me greatly. Was I actually now to experience in my own person, and with no possibility of escape, the trying ordeal that bold ghost-hunter went through, under much more favourable circumstances? He at least had his servant with him. He had fuel and a light, and above all, he could get away when he wanted to. I felt I could face any number of spiritual manifestations, if only I had warmth and light. But the icy coldness of the air was eating into my bones, and I shivered until my teeth chattered.

I could not get to sleep. I could not prevent myself listening, and at last I gave up the contest, and let myself listen. But there seemed now nothing to listen to. All the time I had been refusing to let my ears do their office, by putting my handkerchief over one ear, and lying on my arm with the other, a confused noise appeared to reach me, but the moment I turned round and lay on my back, everything seemed quiet. "It's only my fancy after all; the result of cold and want of a good dinner. I will go to sleep." But in spite of this I lay still, listening a little longer. There was the sound of trickling water against the broad bilge of the old hulk, and I knew the tide was rising fast: my thoughts turned to the lost canoe, and to reproaching myself with my stupidity in not allowing enough rope, or looking at it more carefully. Suddenly I became all attention again. An entirely different sound now arrested me. It was distinctly a low groan, and followed almost immediately by heavy blows—blows which fell on a soft substance, and then more groans, and again those sickening blows.

"There must be men here. Where are they? and what is it?" I sat up, and strained my eyes towards where the sound came from. The sounds had ceased again. Should I call out, and let the man or men know that I was here? What puzzled me was the absolute darkness. How could anyone see to hit an object; or do anything else in this dense obscurity? It appalled me. Anything might pass at an inch's distance, and I could not tell who or what it was. But how could anything human find its way about, any more than I could? Perhaps there was a solid bulkhead dividing the forecastle from me. But it would have to be very sound, and with no chink whatever, to prevent a gleam or ray of light finding its way out somewhere. I could not help feeling convinced that the whole hull was open from one end to the other. Was I really dreaming after all? To convince myself that I was wide awake, I felt in my pockets for my notebook, and pulling out my pencil, I opened the book, and holding it in my left hand, wrote as well as I could, by feel alone: "I am wide awake; it is about midnight—Christmas eve, 187_." I found I had got to the bottom of the page, so I shut the book up, resolving to look at it the next morning. I felt curious to see what the writing looked like by daylight.

But all further speculation was cut short by the shuffling and dragging noise beginning again. There was no doubt the sounds were louder, and were coming my way.

I never in all my life felt so uncomfortable—I may as well at once confess it— so frightened. There, in that empty hull, over that boardless floor, over these rotting joists, somebody or something was dragging some heavy weight. What, I could not imagine; only the shrieks, the blows, the groans, the dull thumping sounds, compelled me to suspect the worst;—to feel convinced that I was actually within some few feet of a horrible murder then being committed. I could form no idea of who the victim was, or who was the assassin. That I actually heard the sounds I had no doubt; that they were growing louder and more distinct I felt painfully aware. The horror of the situation was intense. If only I could strike a light, and see what was passing close there—but I had no matches. I could hear a sound as of some one breathing slowly, stertorously, then a dull groan. And once more the cruel sodden blows fell again, followed by a drip, drip, and heavy drop in the dank water below, from which the sickening smell rose, pungent, reeking, horrible.

The dragging shuffling noise now began again. It came quite close to me, so close that I felt I had only to put out my hand to touch, the thing. Good heavens! was it coming to my bunk? The thing passed, and all the time the dull drip, as of some heavy drops, fell into the water below. It was awful. All this time I was sitting up, and holding my gun by its barrel, ready to use it if I were attacked. As the sound passed me at the closest, I put out the gun involuntarily; but it touched nothing, and I shuddered at the thought that *there was no floor over which the weight could be drawn.*

I must be dreaming some terribly vivid dream. It could not be real I pinched myself. I felt I was pinching myself. It was no dream. The sweat poured off my brow, my teeth chattered with the cold. It was terrific in its dreadful mystery.

And now the sounds altered. The noises had reached the companion-ladder. Something was climbing them with difficulty. The old stairs creaked. Bump, thump, the *thing* was dragged up the steps with many pauses, and at last it seemed to have reached the deck. A long pause now followed. The silence grew dense around. I dreaded the stillness-the silence that made itself be heard almost more than the sounds. What new horror would that awful quiet bring forth? What terror was still brooding in the depths of that clinging darkness—darkness that could be felt?

The absolute silence was broken,—horribly broken,—by a dull drip from the stairs, and then the dragging began again. Distant and less distinct, but the steps were louder. They came nearer—over my head—the old boards creaked, and the weight was dragged right over me. I could hear it above my head: for the steps stopped, and two distinct raps, followed by a third heavier one, sounded so clearly above me, that it seemed almost as if it was something striking the rotten wood-work of the berth over my head. The sounds were horribly suggestive of the elbows and head of a body being dropped on the deck.

And now, as if the horrors had not been enough, a fresh ghastliness was added. So close were the raps above me that I involuntarily moved, as if I had been struck by what caused them. As I did so, I felt something drop on to my head and slowly trickle over my forehead: it was too horrible! I sprang up in my disgust, and with a wild cry I stepped forward, and instantly fell between the joists into the rank water below.

The shock was acute. Had I been asleep and dreaming before, this must inevitably have roused me up. I found myself completely immersed in water, and, for a moment, was absolutely incapable of thinking. As it was pitch-dark and my head had gone under, I could not tell whether I was above water or not, as I felt the bottom and struggled and splashed on to my legs. It was only by degrees I knew I must be standing with my head out of the foul mixture, because I was able to breathe easily, although the wet running down from my hair dribbled into my mouth as I stood shivering and gasping. It was astonishing how a physical discomfort overcame a mental terror. Nothing could be more miserable than my present position, and my efforts were at once directed to getting out of this dreadful place. But let anyone who has ever had the ill-luck to fall out of bed in his boyhood try and recollect his sensations. The bewildering realisation that he is not in bed, that he does not know where he is, which way to go, or what to do to get back again; everything he touches seems strange, and one piece of furniture much the same as any other. I well remember such an accident, and how, having rolled under the bed before I was wide awake, I could not for the life of me understand why I could not get up, what it was that kept me down. I had not the least idea which way to get out, and kept going round and round in a circle under my bed for a long time, and should probably have been doing it until daylight, had not my sighs and groans awoke my brother, who slept in the same room, and who came to my help.

If, then, one is so utterly at fault in a room every inch of which one knows intimately, how much more hopeless was my position at the bottom of this old vessel, half immersed in water, and totally without any clue which could help me to get out! I had not the least idea which was the ship's stern or which her stem, and every movement I made with my feet only served to unsteady me, as the bottom was all covered with slime, and uneven with the great timbers of the vessel.

My first thought on recovering my wits was to stretch my arms up over my head, and I was relieved to find that I could easily reach the joists above me. I was always fairly good at gymnastics, and I had not much difficulty in drawing myself up and sitting on the joist, although the weight of my wet clothes added to my exertions considerably. Having so far succeeded, I sat and drained, as it were, into the water below. The smell was abominable. I never disliked myself so much, and I shivered with cold.

As I could not get any wetter, I determined to go on deck somehow, but where was the companion-ladder? I had nothing to guide me. Strange to say, the reality of my struggles had almost made me forget the mysterious phenomena I had been listening to. But now, as I looked round, my attention was caught by a luminous patch which quivered and flickered on my right, at what distance from me I could not tell. It was like the light from a glowworm, only larger and changing in shape; sometimes elongated like a lambent oval, and then it would sway one way or another, as if caught in a draught of air. While I was looking at it and wondering what could cause it, I heard the steps over my head; they passed above me, and then seemed to grow louder on my left. A creeping dread again came over me. If only I could get out of this horrible place—but where were the stairs? I listened. The footfall seemed to be coming down some steps; then the companion-ladder must be on my left. But if I moved that way I should meet the Thing, whatever it was, that was coming down. I shuddered at the thought. However, I made up my mind. Stretching out my hand very carefully, I felt for the next joist, reached it, and crawled across. I stopped to listen. The steps were coming nearer. My hearing had now become acute; I could almost tell the exact place of each footfall. It came closer—closer,— quite close, surely—on the very joist on which I was sitting. I thought I could feel the joist quiver, and involuntarily moved my hand to prevent the heavy tread falling on it. The steps passed on, grew fainter, and ceased, as they drew near the pale lambent light. One thing I noticed with curious horror, and that was, that although the thing must have passed between me and the light, yet it was never for a moment obscured, which it must have been had any body or substance passed between, and yet I was certain that the steps went directly from me to it.

It was all horribly mysterious; and what had become of the other sound— the thing that was being dragged? An irresistible shudder passed over me; but

I determined to pursue my way until I came to something. It would never do to sit still and shiver there.

After many narrow escapes of falling again, I reached a bulkhead, and cautiously feeling along it, I came to an opening. It was the companion-ladder. By this time my hands, by feeling over the joists, had become dry again. I felt along the step to be quite sure that it was the stairs, and in so doing I touched something wet, sticky, clammy. Oh, horror! what was it? A cold shiver shook me nearly off the joist, and I felt an unutterable sense of repulsion to going on. However, the fresher air which came down the companion revived me, and, conquering my dread, I clambered on to the step. It did not take long to get upstairs and stand on the deck again.

I think I never in all my life experienced such a sense of joy as I did on being out of that disgusting hole. It was true I was soaking wet, and the night wind cut through me like a knife; but these were things I could understand, and were matter of common experience. What I had gone through might only be a question of nerves, and had no tangible or visible terror; but it was none the less very dreadful, and I would not go through such an experience again for worlds. As I stood cowering under the lee of the bulwark, I looked round at the sky. There was a pale light as if of daybreak away in the east, and it seemed as if all my troubles would be over with the dawn. It was bitterly cold. The wind had got round to the north, and I could faintly make out the low shore astern.

While I stood shivering there, a cry came down the wind. At first I thought it was a sea-bird, but it sounded again. I felt sure it was a human voice. I sprang up on to the taffrail, and shouted at the top of my lungs, then paused. The cry came down clearer and distinct. It was Jones's voice—had he heard me? I waved my draggled pocket-handkerchief and shouted again. In the silence which followed, I caught the words, "We are coming." What joyful words! Never did shipwrecked mariner on a lonely isle feel greater delight. My misery would soon be over. Anyhow, I should not have to wait long.

Unfortunately the tide was low, and was still falling. Nothing but a boat could reach me, I thought, and to get a boat would take some time. I therefore stamped up and down the deck to get warm; but I had an instinctive aversion for the companion-ladder, and the deep shadows of the forepart of the vessel.

As I turned round in my walk, I thought I saw something moving over the mud. I stopped. It was undoubtedly a figure coming towards me. A voice hailed me in gruff accents—

"*Lily*, ahoy! Be anyone aboard?"

Was anyone aboard? What an absurd question! and here had I been shouting myself hoarse. However, I quickly reassured him, and then understood why my rescuer did not sink in the soft mud. He had mud-pattens on. Coming up as close as he could, he shouted to me to keep clear, and then threw first one, then the other, clattering wooden board on to the deck. I found them, and under the instructions of my friend, I did not take long in putting them on. The man was giving me directions as to how to manage; but I did not care how much wetter I got, and dropped over the side into the slime. Sliding and straddling, I managed to get up to my friend, and then together we skated, as it were, to the shore—although skating very little represents the awkward splashes and slips I made on my way to land. I found quite a little crowd awaiting me on the bank; but Jones, with ready consideration, hurried me off to a cart he had in a lane near, and drove me home.

I told him the chief points of the adventure on our way; but did not say anything of the curious noises. It is odd how shy a man feels at telling what he knows people will never believe. It was not until the evening of the next day that I began to tell him, and then only after I was fortified by an excellent dinner, and some very good claret. Jones listened attentively. He was far too kindly and well bred to laugh at me; but I could see he did not believe one word as to the reality of the occurrence. "Very strange!"

"How remarkable!" "Quite extraordinary!" he kept saying, with evident interest. But I was sure he put it all down to my fatigue and disordered imagination. And so, to do him justice, has everybody else to whom I have told the tale since.

The fact is, we cannot, in this prosaic age, believe in anything the least approaching the supernatural. Nor do I. But nevertheless I am as certain as I am that I am writing these words, that the thing did really happen, and will happen again, may happen every night for all I know, only I don't intend to try and put my belief to the test. I have a theory which of course will be laughed at, and as I am not in the least scientific, I cannot bolster it up by scientific arguments. It is this: As Mr. Edison has now discovered that by certain simple processes human sounds can be reproduced at any future date, so accidentally, and owing to the combination of most curious coincidences, it might happen that the agonised cries of some suffering being, or the sounds made by one at a time when all other emotions are as nothing compared to the supreme sensations of one committing some awful crime, could be impressed on the atmosphere or surface of an enclosed building, which could be reproduced by a current of air passing into that building under the same atmospheric conditions. This is the vague explanation I have given to myself.

However, be the explanation what it may, the facts are as I have stated them. Let those laugh who did not experience them. To return to the end of the story. There were two things I pointed out to Jones as conclusive that I was not dreaming. One was my pocket-book. I showed it him, and the words were quite clear—only, of course, very straggling. This is a facsimile of the writing, but I cannot account for the date being 1837—

I am wide awake it is about midnight Christmas Eve 1837

The other point was the horrible stains on my hands and clothes. A foul-smelling dark chocolate stain was on my hair, hands, and clothes. Jones said, of course, this was from the rust off the mouldering iron-work, some of which no doubt had trickled down, owing to the heavy rain, through the defective caulking of the deck. The fact is, there is nothing that an ingenious mind cannot explain; but the question is, Is the explanation the right one?

I could easily account for the phosphorescent light. The water was foul and stagnant, and. it was no doubt caused by the same gases which produce the well-known *ignis-fatuus* or Will-o'-the-wisp.

We visited the ship, and I recovered my gun. There were the same stains on the deck as there were on my clothes; and curiously enough they went in a nearly straight line over the place where I lay, from the top of the companion to the starboard bulwark.

We carefully examined the forepart of the ship: it was as completely gutted as the rest of her. Jones was glad to get on deck again, as the atmosphere was very unpleasant, and I had no wish to stay.

At my request Jones made every inquiry he could about the old hulk. Not much was elicited. It bore an evil name, and no one would go on board who could help it. So far it looked as if it were credited with being haunted. The owner, who had been the captain of her, had died about three years before. His character did not seem amiable; but as he had left his money to the most influential farmer in the district, the country-people were unwilling to talk against him.

I went with Jones to call on the farmer, and asked him point-blank if he had ever heard whether a murder had been committed on board the *Lily*. He stared at me, and then laughed. "Not as I know of" was all his answer—and I never got any nearer than that.

I feel that this is all very unsatisfactory. I wish I could give some thrilling and sensational explanation. I am sorry I cannot. My imagination suggests many, as no doubt it will to each of my readers who possesses that faculty; but I have only written this to tell the actual facts, not to add to our superabundant fiction.

If ever I come across any details bearing upon the subject, I will not fail to communicate them at once. The vessel I found was the *Lily of Goole*, owned by one Master Gad Earwaker, and built in 1801.

The True Fate of the Flying Dutchman

by George Griffith

There is nothing original about the following story as far as I am concerned, and therefore I cannot of course be expected to vouch for the truth of it. I merely retail it to you as nearly as possible as I had it from the man who gave it to me, an ancient shellback very much on his beam ends, as the nautical saying goes, to whom I once had an opportunity of doing a good turn, as a set-off to which, like the ancient mariner in Gilbert's burlesque of Coleridge's masterpiece, "he spun me this painful yarn".

"As I was telling you, Sir," taking a fresh nip of the grog wherewith I had loosened his tongue, "until three or four year ago, when I got laid by for good, I'd been following the sea, man and boy, for something going on for sixty years, and, as you rightly guessed, I've seen one or two queer sorts of things in my time.

"It's the fashion nowadays for folk to turn up their eddicated noses at things that isn't plain for 'em to see in all their bearings with the naked eye a fathom in front of them, but for all that there's things as true as any that ye reads in the papers, and a bit truer, some of 'em, that happens away out there in the big wide sea that few folks ever 'ears of, and when they do 'ear of 'em, as I say, they just turns their noses up at 'em in a superior sort of way and calls 'em lies."

"Like the story of the *Flying Dutchman* for instance?" I said, drawing a sympathetic bow at a venture, and, as it happened, hitting the mark.

The old man's jaw dropped for a moment and the wrinkles round his still bright grey eyes contracted. Then he rapped gently on the table with the little blackened stump of a clay pipe that he was smoking, and said in a half-startled, half-dreamy sort of voice:

"You've hit it, Mister. I don't know how you've come to do it, but it's just about that that I'm going to spin you this yarn you asked for. It's no lie that story about Vanderdecken and the old galliot that he boxed about the Cape in for pretty near three hundred years, because, mister, as true as I'm sitting here"—and again he rapped on the table with his pipe—"I've seen him, and, what's more, I believe I'm the only man living, ashore or afloat, that saw the last of him and his old broad-bottomed hooker, or what was left of him."

To have expressed doubt at such a juncture would have been fatal, so I simply said:

"Then if that's so you must have as queer a yarn to spin as ever man told. Help yourself and reel it out."

He accepted the invitation and got under weigh again.

"It's getting on for five-and-forty years now that I, a British born boy hailing from Falmouth, had the bad luck to find myself cabin-boy and general knock-about on the *Prairie Flower*, a Yankee China tea-clipper, sailing out of Baltimore. I say 'bad luck' because if ever a harmless, willing lad led a dog's life on board a floating workhouse that was me on the *Prairie Flower*.

"The Skipper, Dave Schuyler was his name, was a good seaman of the old driving sort, but as big a brute as ever thought himself the Lord Almighty because he had command of a smart ship. He was a half-Yankee, half-Dutchman, as you might guess from his name, and he was wicked enough to sink a ship twice the tonnage of the *Prairie Flower*.

"There was another boy on board beside me, a little fellow with a spirit of a lion and a body of a mouse, so to speak, and we hadn't been at sea a week before the skipper took a deadly hate against him because he answered him back once instead of cringing to him like a kicked dog as he expected everyone aboard the ship to do. After that he never lost a chance of hazing the poor lad—that's the sea term for "sitting on him" you know, Sir—and at last one bitter cold night down in the Forties he found some fault with him and for a punishment sent him up to the foretop-gallant yard and told him to stop there till he told him to come down.

"He never did come down, leastways not in the regular way, for when it got daylight there was no one on the yard and I was the only boy on board the ship. Of course the poor little chap had either been jerked off the yard by the rolling of the ship or else he'd got half-frozen and half-stupid with the cold and just dropped overboard. It was put down against his name in the log-book 'Fallen overboard from aloft', and it was an accident for all anyone knew except the skipper and me and a young long-shoreman named Frank Peters, who had been sent by the owners as supercargo or ship's husband, as we used to call 'em in those days.

"The skipper didn't know that I knew anything about it; he didn't see that I wasn't below when he sent Slim Jim aloft to sit on the yard. If he had done I shouldn't have seen the end of the voyage, but Mr. Peters heard him give the order and saw the kick that he helped him off the poop with, and the next morning when he was missing he up and told him that it was nothing less than manslaughter and he should report him at the first port the ship touched at. The skipper didn't say much, but he thought a lot, and what he thought wasn't very healthy for Mr. Peters.

"We had a rough baddish lot in the fo'castle—just such a lot as yer might expect to sail with such a skipper—and as we had a lot of bad luck one way and another after the lad fell overboard, he hadn't much trouble in persuading them that the super-cargo was an out-and-out Jonah and was bringing all the bad time on to 'em. We hadn't got many days' runs behind us before poor Peters was hated fore and aft, and there were a good many of the chaps for'ard and who'd have helped him overboard for an extra tot of grog.

"We went hammering away down the Forties and at last got round the Cape, and one bright windy moonlight night the lookout sung out:

"'A sail on the starboard bow—and a queer one she looks too.'

"Queer she did look, I can tell you, lying right in the track of the moon's light over the water, rising and falling to the waves with a slow heavy motion that showed she was a dull sailor, whatever else she was. You've seen those square-bowed square-sterned slab-sided Dutchmen that used to sail out of Rotterdam and Amsterdam a few years ago?

"Well, build up a great high sort of castle on the stern with galleries running out aft at the sides and big square lanterns like they have now in the streets stuck up at the corners, cut the bow down low, run the bowsprit up about as steep again as we have them now, and put a square sail underneath it on the martingale and rig the masts and yards in the most antediluvian style you can think of—and that's the sort of craft that we saw lying between us and the moonlight that night.

"There was a flag hanging half-mast high from his foremast and his sails were flapping about just as though there wasn't a catspaw of wind, and yet we were beating up under short sail against a ten-knot breeze from the nor'east. The skipper got his glass on him in a minute, and when he took it down from his eye he said with words that I won't repeat to you, Sir:

"'If that's not old Vanderdecken himself may I be drowned with my head in a slush bucket. Haul round the fore-yard there, and let her fall off a bit. We'll see if the old Dutchman has anything to say. P'raps he can tell us what to do with this ——— Jonah that we've got aboard.'

"It wasn't a job that any man aboard the ship liked, but Dave Schuyler was in a mood that it wouldn't do to fool with. When the yards were round he called the boat's crew aft, ordered the steward to serve out a double tot of rum, and then told them to lower away the quarter-boat, as he wanted to take Jonah to pay a visit to Vanderdecken.

"'We'll send bad luck to bad luck, boys,' he said, 'and then p'raps we'll be rid of it. What do you say? He might be able to show old Vanderdecken the way into Table Bay.'

"It was a horrible cruel ghastly sort of notion, but as soon as they'd got the grog into them the men jumped at it and went to clear away the boat, swearing that Jonah had better sink the Dutchman than them. The skipper had a word or two with the mate, nearly as big a brute and bully as himself, and by the time the boat was clear poor Peters was brought up on deck out of his bunk, and Schuyler showed him the queer craft that was bobbing about under half a mile from us and said in a mocking politeful sort of voice:

"'There, Mr. Peters, Sir, allow me to introduce you to an old pal and country-man of mine, Philip Vanderdecken, better known as the Flying Dutchman. You've brought us a blamed sight of bad luck since you've been on board the *Prairie Flower*, and as I think we shall get to China better without you than with you I am going to take you aboard in the boat and ask Vanderdecken to give you a passage home.'

"The poor chap looked at the strange uncanny craft abeam and then at the skipper in a mute beseeching sort of way. Then he lost his nerve, as any other man might have done in the same fix, and fell on his knees and started out to beg for mercy, but Schuyler wasn't that sort.

"He sung out to a couple of the chaps at the davits and they picked up poor Peters, whipped a line round his hands and feet and bundled him into the boat without any more fuss. Then he sent me down into the supercargo's cabin to fetch up some of his clothes, saying with a laugh that he might find it cold and want them before he got home. I went down and fetched up all I could lay my hands on.

"Now I ought to have said that this Peters was a Roman Catholic, and on his table I found a little silver crucifix with a silver chain to it. Something told me to take this up too, I thought it might sort of comfort him. When I got on deck the boat was in the water and the skipper pretty nearly frightened the life out of me by telling me to shin down the tackles and take the gentleman his clo'es, as he said.

"I had to go, though I think I'd sooner have jumped overboard than get into a boat going to that ghostly-looking ship; but when I got down and showed poor Peters his crucifix, his face lit up so that I was almost glad I'd come. He asked me to hang it round his neck, and I did.

"As we approached, the most awful-looking faces mortal eyes ever looked at showed themselves over the bulwarks, staring down at us, but there was never a word or a sound out of any of 'em. On the big high stern there was a tall figure with long white hair and a long ragged white beard, and he was dressed just like the sailors you see in some of the old pictures at Grinnidge Hospital.

"When we ran alongside under her high quarter the faces of the boat's crew were almost as white as the ghostly things that were looking at us over the side, but the skipper didn't seem to have a bit of fear about him. He stood up in the stern sheets and hailed in Dutch, and there came back something that sounded like the same language, only far away as though the voice had dropped from the clouds.

"The tall figure came down from the quarter-deck and then a crazy old rope ladder all covered with dried green slime, like the ship's sides were, tumbled out of the gangway port. All he could do the skipper couldn't persuade one of the men to go up that ladder. They told him straight they'd see him further first, only in a lot stronger words than that, and so he cursed them for a lot of white-livered chicken-hearted swabs and swarmed up himself.

"We held our breath and heard him saying something to the old fellow with the white hair and beard that we knew by this time must be Vanderdecken himself. Then he came to the gangway and slung a rope over and told us to make it fast round the supercargo's shoulders. The men wanted to be away again, and they did it without any more telling, in spite of the poor fellow's shrieks and prayers for mercy. Then the skipper, and maybe some of them on board, toiled on the rope and hauled poor Peters, struggling and yelling like a madman, up over the side. They had scarcely got him on deck when Schuyler called to me and told me to bring his clothes up.

"I was so struck with fright that I couldn't move, and when the skipper saw this he swore that if I didn't come up sharp he'd haul me up after Peters and leave me with him. Then one of the chaps in the boat told me to hurry up and hoist myself aboard, or they'd sling me up, for they didn't want to stop there all night, and the end of it was that I slung the bundle of Peter's clothes round my neck and swarmed up, feeling every moment as I should drop into the water again.

"It's no use telling you what I saw on deck, because if I did you wouldn't believe me. If ever there was a ghost-ship with real timbers, and cordage, and sails, and a crew of ghosts, that was her. The skipper had untied Peters's legs and arms and was just telling him that he might like to walk about a bit and get acquainted with his new shipmates as I reached the deck. Then he slung his bag of clothes at him with a horrible oath, knocking the poor chap over like a nine-pin he was that weak with fright, and after he'd done it he did what I couldn't have believed even he'd do if I hadn't seen it—he held out his hand to Vanderdecken's ghost and said what I expect was good-bye in Dutch.

"Vanderdecken took it, and said something in his queer, far-away voice that made Schuyler drop his hand as if it had been red-hot instead of ice-cold as I expect it was, and he was almost as white as Vanderdecken himself when he stumbled to the gangway and scrambled down the ladder as hard as he could go. I needn't tell you I followed him as sharp as I could, Peters cursing Schuyler from the bulwarks.

"As we were pulling away from the side those queer ghostly faces came and looked over at us, and among them was poor Peters's, and it was as white and ghostly as any of 'em, but they were quiet and he wasn't. He shook his fists above his head and screamed out words that were a lot awfuller than swearing from the way he said 'em, and the last words we heard were:

"'We'll meet again yet, David Schuyler, and when we do I'll take you with me to the judgment of God. Remember that.'

"And then there came a long scream like the whistle of the wind through cordage in a living gale, and we all shut our eyes and the chaps at the oars pulled as if old Vanderdecken himself was coming after 'em to fetch 'em back.

"By the time we got to the ship again and had her under weigh the Dutchman had got all his sails drawing and was bumping away over the short seas to the nor'ard and west'ard heading straight for Table Bay. The *Prairie Flower* never got to China, but that's not in the story so I can make it short. We ran ashore on one of the islands in the Malacca Straits one dark night when it was blowing fit to blow the beard off a Turk. Not a soul of the crew were saved but the skipper and me.

*   *   *

"It was nearly fifteen years after we parted company that time that I saw Dave Schuyler again. It was on the wharf at Hoboken and he knew me at once, although I had grown from a boy to a man. He wasn't much changed except he looked a good bit soberer and quieter. He came and spoke to me quite friendly like and we soon got into conversation, and he told me he'd got converted and found religion, or something of that sort, and had repented of his past life and was doing very well.

"Then he told me that he had a great scheme on hand, that there was millions in it if it could only be worked proper like, and he asked me to go to his house that night and he'd tell me all about it. I was out of a job just then, although I'd got my master's certificate, and to tell you the truth I was mortal hard up. I'd almost forgotten, not the *Flying Dutchman*, but what took us on board of him, for I'd seen so many other queer things done at sea since then that it didn't seem anything particular, so I said yes, and when I got to Schuyler's house that evening he spread out a chart of the middle Atlantic on his table, clapped his fore-finger down on it and said:

"'There, Tom lad, that's where we're going.'

"I looked down and saw that he'd put his finger on the big patch in the centre of the North Atlantic that's called the Sargasso Sea.

"'I never knew there were any millions in seaweed before,' I said looking up at him with a bit of a grin.

"'No,' he said, 'no more there aren't, and it isn't seaweed we're goin' for. You know enough not to need me to tell you that's a patch of still water made by the meeting of a lot of currents. No ship ever goes there, leastways if it can help it, but lot's go there as can't help it. Don't yer see that pretty near all the derelicts and missing ships in the North Atlantic that don't go down there must get taken there by the currents some time or other? Some of 'em have good cargoes that won't spoil by water. Most of 'em have money and valuables aboard and some of 'em have hundredweights of specie and bullion—and that's what we're going after.'

"'That looks as if there might be money in it,' I said after thinkin' a bit quietly and really it did seem very reasonable when you came to look at it. 'How are you goin' to get there?' I said, looking at it all practical like.

"'Well, I've had this scheme in my head some years and now I've got a little three-hundred-ton steamer and we're going to drive her slap into the middle, seaweed or no seaweed, and if you like to be first officer of that steamer, well you can be and you shall have your share of the plunder if there is any and good wages as well.'

"'I'm with you, Schuyler,' says I. And so it was settled.

"I needn't tell you how long we were getting the *Gold Seeker*—that was the name of our steamer—into the middle of those hundreds of miles of seaweed or what day-and-night labour we had to shove her through it, for it was about time I was hauling in the slack of this yarn, so I'll get on to the end.

"Never did mortal eyes look on such a collection of old weather-battered hulks and rusty iron floating coffins as we found jammed up together in that patch of sea and weed. We sighted 'em first at night and for all the world they looked in the gloom like a lot of ghost-ships that had started out to sail to the other world and never got there.

"We lay to for the light, and when it came what should be the first ship that I clapped eyes on lying broad abeam of us and only two or three hundred yards away but old Vanderdecken's craft, the *Flying Dutchman*. He'd got round the Cape at last, and this was the end of his three-hundred-year voyage.

"There was no mistaking him, although the ropes and chains had rotted and rusted through, and the yards had fallen down on deck, and the fore and aft sails were falling in tatters, and the timbers were that full of worm holes that they might have been riddled with small shot. As I was standing looking at her Schuyler came up from below.

"I didn't turn to look at him; I daren't, but I felt a trembling hand laid on my shoulder and heard his voice say in a hoarse shaking whisper:

"'My God, Tom, that's her again! You remember what Peters said when we left him on board of her. I knew it'd come—I've dreamt of it and I've heard his voice calling to me when I've been broad awake. It's got to be and I've got to go. Lower the boat, Tom, and come with me.'

"I tried to persuade him out of it but it was no good. He swore he'd jump overboard and swim to her; so at last I gave in, hoping that after all it might be some other old craft like the Dutchman that had got fastened up here for hundreds of years. We had the gig out with a couple of men to pull her, and in a few minutes we were once more standing on the deck where we'd left poor Peters.

"There was no mistake about it, it was the same ship, only there was this difference, there was no captain and no crew. A few grey crumbling bones were lying about the cracked curled up decks and that was all. Schuyler gave one look round and then made straight for the cabin under the high quarter-deck. I followed him, and there, sitting at each end of the table with their heads bent forward on their folded arms were the bodies of Philip Vanderdecken and poor Frank Peters.

"They were dried to mummies, but still horribly life-like, and round Frank's neck was hanging the little silver chain with the crucifix lying on the table in front of him. We stared at 'em speechless with horror and then Schuyler gasped out:

"'I knew it, Tom, he's fetched me here and here I'll have to die. What's that?'

"As he spoke a shiver seemed to run through the old hulk and we heard a queer crackling creaking noise and the sound of something falling on deck. Then Schuyler turned to me and whispered, for fear hadn't left him any better voice:

"'Run, Tom, run for the boat! She's breaking up at last.'

"I took him by the arm and tried to drag him out with me, but as soon as I got him to the door he broke away and ran back and threw himself on his knees at the table. Just then the old craft gave a heave and my own fear got the best of me and I ran on deck.

"The fellows in the boat were shouting for us and I shouted back to 'em to come and help me bring the Skipper out. But before one of 'em could get up the side the main-mast fell aft crashing through the rotten timbers of the quarter-deck and blocking the way to the cabin. Then a great split opened right across the deck and I bundled into the boat and we pulled away as fast as the weed would let us.

"We hadn't got twenty yards off when the old craft broke up as though a broadside of big guns had been fired into her. She seemed to go right to pieces where she lay and the last of her that we saw was the high stern heeling over and going down, dragging the weeds with it. That was the last that any man, saw or ever will see of the *Flying Dutchman*."

"And what about the *Gold Seeker*?" I asked. "Did you get your millions?"

"Yes. The men wouldn't go back when we'd taken so much trouble to get there, and in less than a fortnight we got tons of treasure; but it never did us any good. No ship ever sighted the *Flying Dutchman* and got back safe to port. We broke our shaft getting out of the weed and knocked about for a month under what sail we could carry, then we drifted into the hurricane area and the last of the *Gold Seeker* was that she was smashed to pieces on one of the Keys of the Bahamas. I was the only one of her crew that was saved, and that's why I'm the only man alive that knows the true story of the fate of the *Flying Dutchman*."

A Matter of Fact

(excerpt)

by Rudyard Kipling

And if ye doubt the tale I tell,
Steer through the South Pacific swell;
Go where the branching coral hives
Unending strife of endless lives,
Where, leagued about the 'wildered boat,
The rainbow jellies fill and float;
And, lilting where the laver lingers,
The starfish trips on all her fingers;
Where, 'neath his myriad spines ashock,
The sea-egg ripples down the rock;
An orange wonder dimly guessed,
From darkness where the cuttles rest,
Moored o'er the darker deeps that hide
The blind white Sea-snake and his bride
Who, drowsing, nose the long-lost ships
Let down through darkness to their lips.

—*THE PALMS.*

Once a priest, always a priest; once a Mason, always a Mason; but once a journalist, always and for ever a journalist.

There were three of us, all newspaper men, the only passengers on a little tramp steamer that ran where her owners told her to go. She had once been in the Bilbao iron ore business, had been lent to the Spanish Government for service at Manilla; and was ending her days in the Cape Town coolie-trade, with occasional trips to Madagascar and even as far as England. We found her going to Southampton in ballast, and shipped in her because the fares were nominal. There was Keller, of an American paper, on his way back to the States from palace executions in Madagascar; there was a burly half-Dutchman, called Zuyland, who owned and edited a paper up country near Johannesburg; and there was myself, who had solemnly put away all journalism, vowing to forget that I had ever known the difference between an imprint and a stereo advertisement.

Ten minutes after Keller spoke to me, as the *Rathmines* cleared Cape Town, I had forgotten the aloofness I desired to feign, and was in heated discussion on the immorality of expanding telegrams beyond a certain fixed point. Then Zuyland came out of his cabin, and we were all at home instantly, because we were men of the same profession needing no introduction. We annexed the boat formally, broke open the passengers' bath-room door—on the Manilla lines the Dons do not wash—cleaned out the orange-peel and cigar-ends at the bottom of the bath, hired a Lascar to shave us throughout the voyage, and then asked each other's names.

Three ordinary men would have quarrelled through sheer boredom before they reached Southampton. We, by virtue of our craft, were anything but ordinary men. A large percentage of the tales of the world, the thirty-nine that cannot be told to ladies and the one that can, are common property coming of a common stock. We told them all, as a matter of form, with all their local and specific variants which are surprising. Then came, in the intervals of steady card-play, more personal histories of adventure and things seen and suffered: panics among white folk, when the blind terror ran from man to man on the Brooklyn Bridge, and the people crushed each other to death they knew not why; fires, and faces that opened and shut their mouths horribly at red-hot window frames; wrecks in frost and snow, reported from the sleet-sheathed rescue-tug at the risk of frostbite; long rides after diamond thieves; skirmishes on the veldt and in municipal committees with the

Boers; glimpses of lazy tangled Cape politics and the mule-rule in the Transvaal; card-tales, horse-tales, woman-tales, by the score and the half hundred; till the first mate, who had seen more than us all put together, but lacked words to clothe his tales with, sat open-mouthed far into the dawn.

When the tales were done we picked up cards till a curious hand or a chance remark made one or other of us say, "That reminds me of a man who—or a business which—" and the anecdotes would continue while the *Rathmines* kicked her way northward through the warm water.

In the morning of one specially warm night we three were sitting immediately in front of the wheel-house, where an old Swedish boatswain whom we called "Frithiof the Dane" was at the wheel, pretending that he could not hear our stories. Once or twice Frithiof spun the spokes curiously, and Keller lifted his head from a long chair to ask, "What is it? Can't you get any steerage-way on her?"

"There is a feel in the water," said Frithiof, "that I cannot understand. I think that we run downhills or somethings. She steers bad this morning."

Nobody seems to know the laws that govern the pulse of the big waters. Sometimes even a lands-man can tell that the solid ocean is atilt, and that the ship is working herself up a long unseen slope; and sometimes the captain says, when neither full steam nor fair wind justifies the length of a day's run, that the ship is sagging downhill; but how these ups and downs come about has not yet been settled authoritatively.

"No, it is a following sea," said Frithiof; "and with a following sea you shall not get good steerage-way."

The sea was as smooth as a duck-pond, except for a regular oily swell. As I looked over the side to see where it might be following us from, the sun rose in a perfectly clear sky and struck the water with its light so sharply that it seemed as though the sea should clang like a burnished gong. The wake of the screw and the little white streak cut by the log-line hanging over the stern were the only marks on the water as far as eye could reach.

Keller rolled out of his chair and went aft to get a pine-apple from the ripening stock that was hung inside the after awning.

"Frithiof, the log-line has got tired of swimming. It's coming home," he drawled.

"What?" said Frithiof, his voice jumping several octaves.

"Coming home," Keller repeated, leaning over the stern. I ran to his side and saw the log-line, which till then had been drawn tense over the stern railing, slacken, loop, and come up off the port quarter. Frithiof called up the speaking-tube to the bridge, and the bridge answered, "Yes, nine knots." Then Frithiof spoke again, and the answer was, "What do you want of the skipper?" and Frithiof bellowed, "Call him up."

By this time Zuyland, Keller, and myself had caught something of Frithiof's excitement, for any emotion on shipboard is most contagious. The captain ran out of his cabin, spoke to Frithiof, looked at the log-line, jumped on the bridge, and in a minute we felt the steamer swing round as Frithiof turned her.

"Going back to Cape Town?" said Keller.

Frithiof did not answer, but tore away at the wheel. Then he beckoned us three to help, and we held the wheel down till the *Rathmines* answered it, and we found ourselves looking into the white of our own wake, with the still oily sea tearing past our bows, though we were not going more than half steam ahead.

The captain stretched out his arm from the bridge and shouted. A minute later I would have given a great deal to have shouted too, for one-half of the sea seemed to shoulder itself above the other half, and came on in the shape of a hill. There was neither crest, comb, nor curl-over to it; nothing but black water with little waves chasing each other about the flanks. I saw it stream past and on a level with the *Rathmines'* bow-plates before the steamer hove up her bulk to rise, and I argued that this would be the last of all earthly voyages for me. Then we lifted for ever and ever and ever, till I heard Keller saying in my ear, "The bowels of the deep, good Lord!" and the *Rathmines* stood poised, her screw racing and drumming on the slope of a hollow that stretched downwards for a good half-mile.

We went down that hollow, nose under for the most part, and the air smelt wet and muddy, like that of an emptied aquarium. There was a second hill to climb; I saw that much: but the water came aboard and carried me aft till it jammed me against the wheel-house door, and before I could catch breath or clear my eyes again we were rolling to and fro in torn water, with the scuppers pouring like eaves in a thunderstorm.

"There were three waves," said Keller; "and the stokehold's flooded."

The firemen were on deck waiting, apparently, to be drowned. The engineer came and dragged them below, and the crew, gasping, began to work the clumsy Board of Trade pump. That showed nothing serious, and when I understood that the *Rathmines* was really on the water, and not beneath it, I asked what had happened.

"The captain says it was a blow-up under the sea—a volcano," said Keller.

"It hasn't warmed anything," I said. I was feeling bitterly cold, and cold was almost unknown in those waters. I went below to change my clothes, and when I came up everything was wiped out in clinging white fog.

"Are there going to be any more surprises?" said Keller to the captain.

"I don't know. Be thankful you're alive, gentlemen. That's a tidal wave thrown up by a volcano. Probably the bottom of the sea has been lifted a few feet some-where or other. I can't quite understand this cold spell. Our sea-thermometer says the surface water is 44°, and it should be 68° at least."

"It's abominable," said Keller, shivering. "But hadn't you better attend to the fog-horn? It seems to me that I heard something."

"Heard! Good heavens!" said the captain from the bridge, "I should think you did." He pulled the string of our fog-horn, which was a weak one. It sputtered and choked, because the stokehold was full of water and the fires were half-drowned, and at last gave out a moan. It was answered from the fog by one of the most appalling steam-sirens I have ever heard. Keller turned as white as I did, for the fog, the cold fog, was upon us, and any man may be forgiven for fearing a death he cannot see.

"Give her steam there!" said the captain to the engine-room. "Steam for the whistle, if we have to go dead slow."

We bellowed again, and the damp dripped off the awnings on to the deck as we listened for the reply. It seemed to be astern this time, but much nearer than before.

"The *Pembroke Castle* on us!" said Keller; and then, viciously, "Well, thank God, we shall sink her too."

"It's a side-wheel steamer," I whispered. "Can't you hear the paddles?"

This time we whistled and roared till the steam gave out, and the answer nearly deafened us. There was a sound of frantic threshing in the water, apparently about fifty yards away, and something shot past in the whiteness that looked as though it were gray and red.

"The *Pembroke Castle* bottom up," said Keller, who, being a journalist, always sought for explanations. "That's the colours of a Castle liner. We're in for a big thing."

"The sea is bewitched," said Frithiof from the wheel-house. "There are *two* steamers!"

Another siren sounded on our bow, and the little steamer rolled in the wash of something that had passed unseen.

"We're evidently in the middle of a fleet," said Keller quietly. "If one doesn't run us down, the other will. Phew! What in creation is that?"

I sniffed, for there was a poisonous rank smell in the cold air—a smell that I had smelt before.

"If I was on land I should say that it was an alligator. It smells like musk," I answered.

"Not ten thousand alligators could make that smell," said Zuyland; "I have smelt them."

"Bewitched! Bewitched!" said Frithiof. "The sea she is turned upside down, and we are walking along the bottom."

Again the *Rathmines* rolled in the wash of some unseen ship, and a silver-gray wave broke over the bow, leaving on the deck a sheet of sediment—the gray broth that has its place in the fathomless deeps of the sea. A sprinkling of the wave fell on my face, and it was so cold that it stung as boiling water stings. The dead and most untouched deep water of the sea had been heaved to the top by the submarine volcano—the chill still water that kills all life and smells of desolation and emptiness. We did not need either the blinding fog or that indescribable smell of musk to make us unhappy—we were shivering with cold and wretchedness where we stood.

"The hot air on the cold water makes this fog," said the captain; "it ought to clear in a little time."

"Whistle, oh! whistle, and let's get out of it," said Keller.

The captain whistled again, and far and far astern the invisible twin steam-sirens answered us. Their blasting shriek grew louder, till at last it seemed to tear out of the fog just above our quarter, and I cowered while the *Rathmines* plunged bows under on a double swell that crossed.

"No more," said Frithiof, "it is not good any more. Let us get away, in the name of God."

"Now if a torpedo-boat with a *City of Paris* siren went mad and broke her moorings and hired a friend to help her, it's just conceivable that we might be carried as we are now. Otherwise this thing is—"

The last words died on Keller's lips, his eyes began to start from his head, and his jaw fell. Some six or seven feet above the port bulwarks, framed in fog, and as utterly unsupported as the full moon, hung a Face. It was not human, and it certainly was not animal, for it did not belong to this earth as known to man. The mouth was open, revealing a ridiculously tiny tongue—as absurd as the tongue of an elephant; there were tense wrinkles of white skin at the angles of the drawn lips, white feelers like those of a barbel sprung from the lower jaw, and there was no sign of teeth within the mouth. But the horror of the face lay in the eyes, for those were sightless—white, in sockets as white as scraped bone, and blind. Yet for all this the face, wrinkled as the mask of a lion is drawn in Assyrian sculpture, was alive with rage and terror. One long white feeler touched our bulwarks. Then the face disappeared with the swiftness of a blindworm popping into its burrow, and the next thing that I remember is my own voice in my own ears, saying gravely to the mainmast, "But the air-bladder ought to have been forced out of its mouth, you know."

Keller came up to me, ashy white. He put his hand into his pocket, took a cigar, bit it, dropped it, thrust his shaking thumb into his mouth and mumbled, "The giant gooseberry and the raining frogs! Gimme a light—gimme a light! Say, gimme a light." A little bead of blood dropped from his thumb joint.

I respected the motive, though the manifestation was absurd. "Stop, you'll bite your thumb off," I said, and Keller laughed brokenly as he picked up his cigar. Only Zuyland, leaning over the port bulwarks, seemed self-possessed. He declared later that he was very sick.

"We've seen it," he said, turning round. "That is it."

"What?" said Keller, chewing the unlighted cigar.

As he spoke the fog was blown into shreds, and we saw the sea, gray with mud, rolling on every side of us and empty of all life. Then in one spot it bubbled and became like the pot of ointment that the Bible speaks of. From that wide-ringed trouble a Thing came up—a gray and red Thing with a neck—a Thing that bellowed and writhed in pain. Frithiof drew in his breath and held it till the red letters of the ship's name, woven across his jersey, straggled and opened out as though they had been type badly set. Then he said with a little cluck in his throat, "Ah me! It is blind. *Hur illa*! That thing is blind," and a murmur of pity went through us all, for we could see that the thing on the water was blind and in pain. Something had gashed and cut the great sides cruelly and the blood was spurting out. The gray ooze of the undermost sea lay in the monstrous wrinkles of the back, and poured away in sluices. The blind white head flung back and battered the wounds, and the body in its torment rose clear of the red and gray waves till we saw a pair of quivering shoulders streaked with weed and rough with shells, but as white in the clear spaces as the hairless, maneless, blind, toothless head. Afterwards, came a dot on the horizon and the sound of a shrill scream, and it was as though a shuttle shot all across the sea in one breath, and a second head and neck tore through the levels, driving a whispering wall of water to right and left. The two Things met—the one untouched and the other in its death-throe— male and female, we said, the female coming to the male. She circled round him bellowing, and laid her neck across the curve of his great turtle-back, and he disappeared under water for an instant, but flung up again, grunting in agony while the blood ran. Once the entire head and neck shot clear of the water and stiffened, and I heard Keller saying, as though he was watching a street accident, "Give him air. For God's sake, give him air." Then the death-struggle began, with crampings and twistings and jerkings of the white bulk to and fro, till our little steamer rolled again, and each gray wave coated her plates with the gray slime. The sun was clear, there was no wind, and we watched, the whole crew, stokers and all, in wonder and pity, but chiefly pity. The Thing was so helpless, and, save for his mate, so alone. No human eye should have beheld him; it was monstrous and indecent to exhibit him there in trade waters between atlas degrees of latitude. He had been spewed up, mangled and dying, from his rest on the sea-floor, where he might have lived till the Judgment Day, and we saw the tides of his life go from him as an angry tide goes out across rocks in the teeth of a landward gale. His mate lay rocking on the water a little distance off, bellowing continually, and the smell of musk came down upon the ship making us cough.

At last the battle for life ended in a batter of coloured seas. We saw the writhing neck fall like a flail, the carcase turn sideways, showing the glint of a white belly and the inset of a gigantic hind leg or flipper. Then all sank, and sea boiled over it, while the mate swam round and round, darting her head in every direction. Though we might have feared that she would attack the steamer, no power on earth could have drawn any one of us from our places that hour. We watched, holding our breaths. The mate paused in her search; we could hear the wash beating along her sides; reared her neck as high as she could reach, blind and lonely in all that loneliness of the sea, and sent one desperate bellow booming across the swells as an oyster-shell skips across a pond. Then she made off to the westward, the sun shining on the white head and the wake behind it, till nothing was left to see but a little pin point of silver on the horizon. We stood on our course again; and the *Rathmines*, coated with the sea-sediment from bow to stern, looked like a ship made gray with terror.

The Ballad of Carmilhan

by Henry Wadsworth Longfellow

I

At Stralsund, by the Baltic Sea,
Within the sandy bar,
At sunset of a summer's day,
Ready for sea, at anchor lay
The good ship *Valdemar*.

The sunbeams danced upon the waves,
And played along her side;
And through the cabin windows streamed
In ripples of golden light, that seemed
The ripple of the tide.

There sat the captain with his friends,
Old skippers brown and hale,
Who smoked and grumbled o'er their grog,
And talked of iceberg and of fog,
Of calm and storm and gale.

And one was spinning a sailor's yarn
About Klaboterman,
The Kobold of the sea; a spright
Invisible to mortal sight,
Who o'er the rigging ran.

Sometimes he hammered in the hold,
Sometimes upon the mast,
Sometimes abeam, sometimes abaft,
Or at the bows he sang and laughed,
And made all tight and fast.

He helped the sailors at their work,
And toiled with jovial din;
He helped them hoist and reef the sails,
He helped them stow the casks and bales,
And heave the anchor in.

But woe unto the lazy louts,
The idlers of the crew;
Them to torment was his delight,
And worry them by day and night,
And pinch them black and blue.

And woe to him whose mortal eyes
Klaboterman behold.
It is a certain sign of death!—
The cabinboy here held his breath,
He felt his blood run cold.

II

The jolly skipper paused awhile,
And then again began;
"There is a Spectre Ship," quoth he,
"A ship of the Dead. that sails the sea,
And is called the *Carmilhan.*

"A ghostly ship, with a ghostly crew,
In tempests she appears;
And before the gale, or against the gale,
She sails without a rag of sail,
Without a helmsman steers.

"She haunts the Atlantic north and south,
But mostly the midsea,
Where three great rocks rise bleak and bare
Like furnace chimneys in the air,
And are called the Chimneys Three.

"And ill betide the luckless ship
That meets the *Carmilhan*;
Over her decks the seas will leap,
She must go down into the deep,
And perish mouse and man."

The captain of the *Valdemar*
Laughed loud with merry heart.
"I should like to see this ship," said he;
"I should like to find these Chimneys Three
That are marked down in the chart.

"I have sailed right over the spot," he said,
"With a good stiff breeze behind,
When the sea was blue, and the sky was clear,—
You can follow my course by these pinholes here,—
And never a rock could find."

And then he swore a dreadful oath,
He swore by the Kingdoms Three,
That, should he meet the *Carmilhan*,
He would run her down, although he ran
Right into Eternity!

All this, while passing to and fro,
The cabinboy had heard;
He lingered at the door to hear,
And drank in all with greedy ear,
And pondered every word.

He was a simple country lad,
But of a roving mind.
"Oh, it must be like heaven," thought he,
"Those faroff foreign lands to see,
And fortune seek and find!"

But in the fo'castle, when he heard
The mariners blaspheme,
He thought of home, he thought of God,
And his mother under the churchyard sod,
And wished it were a dream.

One friend on board that ship had he;
'Twas the Klaboterman,
Who saw the Bible in his chest,
And made a sign upon his breast,
All evil things to ban.

III

The cabin windows have grown blank
As eyeballs of the dead;
No more the glancing sunbeams burn
On the gilt letters of the stern,
But on the figure-head;

On Valdemar Victorious,
Who looketh with disdain
To see his image in the tide
Dismembered float from side to side,
And reunite again.

"It is the wind," those skippers said,
"That swings the vessel so;
It is the wind; it freshens fast,
'Tis time to say farewell at last,
'Tis time for us to go."

They shook the captain by the hand,
"Good luck! good luck!" they cried;
Each face was like the setting sun,
As, broad and red, they one by one
Went o'er the vessel's side.

The sun went down, the full moon rose,
Serene o'er field and flood;
And all the winding creeks and bays
And broad seameadows seemed ablaze,
The sky was red as blood.

The southwest wind blew fresh and fair,
As fair as wind could be;
Bound for Odessa, o'er the bar,
With all sail set, the *Valdemar*
Went proudly out to sea.

The lovely moon climbs up the sky
As one who walks in dreams;
A tower of marble in her light,
A wall of black, a wall of white,
The stately vessel seems.

Low down upon the sandy coast
The lights begin to burn;
And now, uplifted high in air,
They kindle with a fiercer glare,
And now drop far astern.

The dawn appears, the land is gone,
The sea is all around;
Then on each hand low hills of sand
Emerge and form another land;
She steereth through the Sound.

Through Kattegat and Skagerrack
She flitteth like a ghost;
By day and night, by night and day,
She bounds, she flies upon her way
Along the English coast.

Cape Finisterre is drawing near,
Cape Finisterre is past;
Into the open ocean stream
She floats, the vision of a dream
Too beautiful to last.

Suns rise and set, and rise, and yet
There is no land in sight;
The liquid planets overhead
Burn brighter now the moon is dead,
And longer stays the night.

IV

And now along the horizon's edge
Mountains of cloud uprose,
Black as with forests underneath,
Above, their sharp and jagged teeth
Were white as drifted snows.

Unseen behind them sank the sun,
But flushed each snowy peak
A little while with rosy light,
That faded slowly from the sight
As blushes from the cheek.

Black grew the sky,—all black, all black;
The clouds were everywhere;
There was a feeling of suspense
In nature, a mysterious sense
Of terror in the air.

And all on board the *Valdemar*
Was still as still could be;
Save when the dismal shipbell tolled,
As ever and anon she rolled,
And lurched into the sea.

The captain up and down the deck
Went striding to and fro;
Now watched the compass at the wheel,
Now lifted up his hand to feel
Which way the wind might blow.

And now he looked up at the sails,
And now upon the deep;
In every fibre of his frame
He felt the storm before it came,
He had no thought of sleep:

Eight bells! and suddenly abaft,
With a great rush of rain,
Making the ocean white with spume,
In darkness like the day of doom,
On came the hurricane.

The lightning flashed from cloud to cloud,
And rent the sky in two;
A jagged flame, a single jet
Of white fire, like a bayonet,
That pierced the eyeballs through.

Then all around was dark again,
And blacker than before;
But in that single flash of light
He had beheld a fearful sight,
And thought of the oath he swore.

For right ahead lay the Ship of the Dead,
The ghostly *Carmilhan*!
Her masts were stripped, her yards were bare,
And on her bowsprit, poised in air,
Sat the Klaboterman.

Her crew of ghosts was all on deck
Or clambering up the shrouds;
The boatswain's whistle, the captain's hail
Were like the piping of the gale,
And thunder in the clouds.

And close behind the *Carmilhan*
There rose up from the sea,
As from a foundered ship of stone,
Three bare and splintered masts alone:
They were the Chimneys Three.

And onward dashed the *Valdemar*
And leaped into the dark;
A denser mist, a colder blast,
A little shudder, and she had passed
Right through the Phantom Bark.

She cleft in twain the shadowy hulk,
But cleft it unaware;
As when, careering to her nest,
The seagull severs with her breast
The unresisting air.

Again the lightning flashed; again
They saw the *Carmilhan*,
Whole as before in hull and spar;
But now on board of the *Valdemar*
Stood the Klaboterman.

And they all knew their doom was sealed;
They knew that death was near;
Some prayed who never prayed before,
And some they wept, and some they swore,
And some were mute with fear.

Then suddenly there came a shock,
And louder than wind or sea
A cry burst from the crew on deck,
As she dashed and crashed, a hopeless wreck,
Upon the Chimneys Three.

The storm and night were passed, the light
To streak the east began;
The cabinboy, picked up at sea.
Survived the wreck, and only he,
To tell of the *Carmilhan*.

Guests from Gibbet Island

A Legend of Communipaw

by Washington Irving

Found Among the Knickerbocker Papers at Wolfert's Roost

Whoever has visited the ancient and renowned village of Communipaw may have noticed an old stone building, of most ruinous and sinister appearance. The doors and window-shutters are ready to drop from their hinges; old clothes are stuffed in the broken panes of glass, while legions of half-starved dogs prowl about the premises, and rush out and bark at every passer-by, for your beggarly house in a village is most apt to swarm with profligate and ill-conditioned dogs. What adds to the sinister appearance of this mansion is a tall frame in front, not a little resembling a gallows, and which looks as if waiting to accommodate some of the inhabitants with a well-merited airing. It is not a gallows, however, but an ancient sign-post; for this dwelling in the golden days of Communipaw was one of the most orderly and peaceful of village taverns, where public affairs were talked and smoked over. In fact, it was in this very building that Oloffe the Dreamer and his companions concerted that great voyage of discovery and colonization in which they explored Buttermilk Channel, were nearly shipwrecked in the strait of Hell Gate, and finally landed on the island of Manhattan, and founded the great city of New Amsterdam.

Even after the province had been cruelly wrested from the sway of their High Mightinesses by the combined forces of the British and the Yankees, this tavern continued its ancient loyalty. It is true, the head of the Prince of Orange disappeared from the sign, a strange bird being painted over it, with the explanatory legend of "Die Wilde Gans," or, The Wild Goose; but this all the world knew to be a sly riddle of the landlord, the worthy Teunis Van Gieson, a knowing man, in a small way, who laid his finger beside his nose and winked, when, any one studied the signification of his sign, and observed that his goose was hatching, but would join the flock whenever they flew over the water; an enigma which was the perpetual recreation and delight of the loyal but fat-headed burghers of Communipaw.

Under the sway of this patriotic, though discreet and quiet publican, the tavern continued to flourish in primeval tranquillity, and was the resort of true hearted Nederlanders, from all parts of Pavonia; who met here quietly and secretly, to smoke and drink the downfall of Briton and Yankee, and success to Admiral Van Tromp.

The only drawback on the comfort of the establishment was a nephew of mine host, a sister's son, Yan Yost Vanderscamp by name, and a real scamp by nature. This unlucky whipster showed an early propensity to mischief, which he gratified in a small way by playing tricks upon the frequenters of the Wild Goose,—putting gunpowder in their pipes, or squibs in their pockets, and astonishing them with an explosion, while they sat nodding around the fireplace in the bar room; and if perchance a worthy burgher from some distant part of Pavonia lingered until dark over his potation, it was odds but young Vanderscamp would slip a brier under his horses tail, as he mounted, and send him clattering along the road, in neck or nothing style, to the infinite astonishment and discomfiture of the rider.

It may be wondered at, that mine host of the Wild Goose did not turn such a graceless varlet out of doors; but Teunis Van Gieson was an easy-tempered man, and, having no child of his own, looked upon his nephew with almost parental indulgence. His patience and good-nature were doomed to be tried by another inmate of his mansion. This was a cross-grained curmudgeon of a negro, named Pluto, who was a kind of enigma in Communipaw. Where he came from, nobody knew. He was found one morning, after a storm, cast like a sea-monster on the strand, in front of the Wild Goose, and lay there, more dead than alive. The neighbors gathered round, and speculated on his production of the deep; whether it were fish or flesh, or a compound of both, commonly yclept a merman. The kind-hearted Teunis Van Gieson, seeing that he wore the human form, took him into his house, and warmed him into life. By degrees, he showed signs of intelligence, and even uttered sounds very much like language, but which no one in Communipaw could understand. Some thought him a negro just from Guinea, who had either fallen overboard, or escaped from a slave-ship. Nothing, however, could ever draw from him any account of his origin. When questioned on the subject, he merely pointed to Gibbet Island, a small rocky islet which lies in the open bay, just opposite Communipaw, as if that were his native place, though everybody knew it had never been inhabited.

In the process of time, he acquired something of the Dutch language; that is to say, he learnt all its vocabulary of oaths and maledictions, with just words sufficient to string them together. "*Donder en blicksem!*" (thunder and lightning) was the gentlest of his ejaculations. For years he kept about the Wild Goose, more like one of those familiar spirits, or household goblins, we read of, than like a human being. He acknowledged allegiance to no one, but performed various domestic offices, when it suited his humor; waiting occasionally on the guests, grooming the horses, cutting wood, drawing water; and all this without being ordered. Lay any command on him, and the stubborn sea-urchin was sure to rebel. He was never so much at home, however, as when on the water, plying about in skiff or canoe, entirely alone, fishing, crabbing, or grabbing for oysters, and would bring home quantities for the larder of the Wild Goose, which he would throw down at the kitchen-door, with a growl. No Wind nor weather deterred him from launching forth on his favorite element; indeed, the wilder the weather, the more he seemed to enjoy it. If a storm was brewing, he was sure to put off from shore; and would be seen far out in the bay, his light skiff dancing like a feather on the waves, when sea and sky were in a turmoil, and the stoutest ships were fain to lower their sails. Sometimes on such occasions he would be absent for days together. How he weathered the tempest, and how and where he subsisted, no one could divine, nor did any one venture to ask, for all had an almost superstitious awe of him. Some of the Communipaw oystermen declared they had more than once world around him; could navigate from the Hook to

Spiting Devil waves, and after a while come up again, in quite a different part of the bay; whence they concluded that he could live under water like that notable species of wild duck commonly called the bell-diver. All began to consider him in the light of a foul-weather bird, like the Mother Carey's chicken, or stormy petrel; and whenever they saw him putting far out in his skiff, in cloudy weather, made up their minds for a storm.

The only being for whom he seemed to have any liking was Yan Yost Vanderscamp, and him he liked for his very wickedness. He in a manner took the boy under his tutelage, prompted him to all kinds of mischief, aided him in every wild harum scarum freak, until the lad became the complete scapegrace of the village, a pest to his uncle and to every one else. Nor were his pranks confined to the land; he soon learned to accompany old Pluto on the water. Together these worthies would cruise about the broad bay, and all the neighboring straits and rivers; poking around in skiffs and canoes; robbing the set nets of the fishermen; landing on remote. coasts, and laying waste orchards and watermelon patches; in short, carrying on a complete system of piracy, on a small scale. Piloted by Pluto, the youthful Vanderscamp soon became acquainted with all the bays, rivers, creeks, and inlets of the watery seen him suddenly disappear, canoe and all, as if plunged beneath the on the darkest night, and learned to set even the terrors of Hell Gate at defiance.

At length negro and boy suddenly disappeared, and days and weeks elapsed, but without tidings of them. Some said they must have run away and gone to sea; others jocosely hinted that old Pluto, being no other than his namesake in disguise, had spirited away the boy to the nether regions. All, however agreed in one thing, that the village was well rid of them.

In the process of time, the good Teunis Van Gieson slept with his fathers, and the tavern remained shut up, waiting for a claimant, for the next heir was Yan Yost Vanderscamp, and he had not been heard of for years. At length, one day, a boat was seen pulling for shore, from a long, black, rakish-looking schooner, that lay at anchor in the bay. The boat's crew seemed worthy of the craft from which they debarked. Never had such a set of noisy, roistering, swaggering varlets landed in peaceful Communipaw. They were outlandish in garb and demeanor, and were headed by a rough, burly, bully ruffian, with fiery whiskers, a copper nose, a scar across his face, and a great Flaunderish beaver slouched on one side of his head, in whom, to their dismay, the quiet inhabitants were made to recognize their early pest, Yan Yost Vanderscamp. The rear of this hopeful gang was brought up by old Pluto, who had lost an eye, grown grizzly-headed, and looked more like a devil than ever. Vanderscamp renewed his acquaintance with the old burghers, much against their will, and in a manner not at all to their taste. He slapped them familiarly on the back, gave them an iron grip of the hand, and was hail-fellow well-met. According to his own account, he had been all the world over, had made money by bags full, had ships in every sea, and now meant to turn the Wild Goose into a country-seat, where he and his comrades, all rich merchants from foreign parts, might enjoy themselves in the interval of their voyages.

Sure enough, in a little while there was a complete metamorphose of the Wild Goose. From being a quiet, peaceful Dutch public house, it became a most riotous, uproarious private dwelling; a complete rendezvous for boisterous men of the seas, who came here to have what they called a "blow-out" on dry land, and might be seen at all hours, lounging about the door, or lolling out of the windows, swearing among themselves and cracking rough jokes on every passer-by. The house was fitted up, too, in so strange a manner: hammocks slung to the was, instead of bedsteads; odd kinds of furniture, of foreign fashion; bamboo couches, Spanish chairs; pistols, cutlasses, and blunderbusses, suspended on every peg; silver crucifixes on the mantel-pieces, silver candle sticks and porringers on the tables, contrasting oddly with the pewter and Delf ware of the original establishment. And then the strange amusements of these sea-monsters! Pitching Spanish dollars, instead of quoits; firing blunderbusses out of the window; shooting at a mark, or at any unhappy dog, or cat, or pig, or barn-door fowl, that might happen to come within reach.

The only being who seemed to relish their rough waggery was old Pluto; and yet he led but a doles life of it, for they practised all kinds of manual jokes upon him, kicked him about like a foot-ball, shook him by his grizzly mop of wool, and never spoke to him without coupling a curse by way of adjective, to his name, and consigning him to the infernal regions. The old fellow, however, seemed to like them the better the more they cursed him, though his utmost expression of pleasure never amounted to more than the growl of a petted bear, when his ears are rubbed.

Old Pluto was the ministering spirit at the orgies of the Wild Goose; and such orgies as took place there! Such drinking, singing, whooping, swearing; with an occasional interlude of quarrelling and fighting. The noisier grew the revel, the more old Pluto plied the potations, until the guests would become frantic in their merriment, smashing everything to pieces, and throwing the house out of the windows. Sometimes, after a drinking bout, they sallied forth and scoured the village, to the dismay of the worthy burghers, who gathered their women within doors, and would have shut up the house. Vanderscamp, however, was not to be rebuffed. He insisted on renewing acquaintance with his old neighbors, and on introducing his friends, the merchants, to their families; swore he was on the lookout for a wife, and meant, before he stopped, to find husbands for all their daughters. So, will-ye, nill-ye, sociable he was; swaggered about their best parlors, with his hat on one side of his head; sat on the good wife's nicely waxed mahogany table, kicking his heels against the carved and polished leg, kissed and tousled the young *vrows*; and, if they frowned and pouted, gave them a gold rosary, or a sparkling cross, to put them in good-humor again.

Sometimes nothing would satisfy him, but he must have some of his old neighbors to dinner at the Wild Goose. There was no refusing him, for he had the complete upper band of the community, and the peaceful burghers all stood in awe of him. But what a time would the quiet, worthy men have, among these rake-hells, who would delight to astound them with the most extravagant gun-powder tales, embroidered with all kinds of foreign oaths, clink the can with them, pledge them in deep potations, bawl drinking songs in their ears, and occasionally fire pistols over their heads, or under the table, and then laugh in their faces, and ask them how they liked the smell of gunpowder.

Thus was the little village of Communipaw for a time like the unfortunate wight possessed with devils; until Vanderscamp and his brother merchants would sail on another trading voyage, when the Wild Goose would be shut up and everything relapse into quiet, only to be disturbed by his next visitation.

The mystery of all these proceedings gradually dawned upon the tardy intellects of Communipaw. These were the times of the notorious Captain Kidd, when the American harbors were the resorts of piratical adventurers of all kinds, who, under pretext of mercantile voyages, scoured the West Indies, made plundering descents

upon the Spanish Main, visited even the remote Indian Seas, and then came
to dispose of their booty, have their revels, and fit out new expeditions in the
English colonies.

Vanderscamp had served in this hopeful school, and, having risen to importance among the buccaneers, had pitched upon his native village and early home,
as a quiet, out-of-the-way, unsuspected place, where he and his comrades, while
anchored at New York, might have their feasts, and concert their plans, without
molestation.

At length the attention of the British government was called to these piratical
enterprises, that were becoming so frequent and outrageous. Vigorous measures
were taken to check and punish them. Several of the most noted freebooters were
caught and executed, and three of Vanderscam's chosen comrades, the most riotous
swash bucklers of the Wild Goose, were hanged in chains on Gibbet Island, in full
sight of their favorite resort. As to Vanderscamp himself, he and his man Pluto
again disappeared, and it was hoped by the people of Communipaw that he had
fallen in some foreign brawl, or been swung on some foreign gallows.

For a time, therefore, the tranquillity of the village was restored; the worthy
Dutchmen once more smoked their pipes in peace, eying with peculiar compla-
cency their old pests and terrors, the pirates, dangling and drying in the sun, on
Gibbet Island.

This perfect calm was doomed at length to be ruffled. The fiery persecution
of the pirates gradually subsided. Justice was satisfied with the examples that had
been made, and there was no more talk of Kidd, and the other heroes of like
kidney. On a calm summer evening, a boat, somewhat heavily laden, was seen
pulling into Communipaw. What was the surprise and disquiet of the inhabitants
to see Yan Yost Vanderscamp seated at the helm, and his man Pluto tugging at
the oar! Vanderscamp, however, was apparently an altered man. He brought
home with him a wife, who seemed to be a shrew, and to have the upper hand
of him. He no longer was the swaggering, bully ruffian, but affected the regular
merchant, and talked of retiring from business, and settling down quietly, to pass
the rest of his days in his native place.

The Wild Goose mansion was again opened, but with diminished splendor,
and no riot. It is true, Vanderscamp had frequent nautical visitors, and the sound

of revelry was occasionally overheard in his house; but everything seemed to be done under the rose, and old Pluto was the only servant that officiated at these orgies. The visitors, indeed, were by no means of the turbulent stamp of their predecessors; but quiet mysterious traders; full of nods, and winks, and hieroglyphic signs, with whom, to use their cant phrase, "everything was smug." Their ships came to anchor at night, in the lower bay; and, on a private signal, Vanderscamp would launch his boat, and, accompanied solely by his man Pluto, would make them mysterious visits. Sometimes boats pulled in at night, in front of the Wild Goose, and various articles of merchandise were landed in the dark, and spirited away, nobody knew whither. One of the more curious of the inhabitants kept watch, and caught a glimpse of the feature of some of these night visitors, by the casual glance of a lantern, and declared that he recognized more than one of the freebooting frequenters of the Wild Goose, in former times; whence he concluded that Vanderscamp was at his old game, and that this mysterious merchandise was nothing more nor less than piratical plunder. The more charitable opinion, however, was, that Vanderscamp and his comrades, having been driven from their old line of business by the "oppressions of government," had resorted to smuggling to make both ends meet.

Be that as it may, I come now to the extraordinary fact which is the butt-end of this story. It happened, late one night, that Yan Yost Vanderscamp was returning across the broad bay, in his light skiff, rowed by his man Pluto. He had been carousing on board of a vessel, newly arrived, and was somewhat obfuscated in intellect, by the liquor he had imbibed. It was a still, sultry night; a heavy mass of lurid clouds was rising in the west, with the low muttering of distant thunder. Vanderscamp called on Pluto to pull lustily, that they might get home before the gathering storm. The old negro made no reply, but shaped his course so as to skirt the rocky shores of Gibbet Island. A faint creaking overhead caused Vanderscamp to cast up his eyes, when, to his horror, he beheld the bodies of his three pot companions and brothers in iniquity dangling in the moonlight, their rags fluttering, and their chains creaking, as they were slowly swung backward and forward by the rising breeze.

"What do you mean, you blockhead!" cried Vanderscamp, "by pulling so close to the island?"

"I thought you'd be glad to see your old friends once more," growled the negro; "you were never afraid of a living man, what do you fear from the dead?"

"Who's afraid?" hiccoughed Vanderscamp, partly heated by liquor, partly nettled by the jeer of the negro; "who's afraid? Hang me, but I would be glad to see them once more, alive or dead, at the Wild Goose. Come, my lads in the wind!" continued he, taking a draught and flourishing the bottle above his head, "here's fair weather to you in the other world; and if you should be walking the rounds tonight, odds fish! but I'll be happy if you will drop in to supper."

A dismal creaking was the only reply. The wind blew loud and shrill, and as it whistled round the gallows, and among the bones, sounded as if they were laughing and gibbering in the air. Old Pluto chuckled to himself, and now pulled for home. The storm burst over the voyagers, while they were yet far from shore. The rain fell in torrents, the thunder crashed and pealed, and the lightning kept up an incessant blaze. It was stark midnight before they landed at Communipaw.

Dripping and shivering, Vanderscamp crawled homeward. He was completely sobered by the storm, the water soaked from without having diluted and cooled the liquor within. Arrived at the Wild Goose, he knocked timidly and dubiously at the door; for he dreaded the reception he was to experience from his wife. He had reason to do so. She met him at the threshold, in a precious ill-humor.

"Is this a time," said she, "to keep people out of their beds, and to bring home company, to turn the house upside down?"

"Company?" said Vanderscamp, meekly; "I have brought no company with me, wife."

"No, indeed! they have got here before you, but by your invitation; and blessed-looking company they are, truly!"

Vanderscamp's knees smote together. "For the love of heaven, where are they, wife"

"Where?—why in the blue room, up-stairs, making themselves as much at home as if the house were their own."

Vanderscamp made a desperate effort, scrambled up to the room, and threw open the door. Sure enough, there at a table, on which burned a light as blue as brimstone, sat the three guests from Gibbet Island, with halters round their necks, and bobbing their cups together, as if they were hob-or-nobbing, and trolling the old Dutch freebooter's glee, since translated into English:—

> "For three merry lads be we,
> And three merry lads be we;
> I on the land, and thou on the sand,
> And Jack on the gallows-tree."

Vanderscamp, saw and heard no more. Starting back with horror, he missed his footing on the landing-place, and fell from the top of the stairs to the bottom. He was taken up speechless, either from the fall or the fright, and was buried in the yard of the little Dutch church at Bergen, on the following Sunday.

From that day forward the fate of the Wild Goose was sealed. It was pronounced a *haunted house*, and avoided accordingly. No one inhabited it but Vanderscamp's shrew of a widow and old Pluto, and they were considered but little better than its hobgoblin visitors. Pluto grew more and more haggard and morose, and looked more like an imp of darkness than a human being. He spoke to no one, but went about muttering to himself; or, as some hinted, talking with the devil, who, though unseen, was ever at his elbow. Now and then be was seen pulling about the bay alone in his skiff, in dark weather, or at the approach of nightfall; nobody could tell why, unless, on an errand to invite more guests from the gallows. Indeed, it was affirmed that the Wild Goose still continued to be a house of entertainment for such guests, and that on stormy nights the blue chamber was occasionally illuminated, and sounds of diabolical merriment were overheard, mingling with the howling of the tempest. Some treated these as idle stories, until on one such night, it was about the time of the equinox, there was a horrible uproar in the Wild Goose, that could not be mistaken. It was not so much the sound of revelry, however, as strife, with two or three piercing shrieks, that pervaded every part of the village. Nevertheless, no one thought of hastening to the spot. On the contrary, the honest burghers of Communipaw drew their nightcaps over their ears, and buried their beads under the bedclothes, at the thoughts of Vanderscamp, and his gallows companions.

The next morning some of the bolder and more curious undertook to reconnoitre. All was quiet and lifeless at the Wild Goose. The door yawned wide open, and had evidently been open all night, for the storm had beaten into the house. Gathering more courage from the silence and apparent desertion, they gradually ventured over the threshold. The house had indeed the air of having been possessed by devils. Everything was topsy-turvy, trunks had been broken open, and chests of drawers and comer cupboards turned inside out, as in a time of general sack and pillage; but the most woeful sight was the widow of Yan Yost Vanderscamp, extended a corpse on the floor of the blue chamber, with the marks of a deadly gripe on the windpipe.

All now was conjecture and dismay at Communipaw; and the disappearance of old Pluto, who was nowhere to be found, gave rise to all kinds of wild surmises. Some suggested that the negro had betrayed the house to some of Vanderscamp's buccaneering associates, and that they had decamped together with the booty; others surmised that the negro was nothing more nor less than a devil incarnate, who had now accomplished his ends, and made off with his dues.

Events, however, vindicated the negro from this last implication. His skiff was picked up, drifting about the bay, bottom upward, as if wrecked in a tempest; and his body was found, shortly afterward, by some Communipaw fishermen, stranded among the rocks of Gibbet Island, near the foot of the pirates' gallows. The fishermen shook their heads and observed that old Pluto had ventured once too often to invite Guests from Gibbet Island.

THE DERELICT

BY YOUNG E. ALLISON

Fifteen men on the Dead Man's Chest—
    Yo ho ho and a bottle of rum!
Drink with the Devil had done for the rest—
    Yo ho ho and a bottle of rum!
The mate was fixed by the bo's'n's pike.
The bo's'n brained with a marlinspike!
And Cookey's throat was marked belike.
        It had been gripped
                By finger ten;
        And there they lay,
                All good dead men.
Like break o' day in a boozing ken—
    Yo ho ho and a bottle o' rum!

Fifteen men of a whole ship's list—
    Yo ho ho and a bottle o' rum!
Dead and be-damned and rest gone whist—
    Yo ho ho and a bottle o' rum!

The skipper lay with his nob in gore

Where the scullion's ax, his cheek had shore.

And the scullion, he was stabbed times four.

    And there they lay

        And the soggy skies

    Dripped all day long

        In upstaring eyes:

At murk sunset and at foul sunrise—

    Yo ho ho and a bottle o' rum!

Fifteen men of 'em stiff and stark!

    Yo ho ho and a bottle o' rum!

Ten o' the crew had the murder mark!

    Yo ho ho and a bottle o' rum!

'Twas a cutlass swipe, or an ounce o' lead.

Or a yawing hole in a battered head,

And the scuppers glut with a rotting red;

    And there they lay.

        Aye, damn my eyes!

    All lookouts clapped

        On paradise:

All souls bound just contrariwise—

    Yo ho ho and a bottle o' rum!

Fifteen men of 'em good and true—

    Yo ho ho and a bottle o' rum!

Every man jack could ha' sailed with Old Pew—

    Yo ho ho and a bottle o' rum!

There was chest on chest full of Spanish gold,

With a ton o' plate in the middle hold.

And the cabins riot of loot untold:

    And they lay there

        That had the look the plum.

With sightless glare,
And their lips struck dumb,
While we shared all by the rule of thumb—
Yo ho ho and a bottle o' rum!

More was seen through the sternlight screen—
Yo ho ho and a bottle o' rum!
Chartings no doubt where a woman had been—
Yo ho ho and a bottle o' rum!
A flimsy shift on a bunker cot.
With a thin dirk slot through the bosom spot
And the lace stiff dry in a purplish blot.
Oh, was she wench,
Or some shudderin' maid,
What dared the knife
And that took the blade.
By God! She was stuff for a plucky jade!—
Yo ho ho and a bottle o' rum!

Fifteen men on the Dead Man's Chest—
Yo ho ho and a bottle of rum!
Drink and the Devil had done for the rest—
Yo ho ho and a bottle of rum!
We wrapped 'em all in a mains'l tight.
With twice ten turns of a hawser's bight.
And we heaved 'em o'er and out of sight:
With a Yo heave ho!
And a fare-ye well!
And a sullen plunge
In the sullen swell.
Ten fathoms deep on the road to hell!
Yo ho ho and a bottle o' rum!

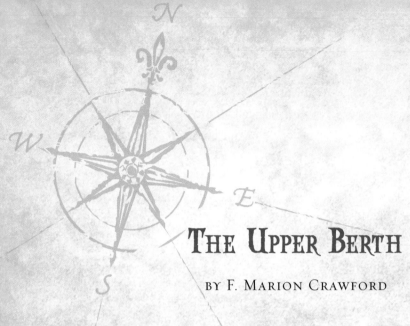

THE UPPER BERTH

by F. Marion Crawford

I

SOMEBODY ASKED FOR THE CIGARS. WE HAD TALKED LONG, AND THE CONVERSATION was beginning to languish; the tobacco smoke had got into the heavy curtains, the wine had got into those brains which were liable to become heavy, and it was already perfectly evident that, unless somebody did something to rouse our oppressed spirits, the meeting would soon come to its natural conclusion, and we, the guests, would speedily go home to bed, and most certainly to sleep. No one had said anything very remarkable; it may be that no one had anything very remarkable to say. Jones had given us every particular of his last hunting adventure in Yorkshire. Mr. Tompkins, of Boston, had explained at elaborate length those working principles, by the due and careful maintenance of which the Atchison, Topeka, and Santa Fé Railroad not only extended its territory, increased its departmental influence, and transported live stock without starving them to death before the day of actual delivery, but, also, had for years succeeded in deceiving those passengers who bought its tickets into the fallacious belief that the corporation aforesaid was really able to transport human life without destroy-ing it. Signor Tombola had endeavoured to persuade us, by arguments which we took no trouble to oppose, that the unity of his country in no way resembled the average modern torpedo, carefully planned, constructed with all the skill of the greatest European arsenals, but, when constructed, destined to be directed by

The steward took my portmanteau, greatcoat, and rug. I shall never forget the expression on his face. Not that he turned pale. It is maintained by the most eminent divines that even miracles cannot change the course of nature. I have no hesitation in saying that he did not turn pale; but, from his expression, I judged that he was either about to shed tears, to sneeze, or to drop my portmanteau. As the latter contained two bottles of particularly fine old sherry presented to me for my voyage by my old friend Snigginson van Pickyns, I felt extremely nervous. But the steward did none of these things.

"Well, I'm damned!" said he in a low voice, and led the way.

I supposed my Hermes, as he led me to the lower regions, had had a little grog, but I said nothing, and followed him. One hundred and five was on the port side, well aft. There was nothing remarkable about the state-room. The lower berth, like most of those upon the *Kamtschatka*, was double. There was plenty of room; there was the usual washing apparatus, calculated to convey an idea of luxury to the mind of a North American Indian; there were the usual inefficient racks of brown wood, in which it is more easy to hang a large-sized umbrella than the common tooth-brush of commerce. Upon the uninviting mattresses were carefully folded together those blankets which a great modern humorist has aptly compared to cold buck-wheat cakes. The question of towels was left entirely to the imagination. The glass decanters were filled with a transparent liquid faintly tinged with brown, but from which an odour less faint, but not more pleasing, ascended to the nostrils, like a far-off sea-sick reminiscence of oily machinery. Sad-coloured curtains half-closed the upper berth. The hazy June daylight shed a faint illumination upon the desolate little scene. Ugh! how I hate that state-room!

The steward deposited my traps and looked at me, as though he wanted to get away—probably in search of more passengers and more fees. It is always a good plan to start in favour with those functionaries, and I accordingly gave him certain coins there and then.

"I'll try and make yer comfortable all I can," he remarked, as he put the coins in his pocket. Nevertheless, there was a doubtful intonation in his voice which surprised me. Possibly his scale of fees had gone up, and he was not satisfied; but on the whole I was inclined to think that, as he himself would have expressed it, he was "the better for a glass". I was wrong, however, and did the man injustice.

II

NOTHING ESPECIALLY WORTHY OF MENTION OCCURRED DURING THAT DAY. WE LEFT the pier punctually, and it was very pleasant to be fairly under way, for the weather was warm and sultry, and the motion of the steamer produced a refreshing breeze. Everybody knows what the first day at sea is like. People pace the decks and stare at each other, and occasionally meet acquaintances whom they did not know to be on board. There is the usual uncertainty as to whether the food will be good, bad, or indifferent, until the first two meals have put the matter beyond a doubt; there is the usual uncertainty about the weather, until the ship is fairly off Fire Island. The tables are crowded at first, and then suddenly thinned. Pale-faced people spring from their seats and precipitate themselves towards the door, and each old sailor breathes more freely as his sea-sick neighbour rushes from his side, leaving him plenty of elbow-room and an unlimited command over the mustard.

One passage across the Atlantic is very much like another, and we who cross very often do not make the voyage for the sake of novelty. Whales and icebergs are indeed always objects of interest, but, after all, one whale is very much like another whale, and one rarely sees an iceberg at close quarters. To the majority of us the most delightful moment of the day on board an ocean steamer is when we have taken our last turn on deck, have smoked our last cigar, and having succeeded in tiring ourselves, feel at liberty to turn in with a clear conscience. On that first night of the voyage I felt particularly lazy, and went to bed in one hundred and five rather earlier than I usually do. As I turned in, I was amazed to see that I was to have a companion. A portmanteau, very like my own, lay in the opposite corner, and in the upper berth had been deposited a neatly-folded rug, with a stick and umbrella. I had hoped to be alone, and I was disappointed; but I wondered who my room-mate was to be, and I determined to have a look at him.

Before I had been long in bed he entered. He was, as far as I could see, a very tall man, very thin, very pale, with sandy hair and whiskers and colourless grey eyes. He had about him, I thought, an air of rather dubious fashion; the sort of man you might see in Wall Street, without being able precisely to say what he was doing there—the sort of man who frequents the Café Anglais, who always seems to be alone and who drinks champagne; you might meet him on a racecourse, but he would never appear to be doing anything there either. A little over-dressed—a little odd. There are three or four of his kind on every ocean steamer. I made up my mind that I did not care to make his acquaintance, and I went to sleep saying to myself that I would study his habits in order to avoid him. If he rose early, I would rise late; if he went to bed late, I would go to bed early. I did not care to know him. If you once know people of that kind they are always turning up. Poor fellow! I need not have taken the trouble to come to so many decisions about him, for I never saw him again after that first night in one hundred and five.

I was sleeping soundly when I was suddenly waked by a loud noise. To judge from the sound, my room-mate must have sprung with a single leap from the upper berth to the floor. I heard him fumbling with the latch and bolt of the door, which opened almost immediately, and then I heard his footsteps as he ran at full speed down the passage, leaving the door open behind him. The ship was rolling a little, and I expected to hear him stumble or fall, but he ran as though he were running for his life. The door swung on its hinges with the motion of the vessel, and the sound annoyed me. I got up and shut it, and groped my way back to my berth in the darkness. I went to sleep again; but I have no idea how long I slept.

When I awoke it was still quite dark, but I felt a disagreeable sensation of cold, and it seemed to me that the air was damp. You know the peculiar smell of a cabin which has been wet with sea-water. I covered myself up as well as I could and dozed off again, framing complaints to be made the next day, and selecting the most powerful epithets in the language. I could hear my room-mate turn over in the upper berth. He had probably returned while I was asleep. Once I thought I heard him groan, and I argued that he was sea-sick. That is particularly unpleasant when one is below. Nevertheless, I dozed off and slept till early daylight.

The ship was rolling heavily, much more than on the previous evening, and the grey light which came in through the porthole changed in tint with every movement according as the angle of the vessel's side turned the glass seawards or skywards. It was very cold—unaccountably so for the month of June. I turned my head and looked at the porthole, and saw to my surprise that it was wide open and hooked back. I believe I swore audibly. Then I got up and shut it. As I turned back I glanced at the upper berth. The curtains were drawn close together; my companion had probably felt cold as well as I. It struck me that I had slept enough. The state-room was uncomfortable, though, strange to say, I could not smell the dampness which had annoyed me in the night. My room-mate was still asleep—excellent opportunity for avoiding him, so I dressed at once and went on deck. The day was warm and cloudy, with an oily smell on the water. It was seven o'clock as I came out—much later than I had imagined. I came across the doctor, who was taking his first sniff of the morning air. He was a young man from the West of Ireland—a tremendous fellow, with black hair and blue eyes, already inclined to be stout; he had a happy-go-lucky, healthy look about him which was rather attractive.

"Fine morning," I remarked, by way of introduction.

"Well," said he, eyeing me with an air of ready interest, "it's a fine morning and it's not a fine morning. I don't think it's much of a morning."

"Well, no—it is not so very fine," said I.

"It's just what I call fuggly weather," replied the doctor.

"It was very cold last night, I thought," I remarked. "However, when I looked about, I found that the porthole was wide open. I had not noticed it when I went to bed. And the state-room was damp, too."

"Damp!" said he. "Whereabouts are you?"

"One hundred and five—"

To my surprise the doctor started visibly, and stared at me.

"What is the matter?" I asked.

"Oh—nothing," he answered; "only everybody has complained of that state-room for the last three trips."

"I shall complain too," I said. "It has certainly not been properly aired. It is a shame!"

"I don't believe it can be helped," answered the doctor. "I believe there is something—well, it is not my business to frighten passengers."

"You need not be afraid of frightening me," I replied. "I can stand any amount of damp. If I should get a bad cold I will come to you."

I offered the doctor a cigar, which he took and examined very critically.

"It is not so much the damp," he remarked. "However, I dare say you will get on very well. Have you a room-mate?"

"Yes; a deuce of a fellow, who bolts out in the middle of the night, and leaves the door open."

Again the doctor glanced curiously at me. Then he lit the cigar and looked grave.

"Did he come back?" he asked presently.

"Yes. I was asleep, but I waked up, and heard him moving. Then I felt cold and went to sleep again. This morning I found the porthole open."

"Look here," said the doctor quietly, "I don't care much for this ship. I don't care a rap for her reputation. I tell you what I will do. I have a good-sized place up here. I will share it with you, though I don't know you from Adam."

I was very much surprised at the proposition. I could not imagine why he should take such a sudden interest in my welfare. However, his manner as he spoke of the ship was peculiar.

"You are very good, doctor," I said. "But, really, I believe even now the cabin could be aired, or cleaned out, or something. Why do you not care for the ship?"

"We are not superstitious in our profession, sir," replied the doctor, "but the sea makes people so. I don't want to prejudice you, and I don't want to frighten you, but if you will take my advice you will move in here. I would as soon see you overboard," he added earnestly, "as know that you or any other man was to sleep in one hundred and five."

"Good gracious! Why?" I asked.

"Just because on the last three trips the people who have slept there actually have gone overboard," he answered gravely.

The intelligence was startling and exceedingly unpleasant, I confess. I looked hard at the doctor to see whether he was making game of me, but he looked perfectly serious. I thanked him warmly for his offer, but told him I intended to be the exception to the rule by which every one who slept in that particular state-room went overboard. He did not say much, but looked as grave as ever, and hinted that, before we got across, I should probably reconsider his proposal. In the course of time we went to breakfast, at which only an inconsiderable number of passengers assembled. I noticed that one or two of the officers who breakfasted with us looked grave. After breakfast I went into my state-room in order to get a book. The curtains of the upper berth were still closely drawn. Not a word was to be heard. My room-mate was probably still asleep.

As I came out I met the steward whose business it was to look after me. He whispered that the captain wanted to see me, and then scuttled away down the passage as if very anxious to avoid any questions. I went toward the captain's cabin, and found him waiting for me.

"Sir," said he, "I want to ask a favour of you."

I answered that I would do anything to oblige him.

"Your room-mate has disappeared," he said. "He is known to have turned in early last night. Did you notice anything extraordinary in his manner?"

The question coming, as it did, in exact confirmation of the fears the doctor had expressed half an hour earlier, staggered me.

"You don't mean to say he has gone overboard?" I asked.

"I fear he has," answered the captain.

"This is the most extraordinary thing—" I began.

"Why?" he asked.

"He is the fourth, then?" I exclaimed. In answer to another question from the captain, I explained, without mentioning the doctor, that I had heard the story concerning one hundred and five. He seemed very much annoyed at hearing that I knew of it. I told him what had occurred in the night.

"What you say," he replied, "coincides almost exactly with what was told to me by the room-mates of two of the other three. They bolt out of bed and run down the passage. Two of them were seen to go overboard by the watch; we stopped and lowered boats, but they were not found. Nobody, however, saw or heard the man who was lost last night—if he is really lost. The steward, who is a superstitious fellow, perhaps, and expected something to go wrong, went to look for him this morning, and found his berth empty, but his clothes lying about, just as he had left them. The steward was the only man on board who knew him by sight, and he has been searching everywhere for him. He has disappeared! Now, sir, I want to beg you not to mention the circumstance to any of the passengers; I don't want the ship to get a bad name, and nothing hangs about an ocean-goer like stories of suicides. You shall have your choice of any one of the officers' cabins you like, including my own, for the rest of the passage. Is that a fair bargain?"

"Very," said I; "and I am much obliged to you. But since I am alone, and have the state-room to myself, I would rather not move. If the steward will take out that unfortunate man's things, I would as lief stay where I am. I will not say anything about the matter, and I think I can promise you that I will not follow my room-mate."

The captain tried to dissuade me from my intention, but I preferred having a state-room alone to being the chum of any officer on board. I do not know whether I acted foolishly, but if I had taken his advice I should have had nothing more to tell. There would have remained the disagreeable coincidence of several suicides occurring among men who had slept in the same cabin, but that would have been all.

That was not the end of the matter, however, by any means. I obstinately made up my mind that I would not be disturbed by such tales, and I even went so far as to argue the question with the captain. There was something wrong about the state-room, I said. It was rather damp. The porthole had been left open last night. My room-mate might have been ill when he came on board, and he might have become delirious after he went to bed. He might even now be hiding somewhere on board, and might be found later. The place ought to be aired and the fastening of the port looked to. If the captain would give me leave, I would see that what I thought necessary was done immediately.

"Of course you have a right to stay where you are if you please," he replied, rather petulantly, "but I wish you would turn out and let me lock the place up, and be done with it."

I did not see it in the same light, and left the captain, after promising to be silent concerning the disappearance of my companion. The latter had had no acquaintances on board, and was not missed in the course of the day. Towards evening I met the doctor again, and he asked me whether I had changed my mind. I told him I had not.

"Then you will before long," he said, very gravely.

III

WE PLAYED WHIST IN THE EVENING, AND I WENT TO BED LATE. I WILL CONFESS now that I felt a disagreeable sensation when I entered my state-room. I could not help thinking of the tall man I had seen on the previous night, who was now dead, drowned, tossing about in the long swell, two or three hundred miles astern. His face rose very distinctly before me as I undressed, and I even went so far as to draw back the curtains of the upper berth, as though to persuade myself that he was actually gone. I also bolted the door of the state-room. Suddenly I became aware that the porthole was open, and fastened back. This was more than I could stand. I hastily threw on my dressing-gown and went in search of Robert, the steward of my passage. I was very angry, I remember, and when I found him I dragged him roughly to the door of one hundred and five, and pushed him towards the open porthole.

"What the deuce do you mean, you scoundrel, by leaving that port open every night? Don't you know it is against the regulations? Don't you know that if the ship heeled and the water began to come in, ten men could not shut it? I will report you to the captain, you blackguard, for endangering the ship!"

I was exceedingly wroth. The man trembled and turned pale, and then began to shut the round glass plate with the heavy brass fittings.

"Why don't you answer me?" I said roughly.

"If you please, sir," faltered Robert, "there's nobody on board as can keep this 'ere port shut at night. You can try it yourself, sir. I ain't a-going to stop hany longer on board o' this vessel, sir; I ain't, indeed. But if I was you, sir, I'd just clear out and go and sleep with the surgeon, or something, I would. Look 'ere, sir, is that fastened what you may call securely, or not, sir? Try it, sir, see if it will move a hinch."

I tried the port, and found it perfectly tight.

"Well, sir," continued Robert triumphantly, "I wager my reputation as a A1 steward that in 'arf an hour it will be open again; fastened back, too, sir, that's the horful thing—fastened back!"

I examined the great screw and the looped nut that ran on it.

"If I find it open in the night, Robert, I will give you a sovereign. It is not possible. You may go."

"Soverin' did you say, sir? Very good, sir. Thank ye, sir. Good-night, sir. Pleasant reepose, sir, and all manner of hinchantin' dreams, sir."

Robert scuttled away, delighted at being released. Of course, I thought he was trying to account for his negligence by a silly story, intended to frighten me, and I disbelieved him. The consequence was that he got his sovereign, and I spent a very peculiarly unpleasant night.

I went to bed, and five minutes after I had rolled myself up in my blankets the inexorable Robert extinguished the light that burned steadily behind the ground-glass pane near the door. I lay quite still in the dark trying to go to sleep, but I soon found that impossible. It had been some satisfaction to be angry with the steward, and the diversion had banished that unpleasant sensation I had at first experienced when I thought of the drowned man who had been my chum; but I was no longer sleepy, and I lay awake for some time, occasionally glancing at the porthole, which I could just see from where I lay, and which, in the darkness, looked like a faintly-luminous soup-plate suspended in blackness. I believe I must have lain there for an hour, and, as I remember, I was just dozing into sleep when I was roused by a draught of cold air, and by distinctly feeling the spray of the sea blown upon my face. I started to my feet, and not having allowed in the dark for the motion of the ship, I was instantly thrown violently across the state-room upon the couch which was placed beneath the port-hole. I recovered myself immediately, however, and climbed upon my knees. The port-hole was again wide open and fastened back!

Now these things are facts. I was wide awake when I got up, and I should certainly have been waked by the fall had I still been dozing. Moreover, I bruised my elbows and knees badly, and the bruises were there on the following morning to testify to the fact, if I myself had doubted it. The porthole was wide open and fastened back—a thing so unaccountable that I remember very well feeling astonishment rather than fear when I discovered it. I at once closed the plate again, and screwed down the loop-nut with all my strength. It was very dark in the state-room. I reflected that the port had certainly been opened within an hour after Robert had at first shut it in my presence, and I determined to watch it, and see whether it would open again. Those brass fittings are very heavy and by no means easy to move. I could not believe that the clamp had been turned by the shaking of the screw. I stood peering out through the thick glass at the alternate white and grey streaks of the sea that foamed beneath the ship's side. I must have remained there a quarter of an hour.

Suddenly, as I stood, I distinctly heard something moving behind me in one of the berths, and a moment afterwards, just as I turned instinctively to look— though I could, of course, see nothing in the darkness—I heard a very faint groan. I sprang across the state-room, and tore the curtains of the upper berth aside, thrusting in my hands to discover if there were any one there. There was someone.

I remember that the sensation as I put my hands forward was as though I were plunging them into the air of a damp cellar, and from behind the curtains came a gust of wind that smelled horribly of stagnant sea-water. I laid hold of something that had the shape of a man's arm, but was smooth, and wet, and icy cold. But suddenly, as I pulled, the creature sprang violently forward against me, a clammy, oozy mass, as it seemed to me, heavy and wet, yet endowed with a sort of supernatural strength. I reeled across the state-room, and in an instant the door opened and the thing rushed out. I had not had time to be frightened, and quickly recovering myself, I sprang through the door and gave chase at the top of my speed, but I was too late. Ten yards before me I could see—I am sure I saw it—a dark shadow moving in the dimly lighted passage, quickly as the shadow of a fast horse thrown before a dog-cart by the lamp on a dark night. But in a moment it had disappeared, and I found myself holding on to the polished rail that ran along the bulkhead where the passage turned towards the companion. My hair stood on end, and the cold perspiration rolled down my face. I am not ashamed of it in the least: I was very badly frightened.

Still I doubted my senses, and pulled myself together. It was absurd, I thought. The Welsh rare-bit I had eaten had disagreed with me. I had been in a nightmare. I made my way back to my state-room, and entered it with an effort. The whole place smelled of stagnant sea-water, as it had when I had waked on the previous evening. It required my utmost strength to go in, and grope among my things for a box of wax lights. As I lighted a railway reading lantern which I always carry in case I want to read after the lamps are out, I perceived that the porthole was again open, and a sort of creeping horror began to take possession of me which I never felt before, nor wish to feel again.

But I got a light and proceeded to examine the upper berth, expecting to find it drenched with sea-water.

But I was disappointed. The bed had been slept in, and the smell of the sea was strong; but the bedding was as dry as a bone. I fancied that Robert had not had the courage to make the bed after the accident of the previous night—it had all been a hideous dream. I drew the curtains back as far as I could and examined the place very carefully. It was perfectly dry. But the porthole was open again. With a sort of dull bewilderment of horror I closed it and screwed it down, and thrusting my heavy stick through the brass loop, wrenched it with all my might, till the thick metal began to bend under the pressure. Then I hooked my reading lantern into the red velvet at the head of the couch, and sat down to recover my senses if I could. I sat there all night, unable to think of rest—hardly able to think at all. But the porthole remained closed, and I did not believe it would now open again without the application of a considerable force.

The morning dawned at last, and I dressed myself slowly, thinking over all that had happened in the night. It was a beautiful day and I went on deck, glad to get out into the early, pure sunshine, and to smell the breeze from the blue water, so different from the noisome, stagnant odour of my state-room. Instinctively I turned aft, towards the surgeon's cabin. There he stood, with a pipe in his mouth, taking his morning airing precisely as on the preceding day.

"Good-morning," said he quietly, but looking at me with evident curiosity.

"Doctor, you were quite right," said I. "There is something wrong about that place."

"I thought you would change your mind," he answered, rather triumphantly. "You have had a bad night, eh? Shall I make you a pick-me-up? I have a capital recipe."

"No, thanks," I cried. "But I would like to tell you what happened."

I then tried to explain, as clearly as possible, precisely what had occurred, not omitting to state that I had been scared as I had never been scared in my whole life before. I dwelt particularly on the phenomenon of the porthole, which was a fact to which I could testify, even if the rest had been an illusion. I had closed it twice in the night, and the second time I had actually bent the brass in wrenching it with my stick. I believe I insisted a good deal on this point.

"You seem to think I am likely to doubt the story," said the doctor, smiling at my detailed account of the state of the porthole. "I do not doubt in the least. I renew my invitation to you. Bring your traps here, and take half my cabin."

"Come and take half of mine for one night," I said. "Help me to get at the bottom of this thing."

"You will get to the bottom of something else if you try," answered the doctor.

"What?" I asked.

"The bottom of the sea. I am going to leave this ship. It is not canny."

"Then you will not help me to find out—"

"Not I," said the doctor quickly. "It is my business to keep my wits about me— not to go fiddling about with ghosts and things."

"Do you really believe it is a ghost?" I enquired, rather contemptuously. But as I spoke I remembered very well the horrible sensation of the supernatural which had got possession of me during the night. The doctor turned sharply on me—

"Have you any reasonable explanation of these things to offer?" he asked. "No, you have not. Well, you say you will find an explanation. I say that you won't, sir, simply because there is not any."

"But, my dear sir," I retorted, "do you, a man of science, mean to tell me that such things cannot be explained?"

"I do," he answered stoutly. "And, if they could, I would not be concerned in the explanation."

I did not care to spend another night alone in the state-room, and yet I was obstinately determined to get at the root of the disturbances. I do not believe there are many men who would have slept there alone, after passing two such nights. But I made up my mind to try it, if I could not get any one to share a watch with me. The doctor was evidently not inclined for such an experiment. He said he was a surgeon, and that in case any accident occurred on board he must be always in readiness. He could not afford to have his nerves unsettled. Perhaps he was quite right, but I am inclined to think that his precaution was prompted by his inclination. On enquiry, he informed me that there was no one on board who would be likely to join me in my investigations, and after a little more conversation I left him. A little later I met the captain, and told him my story. I said that, if no one would spend the night with me, I would ask leave to have the light burning all night, and would try it alone.

"Look here," said he, "I will tell you what I will do. I will share your watch myself, and we will see what happens. It is my belief that we can find out between us. There may be some fellow skulking on board, who steals a passage by frightening the passengers. It is just possible that there may be something queer in the carpentering of that berth."

I suggested taking the ship's carpenter below and examining the place; but I was overjoyed at the captain's offer to spend the night with me. He accordingly sent for the workman and ordered him to do anything I required. We went below at once. I had all the bedding cleared out of the upper berth, and we examined the place thoroughly to see if there was a board loose anywhere, or a panel which could be opened or pushed aside. We tried the planks everywhere, tapped the flooring, unscrewed the fittings of the lower berth and took it to pieces—in short, there was not a square inch of the state-room which was not searched and tested. Everything was in perfect order, and we put everything back in its place. As we were finishing our work, Robert came to the door and looked in.

"Well, sir—find anything, sir?" he asked, with a ghastly grin.

"You were right about the porthole, Robert," I said, and I gave him the promised sovereign. The carpenter did his work silently and skilfully, following my directions. When he had done he spoke.

"I'm a plain man, sir," he said. "But it's my belief you had better just turn out your things, and let me run half a dozen four-inch screws through the door of this cabin. There's no good never came o' this cabin yet, sir, and that's all about it. There's been four lives lost out o' here to my own remembrance, and that in four trips. Better give it up, sir—better give it up!"

"I will try it for one night more," I said.

"Better give it up, sir—better give it up! It's a precious bad job," repeated the workman, putting his tools in his bag and leaving the cabin.

But my spirits had risen considerably at the prospect of having the captain's company, and I made up my mind not to be prevented from going to the end of this strange business. I abstained from Welsh rare-bits and grog that evening, and did not even join in the customary game of whist. I wanted to be quite sure of my nerves, and my vanity made me anxious to make a good figure in the captain's eyes.

IV

THE CAPTAIN WAS ONE OF THOSE SPLENDIDLY TOUGH AND CHEERFUL SPECIMENS OF seafaring humanity whose combined courage, hardihood, and calmness in difficulty leads them naturally into high positions of trust. He was not the man to be led away by an idle tale, and the mere fact that he was willing to join me in the investigation was proof that he thought there was something seriously wrong, which could not be accounted for on ordinary theories, nor laughed down as a common superstition. To some extent, too, his reputation was at stake, as well as the reputation of the ship. It is no light thing to lose passengers overboard, and he knew it.

About ten o'clock that evening, as I was smoking a last cigar, he came up to me, and drew me aside from the beat of the other passengers who were patrolling the deck in the warm darkness.

"This is a serious matter, Mr. Brisbane," he said. "We must make up our minds either way—to be disappointed or to have a pretty rough time of it. You see I cannot afford to laugh at the affair, and I will ask you to sign your name to a statement of whatever occurs. If nothing happens tonight we will try it again tomorrow and next day. Are you ready?"

So we went below, and entered the state-room. As we went in I could see Robert the steward, who stood a little further down the passage, watching us, with his usual grin, as though certain that something dreadful was about to happen. The captain closed the door behind us and bolted it.

"Supposing we put your portmanteau before the door," he suggested. "One of us can sit on it. Nothing can get out then. Is the port screwed down?"

I found it as I had left it in the morning. Indeed, without using a lever, as I had done, no one could have opened it. I drew back the curtains of the upper berth so that I could see well into it. By the captain's advice I lighted my reading lantern, and placed it so that it shone upon the white sheets above. He insisted upon sitting on the portmanteau, declaring that he wished to be able to swear that he had sat before the door.

Then he requested me to search the state-room thoroughly, an operation very soon accomplished, as it consisted merely in looking beneath the lower berth and under the couch below the porthole. The spaces were quite empty.

"It is impossible for any human being to get in," I said, "or for any human being to open the port."

"Very good," said the captain calmly. "If we see anything now, it must be either imagination or something supernatural."

I sat down on the edge of the lower berth.

"The first time it happened," said the captain, crossing his legs and leaning back against the door, "was in March. The passenger who slept here, in the upper berth, turned out to have been a lunatic—at all events, he was known to have been a little touched, and he had taken his passage without the knowledge of his friends. He rushed out in the middle of the night, and threw himself overboard, before the officer who had the watch could stop him. We stopped and lowered a boat; it was a quiet night, just before that heavy weather came on; but we could not find him. Of course his suicide was afterwards accounted for on the ground of his insanity."

"I suppose that often happens?" I remarked, rather absently.

"Not often—no," said the captain; "never before in my experience, though I have heard of it happening on board of other ships. Well, as I was saying, that occurred in March. On the very next trip— What are you looking at?" he asked, stopping suddenly in his narration.

I believe I gave no answer. My eyes were riveted upon the porthole. It seemed to me that the brass loop-nut was beginning to turn very slowly upon the screw— so slowly, however, that I was not sure it moved at all. I watched it intently, fixing its position in my mind, and trying to ascertain whether it changed. Seeing where I was looking, the captain looked too.

"It moves!" he exclaimed, in a tone of conviction. "No, it does not," he added, after a minute.

"If it were the jarring of the screw," said I, "it would have opened during the day; but I found it this evening jammed tight as I left it this morning."

I rose and tried the nut. It was certainly loosened, for by an effort I could move it with my hands.

"The queer thing," said the captain, "is that the second man who was lost is supposed to have got through that very port. We had a terrible time over it. It was in the middle of the night, and the weather was very heavy; there was an alarm that one of the ports was open and the sea running in. I came below and found everything flooded, the water pouring in every time she rolled, and the whole port swinging from the top bolts—not the porthole in the middle. Well, we managed to shut it, but the water did some damage. Ever since that the place smells of sea-water from time to time. We supposed the passenger had thrown himself out, though the Lord only knows how he did it. The steward kept telling me that he cannot keep anything shut here. Upon my word—I can smell it now, cannot you?" he enquired, sniffing the air suspiciously.

"Yes—distinctly," I said, and I shuddered as that same odour of stagnant sea-water grew stronger in the cabin. "Now, to smell like this, the place must be damp," I continued, "and yet when I examined it with the carpenter this morning everything was perfectly dry. It is most extraordinary—hallo!"

My reading lantern, which had been placed in the upper berth, was suddenly extinguished. There was still a good deal of light from the pane of ground glass near the door, behind which loomed the regulation lamp. The ship rolled heavily, and the curtain of the upper berth swung far out into the state-room and back again. I rose quickly from my seat on the edge of the bed, and the captain at the same moment started to his feet with a loud cry of surprise. I had turned with the intention of taking down the lantern to examine it, when I heard his exclamation, and immediately afterwards his call for help. I sprang towards him. He was wrestling with all his might with the brass loop of the port. It seemed to turn against his hands in spite of all his efforts. I caught up my cane, a heavy oak stick I always used to carry, and thrust it through the ring and bore on it with all my strength. But the strong wood snapped suddenly and I fell upon the couch. When I rose again the port was wide open, and the captain was standing with his back against the door, pale to the lips.

"There is something in that berth!" he cried, in a strange voice, his eyes almost starting from his head. "Hold the door, while I look—it shall not escape us, whatever it is!"

But instead of taking his place, I sprang upon the lower bed, and seized something which lay in the upper berth.

It was something ghostly, horrible beyond words, and it moved in my grip. It was like the body of a man long drowned, and yet it moved, and had the strength of ten men living; but I gripped it with all my might—the slippery, oozy, horrible thing—the dead white eyes seemed to stare at me out of the dusk; the putrid odour of rank sea-water was about it, and its shiny hair hung in foul wet curls over its dead face. I wrestled with the dead thing; it thrust itself upon me and forced me back and nearly broke my arms; it wound its corpse's arms about my neck, the living death, and overpowered me, so that I, at last, cried aloud and fell, and left my hold.

As I fell the thing sprang across me, and seemed to throw itself upon the captain. When I last saw him on his feet his face was white and his lips set. It seemed to me that he struck a violent blow at the dead being, and then he, too, fell forward upon his face, with an inarticulate cry of horror.

The thing paused an instant, seeming to hover over his prostrate body, and I could have screamed again for very fright, but I had no voice left. The thing vanished suddenly, and it seemed to my disturbed senses that it made its exit through the open port, though how that was possible, considering the smallness of the aperture, is more than any one can tell. I lay a long time on the floor, and the captain lay beside me. At last I partially recovered my senses and moved, and instantly I knew that my arm was broken—the small bone of my left forearm near the wrist.

I got upon my feet somehow, and with my remaining hand I tried to raise the captain. He groaned and moved, and at last came to himself. He was not hurt, but he seemed badly stunned.

Well, do you want to hear any more? There is nothing more. That is the end of my story. The carpenter carried out his scheme of running half a dozen four-inch screws through the door of one hundred and five; and if ever you take a passage in the *Kamtschatka*, you may ask for a berth in that state-room. You will be told that it is engaged—yes—it is engaged by that dead thing.

I finished the trip in the surgeon's cabin. He doctored my broken arm, and advised me not to "fiddle about with ghosts and things" any more. The captain was very silent, and never sailed again in that ship, though it is still running. And I will not sail in her either. It was a very disagreeable experience, and I was very badly frightened, which is a thing I do not like. That is all. That is how I saw a ghost—if it was a ghost. It was dead, anyhow.

FOG WRAITHS

BY MILDRED HOWELLS

In from the ocean the white fog creeps,
  Blotting out ship, and rock, and tree,
While wrapped in its shroud, from the soundless deeps,
  Back to the land come the lost at sea.

Over the weeping grass they drift
  By well-known paths to their homes again,
To finger the latch they may not lift
  And peer through the glistering window-pane.

Then in the churchyard each seeks the stone
  To its memory raised among the rest,
And they watch by their empty graves alone
  Till the fog rolls back to the ocean's breast.

THE VOICE IN THE NIGHT

BY WILLIAM HOPE HODGSON

It was a dark, starless night. We were becalmed in the Northern Pacific. Our exact position I do not know; for the sun had been hidden during the course of a weary, breathless week, by a thin haze which had seemed to float above us, about the height of our mastheads, at whiles descending and shrouding the surrounding sea.

With there being no wind, we had steadied the tiller, and I was the only man on deck. The crew, consisting of two men and a boy, were sleeping forrard in their den; while Will—my friend, and the master of our little craft—was aft in his bunk on the port side of the little cabin.

Suddenly, from out of the surrounding darkness, there came a hail:

"Schooner, ahoy!"

The cry was so unexpected that I gave no immediate answer, because of my surprise.

It came again—a voice curiously throaty and inhuman, calling from somewhere upon the dark sea away on our port broadside:

"Schooner, ahoy!"

"Hullo!" I sung out, having gathered my wits somewhat. "What are you? What do you want?"

"You need not be afraid," answered the queer voice, having probably noticed some trace of confusion in my tone. "I am only an old man."

The pause sounded oddly; but it was only afterwards that it came back to me with any significance.

"Why don't you come alongside, then?" I queried somewhat snappishly; for I liked not his hinting at my having been a trifle shaken.

"I—I—can't. It wouldn't be safe. I—" The voice broke off, and there was silence.

"What do you mean?" I asked, growing more and more astonished. "Why not safe? Where are you?"

I listened for a moment; but there came no answer. And then, a sudden indefinite suspicion, of I knew not what, coming to me, I stepped swiftly to the binnacle, and took out the lighted lamp. At the same time, I knocked on the deck with my heel to waken Will. Then I was back at the side, throwing the yellow funnel of light out into the silent immensity beyond our rail. As I did so, I heard a slight, muffled cry, and then the sound of a splash as though someone had dipped oars abruptly. Yet I cannot say that I saw anything with certainty; save, it seemed to me, that with the first flash of the light, there had been something upon the waters, where now there was nothing.

"Hullo, there!" I called. "What foolery is this!'

But there came only the indistinct sounds of a boat being pulled away into the night.

Then I heard Will's voice, from the direction of the after scuttle:

"What's up, George?"

"Come here, Will!" I said.

"What is it?" he asked, coming across the deck.

I told him the queer thing which had happened. He put several questions; then, after a moment's silence, he raised his hands to his lips, and hailed:

"Boat, ahoy!"

From a long distance away there came back to us a faint reply, and my companion repeated his call. Presently, after a short period of silence, there grew on our hearing the muffled sound of oars; at which Will hailed again.

This time there was a reply:

"Put away the light."

"I'm damned if I will," I muttered; but Will told me to do as the voice bade, and I shoved it down under the bulwarks.

"Come nearer," he said, and the oar-strokes continued. Then, when apparently some half-dozen fathoms distant, they again ceased.

"Come alongside," exclaimed Will. "There's nothing to be frightened of aboard here!"

"Promise that you will not show the light?"

"What's to do with you," I burst out, "that you're so infernally afraid of the light?"

"Because," began the voice, and stopped short.

"Because what?" I asked quickly.

Will put his hand on my shoulder.

"Shut up a minute, old man," he said, in a low voice. "Let me tackle him."

He leant more over the rail.

"See here, Mister," he said, "this is a pretty queer business, you coming upon us like this, right out in the middle of the blessed Pacific. How are we to know what sort of a hanky-panky trick you're up to? You say there's only one of you. How are we to know, unless we get a squint at you—eh? What's your objection to the light, anyway?"

As he finished, I heard the noise of the oars again, and then the voice came; but now from a greater distance, and sounding extremely hopeless and pathetic.

"I am sorry—sorry! I would not have troubled you, only I am hungry, and—so is she."

The voice died away, and the sound of the oars, dipping irregularly, was borne to us.

"Stop!" sung out Will. "I don't want to drive you away. Come back! We'll keep the light hidden, if you don't like it."

He turned to me:

"It's a damned queer rig, this; but I think there's nothing to be afraid of?

There was a question in his tone, and I replied.

"No, I think the poor devil's been wrecked around here, and gone crazy."

The sound of the oars drew nearer.

"Shove that lamp back in the binnacle," said Will; then he leaned over the rail and listened. I replaced the lamp, and came back to his side. The dipping of the oars ceased some dozen yards distant.

"Won't you come alongside now?" asked Will in an even voice. "I have had the lamp put back in the binnacle."

"I—I cannot," replied the voice. "I dare not come nearer. I dare not even pay you for the—the provisions."

"That's all right," said Will, and hesitated. "You're welcome to as much grub as you can take—" Again he hesitated.

"You are very good," exclaimed the voice. "May God, Who understands everything, reward you—" It broke off huskily.

"The—the lady?" said Will abruptly. "Is she—"

"I have left her behind upon the island," came the voice.

"What island?" I cut in.

"I know not its name," returned the voice. "I would to God—!" it began, and checked itself as suddenly.

"Could we not send a boat for her?" asked Will at this point.

"No!" said the voice, with extraordinary emphasis. "My God! No!" There was a moment's pause; then it added, in a tone which seemed a merited reproach:

"It was because of our want I ventured—because her agony tortured me."

"I am a forgetful brute," exclaimed Will. "Just wait a minute, whoever you are, and I will bring you up something at once."

In a couple of minutes he was back again, and his arms were full of various edibles. He paused at the rail.

"Can't you come alongside for them?" he asked.

"No—I dare not,' replied the voice, and it seemed to me that in its tones I detected a note of stifled craving—as though the owner hushed a mortal desire. It came to me then in a flash, that the poor old creature out there in the darkness, was suffering for actual need of that which Will held in his arms; and yet, because of some unintelligible dread, refraining from dashing to the side of our little schooner, and receiving it. And with the lightning-like conviction, there came the knowledge that the Invisible was not mad; but sanely facing some intolerable horror.

"Damn it, Will!" I said, full of many feelings, over which predominated a vast sympathy. "Get a box. We must float off the stuff to him in it."

This we did—propelling it away from the vessel, out into the darkness, by means of a boathook. In a minute, a slight cry from the Invisible came to us, and we knew that he had secured the box.

A little later, he called out a farewell to us, and so heartful a blessing, that I am sure we were the better for it. Then, without more ado, we heard the ply of oars across the darkness.

"Pretty soon off," remarked Will, with perhaps just a little sense of injury.

"Wait," I replied. "I think somehow he'll come back. He must have been badly needing that food."

"And the lady," said Will. For a moment he was silent; then he continued:

"It's the queerest thing ever I've tumbled across, since I've been fishing."

"Yes," I said, and fell to pondering.

And so the time slipped away—an hour, another, and still Will stayed with me; for the queer adventure had knocked all desire for sleep out of him.

The third hour was three parts through, when we heard again the sound of oars across the silent ocean.

"Listen!" said Will, a low note of excitement in his voice.

"He's coming, just as I thought," I muttered.

The dipping of the oars grew nearer, and I noted that the strokes were firmer and longer. The food had been needed.

They came to a stop a little distance off the broadside, and the queer voice came again to us through the darkness:

"Schooner, ahoy!"

"That you?" asked Will.

"Yes," replied the voice. "I left you suddenly; but—but there was great need."

"The lady?" questioned Will.

"The—lady is grateful now on earth. She will be more grateful soon in—in heaven."

Will began to make some reply, in a puzzled voice; but became confused, and broke off short. I said nothing. I was wondering at the curious pauses, and, apart from my wonder, I was full of a great sympathy.

The voice continued:

"We—she and I, have talked, as we shared the result of God's tenderness and yours—"

Will interposed; but without coherence.

"I beg of you not to—to belittle your deed of Christian charity this night," said the voice. "Be sure that it has not escaped His notice."

It stopped, and there was a full minute's silence. Then it came again:

"We have spoken together upon that which—which has befallen us. We had thought to go out, without telling any, of the terror which has come into our—lives. She is with me in believing that to-night's happenings are under a special ruling, and that it is God's wish that we should tell to you all that we have suffered since—since—"

"Yes?" said Will softly.

"Since the sinking of the *Albatross*."

"Ah!" I exclaimed involuntarily. "She left Newcastle for 'Frisco some six months ago, and hasn't been heard of since."

"Yes," answered the voice. "But some few degrees to the North of the line she was caught in a terrible storm, and dismasted. When the day came, it was found that she was leaking badly, and, presently, it falling to a calm, the sailors took to the boats, leaving—leaving a young lady—my fiancée—and myself upon the wreck.

"We were below, gathering together a few of our belongings, when they left. They were entirely callous, through fear, and when we came up upon the deck, we saw them only as small shapes afar off upon the horizon. Yet we did not despair, but set to work and constructed a small raft. Upon this we put such few matters as it would hold including a quantity of water and some ship's biscuit. Then, the vessel being very deep in the water, we got ourselves on to the raft, and pushed off.

"It was later, when I observed that we seemed to be in the way of some tide or current, which bore us from the ship at an angle; so that in the course of three hours, by my watch, her hull became invisible to our sight, her broken masts remaining in view for a somewhat longer period. Then, towards evening, it grew misty, and so through the night. The next day we were still encompassed by the mist, the weather remaining quiet.

"For four days we drifted through this strange haze, until, on the evening of the fourth day, there grew upon our ears the murmur of breakers at a distance. Gradually it became plainer, and, somewhat after midnight, it appeared to sound upon either hand at no very great space. The raft was raised upon a swell several times, and then we were in smooth water, and the noise of the breakers was behind.

"When the morning came, we found that we were in a sort of great lagoon; but of this we noticed little at the time; for close before us, through the enshrouding mist, loomed the hull of a large sailing-vessel. With one accord, we fell upon our knees and thanked God; for we thought that here was an end to our perils. We had much to learn.

"The raft drew near to the ship, and we shouted on them to take us aboard; but none answered. Presently the raft touched against the side of the vessel, and, seeing a rope hanging downwards, I seized it and began to climb. Yet I had much ado to make my way up, because of a kind of grey, lichenous fungus which had seized upon the rope, and which blotched the side of the ship lividly.

"I reached the rail and clambered over it, on to the deck. Here I saw that the decks were covered, in great patches, with grey masses, some of them rising into nodules several feet in height; but at the time I thought less of this matter than of the possibility of there being people aboard the ship. I shouted; but none answered. Then I went to the door below the poop deck. I opened it, and peered in. There was a great smell of staleness, so that I knew in a moment that nothing living was within, and with the knowledge, I shut the door quickly; for I felt suddenly lonely.

"I went back to the side where I had scrambled up. My—my sweetheart was still sitting quietly upon the raft. Seeing me look down she called up to know whether there were any aboard of the ship. I replied that the vessel had the appearance of having been long deserted; but that if she would wait a little I would see whether there was anything in the shape of a ladder by which she could ascend to the deck. Then we would make a search through the vessel together. A little later, on the opposite side of the decks, I found a rope side-ladder. This I carried across, and a minute afterwards she was beside me.

"Together we explored the cabins and apartments in the after part of the ship; but nowhere was there any sign of life. Here and there within the cabins themselves, we came across odd patches of that queer fungus; but this, as my sweetheart said, could be cleansed away.

"In the end, having assured ourselves that the after portion of the vessel was empty, we picked our ways to the bows, between the ugly grey nodules of that strange growth; and here we made a further search which told us that there was indeed none aboard but ourselves.

"This being now beyond any doubt, we returned to the stern of the ship and proceeded to make ourselves as comfortable as possible. Together we cleared out and cleaned two of the cabins: and after that I made examination whether there was anything eatable in the ship. This I soon found was so, and thanked God in my heart for His goodness. In addition to this I discovered the whereabouts of the fresh-water pump, and having fixed it I found the water drinkable, though somewhat unpleasant to the taste.

"For several days we stayed aboard the ship, without attempting to get to the shore. We were busily engaged in making the place habitable. Yet even thus early we became aware that our lot was even less to be desired than might have been imagined; for though, as a first step, we scraped away the odd patches of growth that studded the floors and walls of the cabins and saloon, yet they returned almost to their original size within the space of twenty-four hours, which not only discouraged us, but gave us a feeling of vague unease.

"Still we would not admit ourselves beaten, so set to work afresh, and not only scraped away the fungus, but soaked the places where it had been, with carbolic, a can-full of which I had found in the pantry. Yet, by the end of the week the growth had returned in full strength, and, in addition, it had spread to other places, as though our touching it had allowed germs from it to travel elsewhere.

"On the seventh morning, my sweetheart woke to find a small patch of it growing on her pillow, close to her face. At that, she came to me, so soon as she could get her garments upon her. I was in the galley at the time lighting the fire for breakfast.

"Come here, John,' she said, and led me aft. When I saw the thing upon her pillow I shuddered, and then and there we agreed to go right out of the ship and see whether we could not fare to make ourselves more comfortable ashore.

"Hurriedly we gathered together our few belongings, and even among these I found that the fungus had been at work; for one of her shawls had a little lump of it growing near one edge. I threw the whole thing over the side, without saying anything to her.

"The raft was still alongside, but it was too clumsy to guide, and I lowered down a small boat that hung across the stern, and in this we made our way to the shore. Yet, as we drew near to it, I became gradually aware that here the vile fungus, which had driven us from the ship, was growing riot. In places it rose into horrible, fantastic mounds, which seemed almost to quiver, as with a quiet life, when the wind blew across them. Here and there it took on the forms of vast fingers, and in others it just spread out flat and smooth and treacherous. Odd places, it appeared as grotesque stunted trees, seeming extraordinarily kinked and gnarled—the whole quaking vilely at times.

"At first, it seemed to us that there was no single portion of the surrounding shore which was not hidden beneath the masses of the hideous lichen; yet, in this, I found we were mistaken; for somewhat later, coasting along the shore at a little distance, we descried a smooth white patch of what appeared to be fine sand, and there we landed. It was not sand. What it was I do not know. All that I have observed is that upon it the fungus will not grow; while everywhere else, save where the sand-like earth wanders oddly, path-wise, amid the grey desolation of the lichen, there is nothing but that loathsome greyness.

"It is difficult to make you understand how cheered we were to find one place that was absolutely free from the growth, and here we deposited our belongings. Then we went back to the ship for such things as it seemed to us we should need. Among other matters, I managed to bring ashore with me one of the ship's sails, with which I constructed two small tents, which, though exceedingly rough-shaped, served the purpose for which they were intended. In these we lived and stored our various necessities, and thus for a matter of some four weeks all went smoothly and without particular unhappiness. Indeed, I may say with much of happiness—for—for we were together.

"It was on the thumb of her right hand that the growth first showed. It was only a small circular spot, much like a little grey mole. My God! how the fear leapt to my heart when she showed me the place. We cleansed it, between us, washing it with carbolic and water. In the morning of the following day she showed her hand to me again. The grey warty thing had returned. For a little while, we looked at one another in silence. Then, still wordless, we started again to remove it. In the midst of the operation she spoke suddenly.

" 'What's that on the side of your face, dear?' Her voice was sharp with anxiety. I put my hand up to feel.

" 'There! Under the hair by your ear. A little to the front a bit.' My finger rested upon the place, and then I knew.

" 'Let us get your thumb done first,' I said. And she submitted, only because she was afraid to touch me until it was cleansed. I finished washing and disinfecting her thumb, and then she turned to my face. After it was finished we sat together and talked awhile of many things for there had come into our lives sudden, very terrible thoughts. We were, all at once, afraid of something worse than death. We spoke of loading the boat with provisions and water and making our way out on to the sea; yet we were helpless, for many causes, and—and the growth had attacked us already. We decided to stay. God would do with us what was His will. We would wait.

"A month, two months, three months passed and the places grew somewhat, and there had come others. Yet we fought so strenuously with the fear that its headway was but slow, comparatively speaking.

"Occasionally we ventured off to the ship for such stores as we needed. There we found that the fungus grew persistently. One of the nodules on the maindeck became soon as high as my head.

"We had now given up all thought or hope of leaving the island. We had realized that it would be unallowable to go among healthy humans, with the things from which we were suffering.

"With this determination and knowledge in our minds we knew that we should have to husband our food and water; for we did not know, at that time, but that we should possibly live for many years.

"This reminds me that I have told you that I am an old man. Judged by the years this is not so. But—but—"

He broke off; then continued somewhat abruptly:

"As I was saying, we knew that we should have to use care in the matter of food. But we had no idea then how little food there was left of which to take care. It was a week later that I made the discovery that all the other bread tanks—which I had supposed full—were empty, and that (beyond odd tins of vegetables and meat, and some other matters) we had nothing on which to depend, but the bread in the tank which I had already opened.

"After learning this I bestirred myself to do what I could, and set to work at fishing in the lagoon; but with no success. At this I was somewhat inclined to feel desperate until the thought came to me to try outside the lagoon, in the open sea.

"Here, at times, I caught odd fish; but so infrequently that they proved of but little help in keeping us from the hunger which threatened.

"It seemed to me that our deaths were likely to come by hunger, and not by the growth of the thing which had seized upon our bodies.

"We were in this state of mind when the fourth month wore out. When I made a very horrible discovery. One morning, a little before midday. I came off from the ship with a portion of the biscuits which were left. In the mouth of her tent I saw my sweetheart sitting, eating something.

"'What is it, my dear?' I called out as I leapt ashore. Yet, on hearing my voice, she seemed confused, and, turning, slyly threw something towards the edge of the little clearing. It fell short, and a vague suspicion having arisen within me, I walked across and picked it up. It was a piece of the grey fungus.

"As I went to her with it in my hand, she turned deadly pale; then rose red.

"I felt strangely dazed and frightened.

"'My dear! My dear!' I said, and could say no more. Yet at words she broke down and cried bitterly. Gradually, as she calmed, I got from her the news that she had tried it the preceding day, and—and liked it. I got her to promise on her knees not to touch it again, however great our hunger. After she had promised she told me that the desire for it had come suddenly, and that, until the moment of desire, she had experienced nothing towards it but the most extreme repulsion.

"Later in the day, feeling strangely restless, and much shaken with the thing which I had discovered, I made my way along one of the twisted paths—formed by the white, sand-like substance—which led among the fungoid growth. I had, once before, ventured along there; but not to any great distance. This time, being involved in perplexing thought, I went much further than hitherto.

"Suddenly I was called to myself by a queer hoarse sound on my left. Turning quickly I saw that there was movement among an extraordinarily shaped mass of fungus, close to my elbow. It was swaying uneasily, as though it possessed life of its own. Abruptly, as I stared, the thought came to me that the thing had a grotesque resemblance to the figure of a distorted human creature. Even as the fancy flashed into my brain, there was a slight, sickening noise of tearing, and I saw that one of the branch-like arms was detaching itself from the surrounding grey masses, and coming towards me. The head of the thing—a shapeless grey ball, inclined in my direction. I stood stupidly, and the vile arm brushed across my face. I gave out a frightened cry, and ran back a few paces. There was a sweetish taste upon my lips where the thing had touched me. I licked them, and was immediately filled with an inhuman desire. I turned and seized a mass of the fungus. Then more and—more. I was insatiable. In the midst of devouring, the remembrance of the morning's discovery swept into my mazed brain. It was sent by God. I dashed the fragment I held to the ground. Then, utterly wretched and feeling a dreadful guiltiness, I made my way back to the little encampment.

"I think she knew, by some marvellous intuition which love must have given, so soon as she set eyes on me. Her quiet sympathy made it easier for me, and I told her of my sudden weakness; yet omitted to mention the extraordinary thing which had gone before. I desired to spare her all unnecessary terror.

"But, for myself, I had added an intolerable knowledge, to breed an incessant terror in my brain; for I doubted not but that I had seen the end of one of those men who had come to the island in the ship in the lagoon; and in that monstrous ending I had seen our own.

"Thereafter we kept from the abominable food, though the desire for it had entered into our blood. Yet our drear punishment was upon us; for, day by day, with monstrous rapidity, the fungoid growth took hold of our poor bodies. Nothing we could do would check it materially, and so—and so—we who had been human, became— Well, it matters less each day. Only—only we had been man and maid!

"And day by day the fight is more dreadful, to withstand the hungerlust for the terrible lichen.

"A week ago we ate the last of the biscuit, and since that time I have caught three fish. I was out here fishing tonight when your schooner drifted upon me out of the mist. I hailed you. You know the rest, and may God, out of His great heart, bless you for your goodness to a—a couple of poor outcast souls."

There was the dip of an oar—another. Then the voice came again, and for the last time, sounding through the slight surrounding mist, ghostly and mournful.

"God bless you! Good-bye!"

"Good-bye," we shouted together, hoarsely, our hearts full of many emotions.

I glanced about me. I became aware that the dawn was upon us.

The sun flung a stray beam across the hidden sea; pierced the mist dully, and lit up the receding boat with a gloomy fire. Indistinctly I saw something nodding between the oars. I thought of a sponge—a great, grey nodding sponge—The oars continued to ply. They were grey—as was the boat—and my eyes searched a moment vainly for the conjunction of hand and oar. My gaze flashed back to the—head. It nodded forward as the oars went backward for the stroke. Then the oars were dipped, the boat shot out of the patch of light, and the—the thing went nodding into the mist.

A LITTLE BIT ABOUT
JOHN RICHARD STEPHENS

John has had many different occupations ranging from driving an armored truck and working as a professional photographer to being a psychiatric counselor at a couple hospitals and a security officer for the U.S. Navy. He was an intelligence officer and squadron commander in the U.S. Air Force before he moved on to writing full time in 1990. Since then, he's written more than three dozen articles, poems, and short stories for newspapers and magazines that range widely from a short story for the literary journal *Nexus* to an article about anti-American propaganda on postage stamps for *Penthouse*. He is a member of the Authors Guild and the Horror Writers Association.

He's the author/editor of the following books:

Weird History 101
Wyatt Earp Speaks!
Wyatt Earp Tells of the Gunfight Near the O.K. Corral (booklet)
Captured by Pirates
Into the Mummy's Tomb
Vampires, Wine and Roses
The King of the Cats and Other Feline Fairy Tales
Mysterious Cat Stories (co-edited with Kim Smith)
The Dog Lover's Literary Companion
The Enchanted Cat

John's books have been selections of the Preferred Choice Book Club, the Quality Paperback Book Club and the Book of the Month Club. His work has been published as far away as India and Singapore and has been translated into Japanese and Finnish. He can be contacted at pirates@ferncanyonpress.com.